Behavior Analysis, Education, and Effective Schooling

Dedication

For our children
Justin and Darcy Fredrick
Joshua, Celia, and Jacob Deitz
Meghann, Jodie, Andrew, and Gregory Hummel

And our favorite adults
George Fredrick, Tricia Deitz
Suzan Bryceland, and Marcia Hummel

Behavior Analysis, Education, and Effective Schooling

Laura D. Fredrick
Samuel M. Deitz
John A. Bryceland
John H. Hummel

CONTEXT PRESS
Reno, Nevada

iv

Fredrick, Laura D.
Behavior Analysis, Education, and Effective Schooling
    p. 226 cm.
    Includes bibliographical references
    ISBN 1-878978-35-7
    1. Behavior Assessment-United States. 2. Education-United States-Philosopy.
    3. Teaching-United States. 4. Classroom management-United States
    5. Educational tests and measurements-United States. 6. Teachers-Training
    of-United States.

I. Fredrick, Laura D. 1948- II. Deitz, Samuel M. 1945- III. Bryceland, John A. 1951-
IV. Hummel, John H. 1948-

CIP Information:
    LB1060.2.B433 2000
    370.15'3--dc21   99-26805
                                CIP

© 2000 Context Press
933 Gear Street, Reno, NV 89503-2729

Printed in the United States of America

Preface

This book is about education, schooling, and behavior analysis. It is more than a book about how behavior analysis can or should be used in schools. It is also about all that schools can or should accomplish and why they are not accomplishing all that is possible. We analyze how teachers are or should be prepared. We discuss how and why behavior analysis does and does not fit within the existing frameworks of American education.

Our overall emphasis is on "research-based education." This concept means that all that occurs in schools and in schools of education should have a research base—data that support the effectiveness of curricula, or methods of discipline, or methods to enhance a child's self concept. Before we expose children to teaching methods or curriculum materials we should have evidence that the methods and materials are effective. That may sound like a fairly prosaic concept—"of course they should work. Who would use materials that do not work?" Unfortunately, education in America is rarely grounded in research-based practice. It is more often based on theoretical assumptions: supporting data are not available for many of these assumptions. We address this dilemma. We present information as to why this is the case and what can be done about it.

Most important, we present a design for changing American education so that it is possible for all our children to achieve excellence. This design will allow our schools to be so effective that we can, in fact, reach the goals of America 2000— American students can be the best educated in the world. Theories, no matter how comfortable, will not get us there. We show how we must rely on data concerning individual achievement—much of which already exist—to establish the kind of effective education all our children so richly deserve.

We would like to thank Claudia McDade who patiently answered questions and provided clarification about her areas of expertise to assist us in editing some of the chapters. In addition, we are grateful to our graduate research assistants, Jamie Hodges and Tracy Boney. Jamie spent countless hours in the library in search of one thing or another and was relentless in her editing early in this project. She passed the job on to Tracy who helped bring this book to completion with her untiring attention to detail and her cheerful willingness to read, edit, and read again.

Laura Fredrick
Samuel Deitz
John Bryceland
John Hummel
April 2000

Contents

Chapter 1

Achieving Educational Success

This is an interesting and controversial time to be in the field of American education or to begin the study of American education. Critics of education are abundant. They cite the many problems in our schools, including declining test scores, the inability of students to enter the work force immediately after high school, their inability to complete college-level work, the standing of our students in science and math compared to students from other countries, and increased violence and teenage pregnancy. These issues have stirred debates over the purpose of school, what should be taught in school, who should be in school, who should control the school, how business and industry should interact with the school, and the role of choice in schooling.

Imagine if you were to create your own school today. What if you had complete freedom to plan every aspect of your school? What would you do? Would you start a private school or a special school with public funding? Which students would you admit? Would you teach only "at-risk" children or "gifted" children, other "special" students, or all types of children? Would you group your students by ability or would you include students of all abilities in the same classes? What subjects would you teach? What materials and texts would you use? How would you incorporate the latest technology in your school? Who would you hire to work in your school? What training would you require of your teachers and administrators? What in-service training would you provide? How would you insure the safety of your students? What would you do about transportation and lunch? How would you evaluate the success of your school? Who would you turn to for advice? These are stimulating questions with very difficult answers. Debate within and beyond the educational community is intense about each of these questions and many more.

Answers to these questions are being proposed by teachers, administrators, university-based educational experts, other academicians, politicians, and the general public. Solutions include a number of possibilities: returning to "the basics" and essentially ignoring the basics; concentrating on understanding, reasoning skills, and problem solving rather than simply facts; using subject-matter experts as teachers and using teachers trained in our colleges of education; freeing teachers to teach as they think best and instructing teachers through exact scripts (or in some cases using technology to create "teacher-free" instructional systems); privatizing American schools and combining small public systems into larger public systems; placing police in every school and removing students with any level of criminal background to special schools; teaching all forms of birth control and safe-sex health systems and disallowing mention of any issue other than abstinence as birth control. The differences among these as well as the many other proposed solutions make for exciting debate. Depending on who you listened to, you could just about do anything and be considered "right" by some expert or another.

Start a Plan Right Now

One way to learn more about education and behavior analysis is to design a plan for your own school in complete detail. As you work through this book, expand this plan. As you progress, you will identify additional issues that have not yet been introduced and add them to your plan. By the time you finish the book, you should have completed a fairly thorough analysis of how you will begin, fund, and conduct your school. You should keep this information in a journal and your first entry is fairly easy: Decide on the name for your school. Other items will become more difficult but as you work through this book, you should be able to come up with ideas for each of the other items.

Education and Schooling

One problem you will immediately confront when planning a school is that education is a much broader category than schooling. **Education** consists of all family and societal factors that influence an individual. **Schooling** consists only of the formal educational structures such as preschools, elementary and secondary schools, vocational schools, and colleges. When we think of the factors that create the unique character of any individual, we must go beyond schools and other formal structures of education. As Graham (1992) stated, "schooling is a vital but limited aspect of education. Among the many agencies that educate—families, media, communities, religious, eleemosynary, and social institutions—schooling is undoubtably much less influential than the cumulative effect of the others" (p. 14). That is not to say that schooling is not influential; rather, when we consider how children become adults, we may find that schooling currently plays a less significant role than the combined effects of these other educational factors.

But schooling is essential. While it may not be more influential than all of the other factors combined, it may be the single most important factor beyond the family. Children begin school by the age of six (many children begin much earlier) and stay in school for a significant portion of their days until the age of eighteen or longer. Many go on to post-secondary vocational education or to colleges or universities. We cannot ignore the effect of schooling on the creation of an individual's unique personality and abilities. In fact, schooling is one of the few factors that can be controlled by society and to some extent standardized. Much of this text will be about how schools work and what can be done to insure that they work better. Some of what we will discuss will show that effective schools can even help overcome the detrimental effects of other factors. For example, children may come to school from families with no access to books and limited communication skills. Effective schools can teach these children and move them to a point where their skills are as distinguished as those of the children who come from privileged backgrounds.

Current Status of the Schools and Educational Reform

How bad are our schools? Most of today's critics would have us think that our schools have experienced severe declines in the last few decades. After all, it is difficult to argue for complete and thorough reform if schools are not in serious trouble. In the decade of the 1980's, dozens of national or state reports attempted to document serious declines in public education. We have reports on education from the U.S. Department of Education, the National Commission for Excellence in Teacher Education, the Carnegie Forum on Education and the Economy, the American Association of Colleges of Teacher Education, the American Association of School Administrators, the Southern Regional Education Board, the Holmes Group of Colleges of Education, and several state legislatures and local school districts. These reports document major problems in American schooling. For example, according to the report by the National Commission for Excellence in Teacher Education, *A Nation at Risk* (1983):

On 19 international academic tests, American students were never first or second, and were last seven times.

Some 23 million Americans are functionally illiterate by the simplest tests of everyday reading, writing, and comprehension.

Average achievement of high school students on most standardized tests is now lower than 26 years ago.

Over half the population of gifted students do not match their tested ability with comparable achievement in school.

SAT scores demonstrate a virtually unbroken decline from 1963 to 1980. (pp. 3-4)

These problems suggest that while we can be proud of what education has accomplished in the United States, "the educational foundations of our society are presently being eroded by a rising tide of mediocrity that threatens our very future as a nation" (National Commission on Excellence in Education, 1983, p. 1).

However, as unpopular as it is to say, we need to question much of the rhetoric of the critics. If we rely on the best available data, American public schools are no worse today than at any other time in this century. Many of the "facts" listed by the critics are not entirely accurate. Several scholars have documented that our public schools are better in many ways than ever before in our history (Bracey, 1991, 1992; Graham, 1992; Jaeger, 1992). We are doing a better job educating previously underserved children. In addition, test scores, when carefully analyzed, have not really declined. As Glickman (1993) stated, "public schools are doing a better job for minority and poor children. Furthermore, there has been no appreciable decline in the achievement, knowledge, or skills of today's students as compared with students of years past" (p. 3).

There are other indications that make it appear as if American education may not be in such serious decline. More children graduate from high school than ever before with a higher overall level of skill. "In the early years of this century, less than 10 percent of American young people graduated from high school, and now more than 85 percent have either a high school diploma or a GED" (Graham, 1992). If we compare the results of schools today with schools at the turn of this century, we find some interesting information. For example, while we consider the inner city schools of today as those presenting the most difficulties, at the turn of the century, city schools were the best. Still, in those "best schools" of the 1000 students who entered first grade, only 263 were still in school in eighth grade and only 56 reached the fourth year of high school (Graham, 1992). This shows that the total dropout rate used to be almost 95%. Today we complain if an inner city drop-out rate approaches even 30% (clearly higher than we would ever approve but much better than we have accomplished in the past).

If schools are not so bad, why is there such a national concern for significant educational reform? There is one clear answer to that question: the skills and abilities required of students at the turn of the century–or even those required of students in the 1950s–are completely inadequate for students who will mature during the 21st Century. It does not matter if today's students are equal to or even a little better than students of yesterday. With the significant increases in the requirements for jobs in the 21st Century, today's students, to be successful, must be far better skilled than ever before. Tomorrow's graduates need to be prepared to use technology, make decisions based on data, and communicate at very high levels.

Graham (1992) explained this issue quite well: "As we move to enhance the education of American children today, we must educate a much higher fraction of the population than previously to much higher levels of attainment than we have reached in the past" (p. 6). She continued, "we now have significantly higher expectations for what all children need to learn than we used to have" (p. 13) and "this is a new goal in American education" (p. 16). Earlier in our history we didn't expect significant success for all children, rather, we worried more about attendance. This is an important difference. We never expected minority students, poor students, or students with disabilities to succeed. We wanted them to stay in school but our expectations were quite low. Today we want *all children* to succeed and to succeed at *very high levels*. Our national goals for American children are now high. American goals for education by the year 2000 were outlined in 1991 in the brief document, *America 2000*:

1. All children in America will start school ready to learn.
2. The high school graduation rate will increase to at least 90 percent.
3. American students will leave grades four, eight, and twelve having demonstrated competency in challenging subject matter including English, mathematics, science, history, and geography; and every school in America will ensure that all students learn to use their minds well, so they may be

prepared for responsible citizenship, further learning, and productive employment in our modern economy.

4. U.S. students will be first in the world in science and mathematics achievement.

5. Every adult American will be literate and will possess the knowledge and skills necessary to compete in a global economy and exercise the rights and responsibilities of citizenship.

6. Every school in America will be free of drugs and violence and will offer a disciplined environment conducive to learning. (p. 19)

These are exceptionally high expectations in such a short period of time, but they are supported and endorsed by government officials at the highest levels. These goals have been approved by the last two Presidents of the United States and by most State Departments of Education. While they are significant goals, in reality, schools are expected to do even more.

Unfortunately, part of the reason why schools are such easy targets for criticism is that their goals are so diffuse and fragmented. We read that schools should have goals that address basic skills, self-esteem, vocational skills, higher-order thinking, health and nutrition, character education, responsible and cooperative behavior, aesthetic appreciation and so on. (Glickman, 1993, p. 7)

A careful examination of the goals listed for America in the year 2000 shows the complaint about "diffuse and fragmented" goals has some merit. While a few goals are fairly clear, many are quite vague and ill-defined. We need to question whether schools can accomplish all of these goals at a very high level, and we need to at least acknowledge that current reform movements have placed a very heavy burden on schooling as the primary source of education in America. Reform movements often consider other factors in education such as families, religious organizations, and the media, but the one component of society over which government has some control is the schools. Schools have been left with a very heavy burden.

The report from the Carnegie Forum on Education and the Economy (1986) clarifies what could happen if schools fail:

If our standard of living is to be maintained, if the growth of a permanent underclass is to be averted, if democracy is to function effectively into the next century, our schools must graduate the vast majority of their students with achievement levels long thought possible for only the privileged few. The American mass education system, designed in the early part of the century for a mass-production economy, will not succeed unless it not only raises but redefines the essential standards of excellence and strives to make quality and equality of opportunity compatible with each other. (p. 3)

If what the Carnegie Report says is true, we have a mandate for comprehensive change. We must make immediate improvements in schools to prepare our children for tomorrow, and tomorrow brings challenges never before considered in the design of American schooling.

What Will You Teach in Your School?

These issues of goals and objectives allow you to begin to think more seriously about your own school. Your graduates must be very well prepared but for what will you prepare them? What subjects will you teach? Will you teach social skills? To what level of excellence will you have *all* your students aspire? Will you expect all your students to reach the same levels? You may want to go to the library and examine the minimum curriculum required in your state but you will find that those documents leave you significant flexibility. This is a most difficult part of school design and one for which little or no data exist to direct you. America's goals are a useful beginning but they do not provide you with the specifics necessary to design your day-to-day objectives.

The Failure of Current Educational Reform Movements

As critics of schools have increased their attacks, educational reform movements have exploded. There have been many recommendations for improving education. Most recommendations have been structural (for example, specific changes in course requirements for graduation) or political (what seems popular for politicians at the moment). Many recommendations are contradictory. Some recommendations are based on beliefs about the development of children, while others are based on assumptions about learning made by professional organizations. Many of these assumptions have led to major changes in how curriculum should be taught. Reviewing and clarifying each of these recommendations is less important than clarifying what is essential to improve American education.

One significant trend in American education is to improve schools through a system of democratic school renewal where school governance is shared by faculty and students, not just left in the hands of the principal. Carl Glickman (1993) delineated several aspects of that system. For democratic renewal, schools need faculty who are dissatisfied with their teaching, who mentor and guide each other, who plan together, and who are treated as colleagues in decision making. Schools also need norms of collegiality for discussion and debate; and to seek, produce, and consume information. These aspects of renewal are important and useful; democratic school renewal procedures can improve schools. But there is one essential aspect that is most often missing from all efforts toward reform in education. That missing ingredient is the attitude that "if the kid hasn't learned, the teacher hasn't taught" (Engelmann, 1992, p. 62). Without the responsibility for success on the teacher, in subtle ways, we "blame the children."

If reform means improvement, success is not likely unless teachers are accountable for improvement. Not surprisingly, few effective changes in education have actually occurred. Changes are not occurring even when so many influential participants in government, business, and education are strongly backing such change. One important reason, leading from the subtle blame on children, is that while our talk is always of equality of ability—"all children can learn"—our action has been to separate children into groups where some get a more demanding education than others. This is not a new trend. As Graham (1992) explained:

> In the early years of this century, the president of Harvard University, Charles William Eliot, addressed a group of educators and advised them: "The teachers of the elementary school ought to sort the pupils and sort them by their evident or probable destinies." Few pieces of advice from Harvard presidents have ever been so widely followed! (p. 23)

While it is popular to state that all children can learn, it is more likely that schools sort children into categories. Engelmann (1992) called this the "Sorting Machine." The sorting machine philosophy allows schools to "do what the schools choose to do, and if kids fail, it's their own fault. Historically, this philosophy was functional. It served to sort out kids so that only a small percentage went to college and beyond" (p. 58). Engelmann (1992) also told us that:

> Reforms are a paradox within the current system because, while rhetoric refers to avant-garde approaches, practices belch from the Model T sorting machine. Changing parts of this system won't work. The sorting machine must be scrapped, from the conceptual level, and replaced with a philosophy of empathy for kids. (p. 67)

The sorting machine has always worked fairly well for middle class children who come to school prepared for success. These children have extensive vocabularies that are compatible with the vocabularies used by most teachers. Often they can already read and they know their numbers. Middle class children accomplish what schools expect, but often not because of what those in the schools do. It is common to hear that middle class children succeed at least at minimal levels "in spite of what teachers do." Middle class children are victims of relatively ineffective instruction used in most schools. They do not progress as rapidly as they could progress. Most do not even approximate the lofty goals of *America 2000* (1991). But they do well enough to succeed and to get into college. They have learned how to get by.

Even though some children are doing better than they were some years ago, the saddest fate of schools is reserved for poor children. Poor children are the true victims of the sorting machine. Missing the essential preschool experiences available to middle class children places poor children behind from the very beginning. Efforts at reform have not helped the poor children, the ones most in need of effective education. Without clearly effective schools—schools that follow the dictum that if the kid hasn't learned, the teacher hasn't taught—these poor children will continue to be sorted into the lowest levels of expectation and achievement.

School reform and school renewal need the support of parents, businesses, and the educational establishment. Democratic school reorganization also will be of use. To reform what happens in American classrooms, school renewal must be driven by data from research on teaching and learning. Engelmann (1991) cautions that very little information based on research related to effective practice is included in deliberations about school change. Without that component, schools will remain as they are—relatively effective for middle class children and clearly unsuccessful for poor children. The implied prediction of the Carnegie Forum on Education and the Economy (1986) could come true—our standard of living could be diminished, a permanent underclass could be expanded, and democracy could become ineffective in the next century.

Behavior Analysis

This book is not just about education and schooling. In this book we explain how the field of behavior analysis clarifies the impact of education and schooling on individual children. **Behavior analysis** is a branch of the natural sciences that helps us understand the complex influences of all educational factors—families, friends, religious organizations, media, schools, curriculum, and teaching methods—on the behavior and development of individual children and adults. Behavior analysis is a science that allows us to comprehend the important but often subtle moment-to-moment effects the world we live in has on how we become who we are and why we do what we do. There are three essential defining features that make behavior analysis a most effective method through which to examine education.

Data-Based Effectiveness

An important defining feature of behavior analysis is **data-based effectiveness**. Educational methods are not chosen by behavior analysts because they fit into some theory. Rather, experimental evidence is collected by researchers and teachers to document whether a method actually works. Teachers are taught to collect and use data to make decisions about teaching. If even the most popular curriculum is found not to be effective, behavior analysts demand that it be excluded from the classroom.

This emphasis on effectiveness should be common in schools. If education were a business, or a field such as medicine, the stress on effectiveness would not be unusual. Accountability is critical to any profession seeking progress. If a doctor touted a cure for AIDS, or an engineer announced a new style of construction, or an inventor introduced a new computer, data concerning effectiveness would be demanded before general acceptance could be gained. However, when an educator introduces a new reading or math curriculum, it is a different story. While all the medical and economic innovations would not be uniformly adopted without rigorous testing, the educational innovation would be accepted if it were based on an acceptable educational theory even in the absence of supporting data. We even accept educational innovations on anecdotal evidence that only shows that students "like" the material or exercise, not that it is effective. These practices have not worked to the advantage of the children in our schools.

Individuals

A second defining feature of behavior analysis that makes it important for education is an emphasis on the **individual**. The research methodology of behavior analysis is often called "single-subject research methodology." This does not mean that behavior analysts study only one person. It means that the results of an intervention—a teaching method, for example—are examined for each and every individual in a classroom. For instance, it may be interesting but not very important if the average for the whole class on a given test rises by some amount when the teacher tries a new instructional method. The average test score for a class of 30 children can rise if 10 children do significantly better, 10 stay the same, and 10 decline a small amount. Twenty of the thirty children either stayed the same or got worse! If that occurred, could you say that the teaching method was effective?

In most educational research, separate analyses of all thirty individual children are not conducted. An evaluation is considered complete and the method is rated as successful if the average score improves significantly—even if the scores of some of the children declined. Behavior analysts do not accept that result. For a method to be rated as effective, it must work with *all* of the children for whom it is intended. One method may not work for every child, but you need to know for which children the method does work. You may need more than one method to teach science or math or social studies and you need to be sure that the ones you choose are effective for the children with whom you use them. Without this form of analysis, we are often just "blaming the victim." Teachers could say, "I taught the lesson but many (even most) of the children did not learn it." That implies that the children are at fault. Unless we insist on finding effective strategies for all individuals, we can blame the children when they are only victims of ineffective teaching. This is not a very good way to run a school.

Practicality

The third defining feature of behavior analysis is an emphasis on factors affecting teaching over which a teacher actually has practical control. **Practicality** is essential since the effectiveness of practice is limited if a teacher cannot control the important factors of instruction. Many important influences affecting children in a classroom or at home cannot be changed by the teacher. If children come from a severely disadvantaged background, it will affect their performance in school. If children have a disability, it can affect parts (surely not all) of their performance in school. If children have been taught poorly in the past, it will affect their performance in the current classroom. Behavior analysts do not ignore these issues—they accept them as important but insist that there are sufficient, powerful influences that remain available to the teacher to allow her to be effective with each individual. Rather than accepting failure because a child comes from a disadvantaged background or has some form of disability, behavior analysts seek teaching methods that can help overcome the initial lack of ability and insure the success of each individual child. Much of this book will be about the ways behavior analysts have discovered to gain success where others only find reasons for failure.

Emphasizing the practical factors that a teacher can use requires the teacher to take responsibility for the success of the children. Since there are ways to arrange a classroom to insure that children learn, the teacher, not the home or the child, becomes accountable for success in school. This is another way behavior analysts avoid "blaming the victim" for failure in school. This level of responsibility for effectiveness is unusual in American education but it is an attitude that will insure greater success in the future.

Success and Evaluation

As you design your school, insure that each of these three factors is a constant part of what you plan. How will you determine and use the measures to quantify your success or failure? Is every part of your experiences for children aimed at the success of each individual? Is what you have your teachers do practical? These will become more difficult questions than you may think as you work through the details of a complete plan for a school.

Behavioral Analysis and the Individual

Behavior analysis achieves these three defining features (data-based effectiveness, emphasis on the individual, and practicality) by presenting a comprehensive, systematic view of the effect of environmental factors, the world in which we live, on our lives. It begins by acknowledging the biological factors that affect individuals, such as the genetic endowment that prepares individuals for life. Behavior analysis acknowledges that health, nutrition, and accidents all affect us in their own unique ways. However, much of what we are is the result of what happens to us during our lifetime. We are shaped and changed by how we are treated by family members, religious leaders, and teachers, and by what we see on television or listen to on the radio. Each small interaction between an individual and a part of the physical or social world changes the individual in some slight way. Behavior analysis gives us the concepts and tools we need to understand this interaction.

Imagine a child born with a unique biological makeup that prepares that child to fall within the "normal" range of development. No major diseases or accidents severely impair the intellectual or physical abilities of the child. What will this child grow up to be like? Some part of that answer comes from the biology of the child. The major part of the answer, however, comes from how that child interacts, often in the smallest, moment-to-moment ways, on a daily basis with each and every component of life. It is not very useful to know just that the child has a "good family." We need to know exactly how the child is treated within that family.

The **history** of children's interactions, along with their biological factors, brings them to where they are today. Effective teaching with individuals requires a thorough understanding of how the unique, individual history has prepared a child. Some of this is deceptively simple. For example, if a child is born to French speaking parents and raised in a French speaking home, we would expect the child to speak French. What if the same child born to French speaking parents was adopted at birth and raised in an English speaking home? Would that child speak French or English? One could argue that the child is biologically "French" but no one would expect the child to speak French (without training in French). The family environment in which the child is raised insures what language the child speaks.

We can make the same argument for other factors as well. Imagine a child raised in a warm and loving family and another child raised in an abusive family. Would you need to know the biological background of these children to be able to predict which would be more socially adjusted? What about the child who watches TV six hours a day, or the child who attends church on a regular basis, or the child raised in a small community where all adults share in child-rearing (an African proverb states, "It takes a whole village to raise a single child."). Would these children be different? Of course they would. It is their day-to-day history that determines much of what they will become. These influences do not randomly affect the child. Rather, they act in quite specific and understandable ways to shape the unique character of each individual. The scientific understanding of how this occurs is embodied by the field of behavior analysis. Character, personality, individuality–whatever we choose to call it–is strongly determined by the social and physical environment in which a child is raised.

In most cases, it is important to break down character, personality, or individuality into smaller units so that we can study the environmental influences on those units. The term we use for those smaller units is **behavior**. When a behavior analyst uses the term behavior it is as a general term describing all forms and types of actions people do. These include observable actions such as walking, crying, and writing as well as less observable behaviors such as talking, feeling, and thinking. Behavior is anything a person does. Behavior does not have to be observable or measurable, although it is much easier to study behavior that is observable and measurable. Behavior, as a general term, is sometimes difficult to understand for those who have not studied the science of behavior. It can be confusing to include a wide range of activities under the term behavior. To many people, behavior refers only to misbehavior or inappropriate activity. That is too restrictive. To other people, behavior means only observable, physical action. That is also too restrictive. Behavior is a comprehensive category that includes all that we do–physically, cognitively, and emotionally.

Behavior analysis is a science that explains exactly how, given our unique biological endowment, the environment in which we live contributes to creating us as individuals. It explains how that environment determines the physical, cognitive, and emotional behavior that defines each of us. Since we are examining education, one way to look at behavior analysis is to consider that it helps us understand how factors related to education can be explained and changed to improve the education of children. There are many details to this science that will be presented in later chapters. We will talk specifically about individual histories of reinforcement and punishment–the consequences of behavior–and about antecedent events–the events that occur before behavior to "guide" behavior. Each of these factors will be explained in considerable detail so you can understand how the environment influences learning.

Behavior Analysis and Education

The approach of behavior analysis has a distinct advantage for education and schooling. Behavior analysis presents a scientifically validated method of effective educational reform for individual children. Americans typically believe that all children *can* learn. But, unless educators know how to arrange schools and classrooms so that the chances of individual success are increased, we will not be able to insure that all children *will* learn. No educational system should accept anything less. Believing that all children *can learn* is very different than insuring that all children *will learn*. If education in our country and around the world is to achieve equity, we must insure that all children are educated equally well. That occurs only when we design systems to insure that all children will learn.

Behavior analysis does not directly address the question of what children need to learn. A science of instruction cannot determine whether children should learn division in fourth grade, or take a foreign language throughout school, or learn how to type on a computer keyboard. Defining the goals of education is a broad social role that should include all segments of society—from parents through future employers. All schools and school systems have goals. The United States has goals clarified through *America 2000* (1991). An examination of these goals will show that there is much expected from schools. We want children to be the best in the world in understanding subject matter; we want safe and drug-free schools; we want all children to be ready to learn when they come to kindergarten. But our goals are not restricted to basic skills. We want children to be able to understand, think critically, reason logically, and solve problems effectively. Educators also want children to be emotionally healthy. We want all children to think well of themselves and to have what is sometimes called a healthy self concept.

How can behavior analysis help education and schooling? If we take the defining principles of data-based effectiveness, emphasis on the individual, and practicality and apply them to education, we can determine ways teachers can insure success in their own classrooms. First, we must acknowledge that most current practice in schools is based on tradition, not on data-based effectiveness. Most often, teachers teach as they have been taught. They do not teach according to any particular theory or any set of effective practices. Change requires simultaneous work in two areas: the basic science of learning and the applied science of teaching.

Since basic science often informs practice, we need to insure that we have a better understanding of the underlying factors of learning. More research is needed to understand the complex process of learning. If we are to understand how to teach, we need to understand how children learn. We need to know how children learn simple facts and how they learn the complex and important varieties of behavior, such as critical thinking, reasoning skills, logic, and problem solving. The beginning of this understanding can be informed by basic scientists who are examining these issues.

We also need to work equally diligently on the applied science of teaching. One important change that would immediately improve education for all children would be to stress data-based practice, rather than theories of education. Schools should only adopt materials derived from any theory for which there are supporting data about their effectiveness. This is not to claim that there are data supporting curriculum in all educational areas. Much more needs to be done. Still, educators need to look less at theory and more closely at practices that have been proven useful in classrooms. There are a number of important reasons for this. As Murray (1989) explained:

> The chief legacy of educational theory has been and will continue to be the development and evaluation of specific training techniques for various school concepts, even if the success of the techniques may be more parsimoniously explained by another theory. The value of a theory, and ultimately its truth, is in the effective uses to which it is put. (p. 11)

For an educator, it is irrelevant from which theory an effective practice was derived. The essential ingredient making behavior analysis useful to education is not its theory of human behavior but its emphasis on effectiveness, individuals, and practicality.

Teaching needs major changes. Teaching today is too often simply unsystematically talking **at** students about information. We tell students about material or rely on having them read material. Then we tell them to study, after which we test them on how much they have learned. This is telling and testing, not teaching—and it has not proven very effective with most children. As Robert Mager (1962), stated:

> Telling isn't the same as teaching. Though it is a remarkable accomplishment to have developed the skills and knowledge needed to be considered competent in one's craft, those skills are not the same as those needed for teaching that craft. Just as an ability to *make* a tuba is not the same as an ability to *play* one, an ability to *play* one is not the same as an ability to *teach* someone else to do likewise. (p. iii)

Mager is also credited with having commented, "If telling were teaching, we'd all be so smart we could hardly stand it." Clearly, we are not that smart even though there are many things we have been told each and every day of our lives.

Teaching is much more than telling (and then testing). Teaching requires the teacher to prepare the lesson so that information is presented and the students become actively involved in the subject. Decisions about what to teach and the order in which to teach it must be made; materials must be sequenced correctly; examples must be chosen carefully; and consequences must be implemented consistently to insure that the subject is learned. Information must be organized and presented in such a way that the chances of learning are improved for each and every individual student. The methods of teaching that are effective with individual children and are practical for the teacher are not always intuitive, and they are often difficult.

There are two excellent examples of teaching (rather than just telling and testing) that have been developed by behavior analysts. We will introduce them here but clarify each in detail later in this book. The first good example of teaching is a data-based instructional system referred to as Direct Instruction. **Direct Instruction** is a teaching method in which very specific instructional principles are used to design exactly how information is presented to the student. It shows teachers how to select examples and how to order those examples to insure that concepts are understood by the students. It shows the teacher what the students need to be doing and how to use consequences to insure that learning occurs. In other words, Direct Instruction shows exactly what teachers need to do to insure students learn specific academic material. Direct Instruction is an explicit method of explicit teaching, not just telling then testing. This is an important contribution, for as Delpit (1988/1993) noted, "unless one has the leisure of a lifetime of 'immersion' to learn . . . explicit presentation makes learning immeasurably easier" (p. 44). By specifying what teachers need to do, Direct Instruction solves the dilemma of other teaching methods. The sequences of education necessary for learning are not left to chance.

A second good example of teaching derived from behavior analysis is called Precision Teaching. **Precision Teaching** uses the methods of Direct Instruction and other effective procedures to present materials, but its major contribution is in the evaluation of learning by individual students. Evaluation in Precision Teaching includes a measure of accuracy and a measure of rate of responding. Students have not mastered material until they can respond correctly at a rate that is considered "fluent." Fluency has always been understood to be the measure of excellence in foreign languages. We now understand that fluency is equally important in understanding math or literature or science. If a student knows and understands some subject matter and knows or understands it with clarity and speed, we can claim that the student is competent. Memorizing and rote learning do not achieve fluency. Fluency comes from responding over and over in various situations. Fluency is a measure of rate typically calculated as number of responses per minute. We work with students until their "rate" of performance is high and their accuracy is unquestioned. Responses that students can produce at a high rate are likely to be remembered and applied long after the initial learning (Haughton, 1980).

Engelmann (1991) suggested five criteria to insure that teaching results in improved performance with individual students.

1. Field testing and revisions of draft versions of instructional programs before they are published.
2. Using information about child failure to modify teaching practices.
3. Testing and evaluating performance so it can be referenced to the curriculum.
4. Placing students at grade appropriate levels.
5. Training and monitoring teacher performance. (pp. 297-298)

We will examine issues relating to these five criteria. Later chapters will explore in detail many other issues in behavior analysis and education. Our goal will be to work toward education and schooling for the next century that accomplishes what Skinner (1968) explained.

There is a simple job to be done . . . The necessary techniques are known . . . We are on the threshold of an exciting and revolutionary period, in which the scientific study of man will be put to work in man's best interests. Education must play its part. It must accept the fact that a sweeping revision of educational practices is possible and inevitable. When it has done this, we may look forward with confidence to a school system which is aware of the nature of its tasks, secure in its methods, and generously supported by the informed and effective citizens whom education itself will create. (p. 28)

Through the remainder of this book, we will elaborate on these issues and document how behavior analysis can assist education and schooling to meet the challenges. The next chapter presents an introduction to four conceptual approaches that characterize current educational theory. This is followed by a brief overview of schools and schooling from the one-room school house of 19th Century American education to the larger more comprehensive schools of today. Chapter 4 introduces the reader to six instructional strategies based on behavior analysis while Chapter 5 presents a behavior-analytic design for classroom management which includes implementing effective teaching practices, arranging a classroom that supports appropriate behavior, and applying consequences. Chapter 6 provides the reader with detailed instructions for collecting data to assess performance and for using the assessments to guide further instruction. A brief history of teacher education is presented in Chapter 7 along with an examination of typical teacher education programs and how an emphasis on behavior analysis might change these programs. Chapter 8 summarizes reasons why we haven't reached excellence in education and what behavior analysts need to do now.

Annotated Bibliography

Engelmann, S., (1992). *War against the schools' academic child abuse.* Portland, OR: Halcyon House.

Presents a clear picture of why schools are failing, and offers specific instructions on how to effectively challenge school board policies and school practices that are not supported by research findings.

Glickman, C. D. (1993). *Renewing America's schools: A guide for school-based action.* San Francisco: Jossey-Bass.

Informs school personnel and the general public of ways to improve our schools and system of education. To reform education we must reconfigure schools to enable students to achieve in our modern world, incorporate society's democratic principles into school governance, and engage students in learning activities associated with authentic issues of life.

Graham, P. A. (1992). *S.O.S.: Sustain our schools.* New York: Hill & Wang.

Focuses on the types of reform that can begin in schools immediately. These include strengthening relationships between public school faculty and higher education professors, increasing interactions between schools and businesses, limiting the number of hours that public school students are allowed to work, increasing the availability of health care for students, making schools and school personnel more "family friendly" (e.g., more flexible with respect to family schedules), and increasing the use of technology in schools.

Murray, F. B. (1989). Explanations in education. In M. C. Reynolds (Ed.), *Knowledge base for the beginning teacher* (pp. 1-12). New York: Pergamon Press.

Suggests we define educational outcomes, practices, and types of learning by how they will be measured, and cautions us to be skeptical of instructional innovations based on theory that has not yet been demonstrated empirically effective.

Skinner, B. F. (1968). *The technology of teaching*. New York: Appleton-Century-Crofts.

Offers a timeless analysis of why our system of schooling is not efficiently producing the caliber of students desired.

Chapter 2

Introduction to Educational Theory

In this chapter we examine four conceptual approaches that characterize current educational theory: humanism, constructivism, developmentalism, and behaviorism. Each is presented as an overview of basic principles that guide educational practice. We clarify what one would expect to find in a classroom designed according to each of these philosophical orientations. Several themes (e.g., history effects, needs assessment, self concept, errors, practice, peers, active learning, child-centered learning, and evaluation) are addressed in each orientation. We then end our presentation of the philosophical orientations by examining the similarities and differences among the themes. It should be noted throughout that while the orientations are different the goal is the same.

> Because many of the opportunities open to a person hinge on educational accomplishment, the American goal of equal opportunity cannot be realized without effective schooling. Among the rights granted to American citizens should be the right to an effective education. (Barrett et al., 1991, p. 80)

It is likely that educators representing all philosophical orientations presented in this chapter would agree with this right. What varies among the philosophical orientations is a commitment to how this right can best be accomplished. In this chapter, as we examine philosophical orientations, the focus is not on a critique of these philosophical orientations, but on how each attempts to provide the right to effective education.

Our public schools are currently facilitating a move "toward two separate societies—one privileged and the other deprived" (Axelrod, 1993, p. 1). Educators from all philosophical orientations have approaches to educational practice they believe will help us correct such a separation. However, there is not much agreement about what the approaches should be, nor is there much attempt to cross philosophical orientations and learn from each other. Possibly we should be more tentative in our positions, willing to consider other orientations, and open to criticism of our own preferences. We should remember that all knowledge is provisional and must be continuously reconsidered.

All who want to grant students the right to effective education would do well to remember that what matters most is not our theoretical and methodological positions, but whether what we derive from these positions is effective practice in the schools (Neuringer, 1991). Theory is of little value if it doesn't result in effective school practices. Murray (1989) advises students preparing to teach "to adopt a skeptical view toward the claims of educational theorists and researchers because, while much is truly known, the discipline of education still is in its earliest period of development" (p. 11). To a large extent, educational theory has been and continues to be filled with fads and fashions that quickly come and go.

What Philosophy Will Guide Your School?

When you design your school will you be guided by a theory or by the effectiveness of the educational practices in teaching all children, in providing safe schools, and in developing healthy self concepts? If your school accomplishes the above, will the theory that drove the practices matter? Is it possible that the practices will come from more than one theory? Will you discard effective practices because the theory they are based on is currently not the most popular theory?

Humanism

The essence of humanism manifested in education is a rational method of inquiry which assumes that knowledge results from human analysis of human observation, that knowledge (information) is a discrete, selected portion of reality, and that it is meaningful only to those who understand its context. (Davis, 1993, p. 155)

Clearly, then, it matters little what information is presented in a humanistic classroom. It will have no meaning until *the learner* gives it meaning. Further, the learner can only give it meaning based on the context in which the learner considers the information. The teacher may tell students water covers 75% of the earth, but as students reflect on that information and come to "know" it, what they come to understand will vary with the context in which they put it. Their only choice is to put it in a familiar context. Possibly, while the teacher is telling students that water covers 75% of the earth, one student is picturing the Atlantic Ocean where she vacations every summer, while another student is picturing a lake where he and his friends skate in winter, and yet another student is picturing the pond where she and her grandfather frequently fish.

According to the humanistic approach, learning is primarily the result of reflection on personal experiences (Kramlinger & Huberty, 1990). Students' personal experiences are the histories they bring to the classroom, these are valued and provide much of the substance for learning. Therefore, when students arrive in the humanistic classroom, teachers do not assess students' needs in terms of skill development, but rather try to determine what students bring to the learning situation that they can use for reflection. Teachers in the humanistic classroom can then respond to students' needs by allowing students to reflect on personal experiences as a means of addressing their own needs (Alam, 1983).

This is often accomplished through **discovery learning**. Discovery learning occurs when students have hands-on experiences with materials and information that allow the students to come to their own understanding of a phenomenon. Often, discovery learning is done in centers where there is a problem to solve and materials available for experimenting so that students can solve the problem. This can be done independently or cooperatively. "The premise of discovery learning is that the information pupils discover for themselves will be learned easier and remembered longer than information acquired in some other way" (Murray, 1989, p. 9). What they discover is guided by the learning centers available in the classroom and by the personal histories students bring to those learning centers. It will not be important or expected, then, that all students come away with the same discoveries. Their discoveries will be the meanings only the students can give to the information initially provided.

This approach requires students to study the human condition (Gregor, 1981) in an educational climate in which students and teachers are seen as equals and treat each other respectfully (Kramlinger & Huberty, 1990). Teachers are not authority figures, but partners in learning. Everyone's experiences are valued in the humanistic classroom and everyone is a partner in the learning process. Such an environment allows and encourages students to study the human condition.

Humanism teaches values and attempts to improve self-concept (Jackard, 1983). "Values involve the 'why' choices in life—the reasons behind the actions people take to achieve their purposes" (Jackard, 1983, p. 20). According to the humanist, a value is a motivator that prompts people to behave in particular ways because of their life experiences. It is not so much what you believe or what you would do in a particular situation, but "why" you would behave this way. The concern is that many people are sure that what they say and do is right, appropriate, correct, or acceptable, but most have never thought about "why" they think it is right, appropriate, correct, or acceptable. It is this "why" that learners come to know through reasoning and problem solving. In the process students come to clarify their own values (Mills, 1985).

Working within a basic premise of humanism that by nature humans are good (Alam, 1983), learners find that their values are good values. All of us already have values we often just have not reflected upon them. We do something in a particular way because we believe it is right, probably because someone taught us to do it that way, or maybe that is the only way we have ever seen it done. When angry, some students may turn and walk away, some may try to reason, some may scream, and others may hit someone or something. The understanding from the humanistic perspective is that while some of these options are more acceptable in our society, none of the students is wrong. Each is only responding the way he or she knows how to respond in that situation. Therefore, even if the behavior is inappropriate, the child is not bad or wrong. The child is being guided by his/her values.

All of what we do is guided by our values. Therefore, it is important that we clarify those values. Once the values are clarified, students may begin to realize that those values were learned and can be changed if we choose to change them. This gives control to the students, enhancing their self-esteem, that is, how they feel about themselves and the choices they make. Teachers in the humanistic classroom are careful to foster the development of self-esteem. They do this by beginning with the notion that the students' values are good and by communicating this notion to the students. They further the development of self-esteem by addressing the students' needs, not the teachers' predetermined objectives. If I am the student and the teacher is addressing my needs, my needs must be important. This helps to develop my self-esteem by validating where I am in my development.

According to humanists, education should be used to help "achieve the utmost development of equality and opportunity in economic, political, and cultural life" (Mills, 1985, p. 109). This is accomplished by developing self-esteem and by encouraging students to read, think, and reflect for themselves. Students are encouraged to pass up textbooks for original writings (Stone, 1988). They do not accept as fact what someone says or writes, but rather must reflect upon readings and constantly question beliefs and convictions, even their own (Mills, 1985). The purpose of education is to help students become all that they are capable of becoming (Stone, 1988) and students must take the responsibility for this through their reading, questioning, and reflecting. This shifts the responsibility for learning from the teacher to the students.

Teachers serve as models for clarifying values and for questioning through their own reading, questioning, and reflecting. The excellent teachers from a humanistic perspective are passionate about teaching, often feeling that teaching is their calling (Goodwin, 1987). They approach teaching with an infectious excitement for developing critical thinking, judgment, and creativity so that students begin to understand the conditions under which learning occurs, and they become able to distinguish important factors from those that are unimportant (Davis, 1993).

This kind of learning requires considerable effort on the part of the learners who are involved in the teaching/learning process from the very beginning when they help to plan the objectives and lessons (Kramlinger & Huberty, 1990). The methods and curriculum are student-oriented (Mills, 1985), beginning with what the students bring to the class and continuing from there to respond to the students' needs. Teachers ask questions to help students solve their own problems or come to their own solutions. These questions are open-ended; that is, they do not have correct and incorrect responses. They are asked in an attempt to help students reflect on their previous learning and personal experiences.

Students bring much knowledge with them into the classroom. The teacher asks questions that stimulate learners to use this knowledge along with new experiences so that they can make new associations from prior knowledge. The teacher's job, then, is "to extract lessons from the learner's own insight and experience–like drawing water from a well" (Kramlinger & Huberty, 1990, p. 42). This is very different from teachers trying to put information into students' heads. For the humanist, this is not possible because the only real learning that occurs, occurs when we discover understandings, connections, and associations for ourselves.

Motivation is internal; the reward for learning is the learning itself. Children typically start school with a strong desire to learn and to know–to make sense out of their experiences. Humanistic education takes advantage of this desire to know and nurtures it by encouraging children to understand their experiences in their own ways, through their own means. It is part of validating who the child is and how the child thinks. When internal motivation is fostered, there is no need for external motivation; there is no threat that when the external motivation is no longer available students will stop learning.

The humanistic classroom is guided by the belief that we are all capable of solving our own problems through reasoning and problem solving (Mills, 1985). Therefore, teachers must allow students to choose their own problems to solve and they must nurture the skills necessary to do so. If students learn to reason and to solve problems they are prepared to be lifelong learners—they have accomplished the goal of a humanistic education.

> If the ordinary person is to live a life that allows the fullest realization of his potential as a human being, that prepares him for immersion into the mainstream of our cultural heritage, that equips him for genuine decision-making on fundamental social and moral questions, and that, above all, makes possible a genuine community—then that person must receive a humanistic education. (Gregor, 1981, p. 208)

Humanism is not currently a driving force in elementary education. It was quite popular in the 1970s and provided educational practices such as learning centers and discovery learning. Today, if one is to see a classroom guided by humanistic principles one will probably have to study high school and college classrooms. In these classrooms, some readings may be assigned by the teacher while others may be identified by the student. To the extent possible they will be primary source readings and not textbooks. Readings will provide focal points for discussions among students and teachers. Teachers will not have definitive answers, only guiding questions so that students can come to their own understandings. Students may be found working cooperatively in small groups and coming to some agreed upon understanding of what they are reading. Through this process students learn that their understandings are always open to other interpretations and they are capable of, and responsible for, those understandings. A humanistic classroom emphasizes free inquiry, reasoning, and problem solving (Mills, 1985).

A Humanistic School?

Does the humanistic classroom sound like the kind of classroom you would want in your school? Will you want it at every level, or only at the high school and college level? Will it be important that students come to the humanistic classroom with a certain set of skills that allow for free inquiry, reasoning, and problem solving? What are those skills? Where, when, and how will students learn them?

Constructivism

There is a formal knowledge base that can and should be an important influence on a preservice or beginning teacher's conceptions of learning and instruction.... "Constructivist" theories of learning and instruction are the centerpiece of this knowledge base, at least at this point in time. (Anderson, 1989, p. 85)

Constructivism is currently a dominant theory in teacher education and in educational practices. However, there is much disagreement among constructivists as to what is actually meant by constructivism (O'Loughlin, 1992). While educators are still coming to terms by what is meant by constructivism, there are some generally agreed upon themes of constructivism. The major theme of constructivism is that "learning is best described not as a process of assimilating knowledge but as one of constructing mental models" (Nickerson, 1988, p. 5). The issue is not whether it is better to learn through constructing our own knowledge than through taking in and storing knowledge provided by others. The constructivist argument is that constructing is what we *do* when we learn and that the learning environment must support that construction (Perkins, 1991). It does not matter what knowledge/information is presented by others, what the students come away with is not *that* knowledge, but their construction of a mental model—that mental model belongs to the students, it is their knowledge. It may or may not resemble the knowledge presented in the learning situation.

The reason the students' knowledge may not resemble the knowledge presented in the learning situation is because the students' knowledge is a result of the interactions of what's in the learning situation with the students' innate abilities. Truths cannot be offered in the environment for students to take in and make their own because "we cannot put ideas in students' heads, they will and must construct their own meanings" (Wheatley, 1991, p. 10). What students construct will be driven primarily by two things—what they bring to the learning situation, and the learning experience itself. "New meanings are created (constructed) *by the learner within the context of her or his current knowledge*" (Poplin, 1988, p. 404). What students bring to the learning situation is a history much like the history that students bring to the humanistic classroom. This history, once again, provides a context for the current experience. The only difference between humanism and constructivism on this point is that constructivists talk of constructing mental models.

All learners bring a specific set of past experiences to any new learning situation. The past experiences have helped the learners create particular understandings of reality and these current understandings guide the construction of new understandings in the new learning experience. One cannot assume that if 25 students are all put in the same learning environment they will all have the same learning experience. The experience that each student has will be driven by individual past experiences and understandings. Therefore, these students who were all put in the same learning environment will not learn the same thing. Each will construct a mental model based on his or her understandings at the time of the learning experience. "A focus on student thinking or sense making is the defining feature of this approach" (Prawat, 1992, p. 364).

This sense making is the result of assimilation and accommodation. When students **assimilate**, they fit their new experiences into their current mental models. When they **accommodate**, they must change their current mental models to make sense of the new experience. For example, let's suppose that Avi is two years old and has an understanding of balls, houses, cars, families, and many other concepts. One day Avi is looking at a picture book and sees an igloo—something she has never seen before. If she decides this is a ball, she simply fits, or assimilates, the concept of igloo into her existing mental model of balls. However, from social interactions with others, such as siblings or parents, Avi may learn that the igloo is a type of house. When this happens, she changes her mental model of houses to accommodate igloos as another type of house.

As humans, we have a basic tendency to try to make sense out of our experiences. Therefore, when we experience something that does not easily fit our current understandings of the world, we are pushed to make sense out of it and as a result we begin to change our understandings.   Prior knowledge determines whether the new experience will put the student in a state of **cognitive conflict** which occurs when we experience something we cannot understand. Experiences that result in cognitive conflict for some will not have the same effect for others. Learning occurs only for those students who experience cognitive conflict. In resolving the conflict, students construct new knowledge—their knowledge.

"There is no shared reality" (Merrill, 1991, p. 46). Therefore, in the constructivist classroom it is inappropriate to look for small unlearned subskills to be taught individually. Instead, the teacher in the constructivist classroom encourages problem-centered learning, which includes tasks, groups, and sharing. The tasks are problematic for the children given their current repertoires. These tasks are completed in small group situations, allowing students to learn from each other and to push each other into new states of cognitive conflict while simultaneously facilitating the resolution of that conflict. Finally, students come together in a large group to share their conclusions.

The teacher is nonjudgmental and if there are disagreements, students must work out the differences and arrive at a consensus. The goal in the constructivist classroom is to show students "how to construct plausible interpretations of their own, using the tools that we have provided" (Cunningham, 1991, p. 16). They do this by taking in some whole, which they break into parts to try to make sense of, and then build back into their own new whole (Poplin, 1988). An example of this may be seen when the teacher "teaches" latitude and longitude. Montell, a student present for the lesson, understands every word spoken by the teacher and every word read in the book so that at the end of class feels he understands latitude and longitude—the whole that he took in during class. The next day, Sally, who was absent for the latitude and longitude lesson, asks Montell to explain what she missed. In trying to explain, it becomes clear to Montell that he didn't really understand the lesson. He then tries to understand by breaking the lesson down into its component parts—what is meant by each term, how each is measured, how each is read, what each is used for, etc. Through this process, Montell comes to understand these concepts better and begins to build a new whole, that is, a new understanding of latitude and longitude. This new whole is a new mental model; it is equal to more than the sum of the parts that he began to understand one at a time.

Activities in a constructivist classroom typically place heavy cognitive demands on the learners as they must face the inconsistencies between their current understandings and what they are contacting in the learning environment. To come to some new understanding, learners must compare and contrast current understandings with new information. It is accomplished in the constructivist classroom by incorporating authentic learning activities as much as possible. This is how students are taught to use the tools that experts in the field typically use in real life learning situations. In an elementary school classroom the problem may be a class party the students want to have. This provides many opportunities for authentic applications of math. When students are left to decide for themselves what food to have, how much they will need, how they will get the food, how much money they will need to collect, how they will collect it, and when they need the money so they can purchase the food, they will not only use their math skills but also cooperative learning skills.

In a constructivist classroom, collaborative activities allow students to test their understandings by sharing and negotiating those understandings with their peers. With such a process, the outcomes of learning will not be known in advance and therefore one would not expect specific learning objectives to be very useful. "Knowledge is a dialect process the essence of which is that individuals have opportunities to test their constructed ideas on others, persuade others of the virtue of their thinking, and be persuaded" (Cognition and Technology Group at Vanderbilt, 1991, p. 16).

However, constructivists caution that some areas of school curriculum may not be suitable for a constructivist approach. For example, phonics as a reading skill, basic operations in math, motor skills such as typing, fundamental concepts in science, and facts in social studies are not considered suitable topics for the constructivist classroom (Molenda, 1991). Constructivists do not focus on things like number facts and spelling, instead they "focus on higher level concepts such as conservation of number or thematic maturity" (Poplin, 1988, p. 409). The intent is for students to grasp the big picture and only then to work towards understanding all the pieces that make up that picture.

For example, in elementary school, constructivists suggest that we wait until students can write the equivalent of five sentences and in secondary school we wait until students can consistently write a 200 word piece in class before we teach grammar and parts of a sentence (Poplin, 1988). In the constructivist classroom, errors are an important part of the learning process. It is in making errors that students realize shortcomings in their understandings, that is, they see the need to construct new knowledge.

The teacher's role in the constructivist classroom is a challenging one. What is in students' minds determines what new information students will learn and how they will learn it (Poplin, 1988). Therefore, teachers must begin by learning what students already know and how they know it. The teacher must determine the **level of actual development** and the **level of potential development**. The level of actual development is what students can do independently. It is something that could be determined by performance on a standardized test. The level of potential development is what students are capable of doing with assistance, that is, if they had someone to model the activity for them or to walk them through the process they would be able to do it, but they cannot yet do it on their own. **The zone of proximal development** is between the level of actual development and the level of potential development. One of the teacher's goals is to provide experiences within the learner's zone of proximal development.

If experiences are geared toward the learner's actual development, the learner is not likely to experience the cognitive conflict necessary for learning to occur. Similarly, if the experience is beyond the learner's level of potential development, the learner is not likely to experience cognitive conflict and even if the conflict is experienced the learner is not expected to be able to learn from the experience. Therefore, experiences are offered within the zone of proximal development and assistance is provided so the learner can be successful. This assistance is called **scaffolding.** Scaffolding is providing any assistance necessary for the learner to be successful. This often occurs in the form of modeling, asking leading questions, or answering questions the learner may have.

Scaffolding can be provided in **reciprocal teaching**. Reciprocal teaching occurs when a more experienced learner guides a more naive learner. The experienced learner's zone of actual development must be at or beyond the naive learner's potential development. Often the experienced learner introduces the naive learner to the tools used by different groups to understand the problem. For example, in studying the economy, the experienced learner may introduce the use of economic indices and trade balances as used by the economist or social class and educational level as used by the sociologist. In this way, the teacher and all more experienced learners are coaches.

All good coaches begin by finding out the players' current level of athletic ability. They must consider issues of physical development such as speed, endurance, and agility, as well as issues of skill development such as dribbling, passing, and scoring. Once the level of athletic ability is determined, the coach puts slightly higher physical demands on the players so that they can work towards and achieve a higher level of performance. This is done both with drills and with scrimmages. Coaches know that if they want players to improve, players should be playing with others who are currently more advanced. The players are being held in their "zone of proximal development." From interaction with the more advanced players they acquire the tools to improve their own play.

Much like players on a playing field for whom advancement will occur only when they actually engage in the play, students in the classroom must actively engage in the experiences for learning to occur. The most precise, exact instructions of how to shoot a foul shot will not result in perfect shooting of foul shots unless the learner practices the shots. Similarly, the learner in the classroom must be actively engaged in learning. "Regardless of how well the ideas are presented, they will not be understood unless students make personal use of them to understand important aspects of their world" (Prawat, 1992, p. 379). However, while active responding is necessary, it is not sufficient for an effective constructivist classroom. Teachers must guard against setting up learning environments in which the teachers know the answer and then guide the students to respond in a way that leads students to construct the same understanding. For constructivism to work in the classroom, students are not to construct what the teachers and/or text direct. Instead, the learner must be "allowed the space to play an active role in developing a personally constructed understanding of the author's or teacher's message through a process of dialogic interchange" (O'Loughlin, 1992, p. 813).

Many of the experiences in the constructivist classroom focus on social interaction. Everyone in the classroom learns from everyone else. This can only occur if there is a sharing of ideas in a nonjudgmental environment. When students express their ideas several things happen. The students' efforts to make sense of the content are supported, teachers are given the opportunity to assess students' current thinking, and all students in the classroom are presented with an experience that either fits their current understandings of things or challenges them to construct new understandings based on their current understandings. "Constructivist-oriented teachers are constantly trying to connect new learning experiences to students' current knowledge and to their present interests and concerns" (Poplin, 1988, p. 410).

Evaluating learning is probably the most difficult aspect of the constructivist classroom (Jonassen, 1991). Given that students are constructing their own knowledge and that what they construct is guided by the mental models or understandings they bring to the learning situation, all students are not expected to come to the same understandings. "There is not a correct meaning that we are striving for" (Duffy & Jonassen, 1991, p. 8). Therefore, it is unreasonable to assume that the learning could be evaluated with some paper and pencil test administered to all students. Instead, evaluation, like the learning in a constructivist classroom, must be authentic.

To evaluate knowledge construction, teachers must evaluate students' ability to solve relevant problems. Solving relevant problems provides authentic evaluation. An authentic evaluation of reading would be for students to go to the library to find information they need to complete a project, read that information, and comprehend it in a way that allows them to finish the project. This is very different from a timed reading comprehension test in which students have a limited time to read a short passage—usually one for which they have little prior knowledge (or a mental model) and then answer questions about the passage. The answers are of no interest to the students because they meet no intellectual need at the time. What is authentic is what is important to the students and what is currently needed for the students to solve their problems.

Evaluation is not something to be done at the end of instruction, it is a continual process. Through continuous evaluation, teachers can identify "partial understandings en route to true comprehension, or incorrect knowledge and misunderstandings that will lead to further learning problems" (Harris & Pressley, 1991, p. 393). During this evaluation process the teacher is not judgmental because there are no "wrong" answers. Students' answers are accurate reflections of students' current understandings.

Suppose, then, that Ms. Ross asks Gordon "What is 1 + 2?" and Gordon responds "5." Is Gordon wrong? The answer is incorrect, but Gordon's thinking is not wrong. That is, Gordon's response is a result of Gordon's current understanding. This information is used by Ms. Ross to determine what Gordon's mental model for addition may be. If Ms. Ross can understand Gordon's current mental model, she has completed an appropriate evaluation of Gordon's learning. This information is then used to guide instruction within Gordon's zone of proximal development.

It should be noted, however, that Ms. Ross would probably not ask for solutions to an assortment of math problems on a sheet of paper. It is more likely in the constructivist classroom that Ms. Ross might say to Gordon, "When you get your paper please get paper for Demarcus and Theresa also." Ms. Ross would watch to see how many pieces of paper Gordon gets. If he does not get three, Ms. Ross needs to figure out why, so that she can understand Gordon's current mental model for addition.

Assessing students' ability to construct plausible solutions to authentic problems can be very subjective evaluation. Therefore, it is determined from many sources of information typically compiled in a **portfolio** of products. A portfolio includes samples of students' work as well as students' reflections on their work and their understandings at different points along the way. This shows the progress students have made and provides a clear picture of what their current thinking is and how they arrived at that thinking.

The constructivist classroom is designed to allow problem solving through the use of tools that experts in the field may use to solve the problems. Remember, it is not designed to teach decoding in reading or possibly any specific reading skills or math facts. You are not likely therefore to find reading groups and math groups or drill and practice in the constructivist's classroom. Rather, there will be primarily large group instruction or presentation of problems that are then solved by students in small cooperative groups. The reading instruction is likely to be **whole language instruction**. Whole language instruction is a philosophy of teaching reading that encourages the teaching of reading as a communicative process rather than as a set of discrete unconnected skills such as decoding, spelling, and grammar. The premise is that we do not learn to speak by being taught the rules of speaking, but rather learn to speak by being spoken to and by trying out our speaking skills. We learn the rules after we learn how to speak. If it is possible to learn to speak this way it should also be possible to learn to read this way.

Therefore, a classroom in which whole language instruction is being utilized will be a classroom rich in print materials. Typically these materials will include trade books and good literature rather than controlled readers that have little or no meaning to the students' experiences. Teachers read to students often, students follow along, and eventually students begin to read for themselves. Along the way if they need assistance in decoding a word the teacher may teach that skill then. However, many teachers who use whole language do not teach decoding skills because it is thought to be an unnatural way to read. Instead the word is often deciphered by fitting it into the context of the material being read.

One is also likely to find frequent writing in a classroom using whole language instruction. Students learn to read by writing and they learn to write by reading. The writing is focused on communicating ideas and not on the mechanics of writing such as spelling and grammar. Students are taught these mechanics later as needed. Math is likely to be centered around problem solving with manipulatives students may use in an assortment of ways to solve the relevant problems. When students are studying science they are likely to be solving science problems using tools a scientist would use. Teachers, knowing students' current mental models, design science problems that are just past students' current understandings, so that students will realize the limitations of their understandings. This realization of limitations is the push to solve the new problem, which is accomplished using the tools of the scientist provided by the teacher. This sounds like an exciting classroom, but how effective is it?

Given that constructivism is currently the dominant force in teaching (Anderson, 1989) one would expect that there is evidence of its effectiveness. However, "as compelling as the arguments of the constructivists may be, there is no empirical evidence in support of their assumptions, and little empirical evidence in support of the instructional design propositions derived from these assumptions" (Merrill, 1991, p. 51). Because most classroom instruction stresses prespecified information or knowledge and the constructivist classroom stresses learning how to learn, an empirical test that compares the effectiveness of the two types of classrooms would be extremely difficult (Duffy & Bednar, 1991).

The implication is that not only is there currently no empirical evidence of the effectiveness of a constructivist approach in the classroom, but there is not likely to be any in the near future because empirical evidence currently does not seem plausible. Rather than conducting research to empirically validate the approach, constructivists "prefer a developmental model where practice in the field is constantly evaluated in a formative sense and the results are applied to examine and adapt the model in a continuous cycle" (Duffy & Bednar, 1991, p. 15).

A Constructivist School?

Is this what you will choose for your school? If you do, will you conduct research on the effectiveness of the practices derived from the theory? What will you do, if in your evaluation of its effectiveness, you learn it did not provide effective education for all your students? Maybe you will save educational practices from constructivist theory until after students become fluent in reading and math to facilitate the use of the tools provided by the experts. If that is the case, maybe you will want to consider developmentalism, which focuses almost exclusively on the early childhood years and then move to constructivism.

Developmentalism

Developmentalism is a philosophy that is "being strongly promoted by all national education associations that have published position statements on early childhood education" (Greenberg, 1990, p. 74). **Developmentalism**, as it applies to education, refers to what is called the developmentally appropriate curriculum and addresses kindergarten through third grade. To be developmentally appropriate when making curriculum decisions, educators review all that has been learned about child development and consider this information in deciding what, when, and how children will learn (Bredekamp, 1991).

In the developmentally appropriate classroom, children are free to choose what they will master and are encouraged to explore and master curricula in many areas (Greenberg, 1990). This means the teacher does not decide the entire curriculum, but allows and encourages the students to decide part of the curriculum. Beyond choosing some of the curriculum, students are encouraged to find their area of interest and to pursue it. These are classrooms that are clearly child-centered rather than teacher-directed. They are also classrooms in which learning is active rather than passive. To be developmentally appropriate "children should manipulate real objects and learn through hands-on, direct experiences rather than be expected to sit and listen for extended periods of time" (NAEYC, 1988, p. 65).

As one might expect in a child-centered classroom, planned and spontaneous individual and small group activities are common. There may be two or three students who discover a common interest and together they work to learn about this interest and to share what they learn. Students then have rich opportunities for learning from peers rather than only from the teacher. This also gives the children an opportunity to be both student and teacher. "In the developmental classroom, independent choice, responsibility for self, finding and solving self-defined problems, and growth through a significant amount of challenging interaction with peers form the bases of the child's daily experience" (Smith, 1990, p. 13).

Developmentally appropriate education takes "advantage of the child's natural abilities, interests, and enthusiasm for learning" (NAEYC, 1988, p. 64). Children start school with a natural curiosity. When the curriculum dictates a set of objectives to be mastered by all children by a certain point in time, many children are robbed of their natural curiosity and their need to know. In the developmentally appropriate classroom children's natural curiosity and need to know are nurtured—they form the basis for learning.

Cognitive, affective, and psychomotor domains are all integrated within a developmentally appropriate classroom. That is, emphasis is placed not only on developing the intellect, but also on social skills and motor skills (NAEYC, 1988). Children need social skills to get along with classmates and to learn how to be a part of a community. Without these skills children may find themselves unable to interact successfully with their peers. This quickly results in negative feelings towards self and before long interferes with cognitive development. Similarly, children need to develop motor skills to feel competent. However, these skills should not be taught separate from other skills. Children use motor skills to learn cognitive skills and they learn social skills while they are learning cognitive skills. Cognitive, affective, and psychomotor skills are all integrated in the developmentally appropriate classroom.

Within the cognitive domain, academic skills are also integrated rather than taught as discrete subjects. In the developmentally appropriate classroom, much curriculum is centered around themes rather than around subject areas. That is, rather than having a time for reading, a time for social studies, and a time for math, all content areas are integrated into a theme. The theme, for example, may be rain forests.

In developing this theme and learning about rain forests, students will be developing academic skills from many subject areas. They will be doing some reading to learn about rain forests and in so doing will be developing and improving reading comprehension skills. The teacher may also be reading to the students or students may be reading to each other. In these situations, students are developing listening skills. If all the reading material is not provided for the students, they will be going to the library to find books that will provide information about rain forests. In so doing, students are learning library skills. Learning about rain forests may result in both a written report and an oral presentation. In writing the report, students will write rough drafts, they will edit, and they will rewrite. They may do the editing for themselves first, then it may be done by other students or by the teacher. In the rewriting from the edited drafts students will learn grammar, punctuation, sentence structure, and spelling—many language arts skills. They have the benefit of doing this with a piece of text that is important to them. They may be allowed, even encouraged, to construct the first draft in a way that permits them to focus on what they want to say rather than on the mechanics of the writing.

In their reading and research they will learn where rain forests are and this will provide important social studies skills, including map reading, and a picture of where rain forests are in relation to where they live. Learning about the people who live in the rain forests, what they eat, how they dress, and what their homes are like provides additional important social studies skills. Science skills are developed as students learn of plants and animals found in the rain forests and similarities among these plants and animals. Calculating amounts of rainfall in the rain forests and percentage of days it rains in the rain forest provides practice in math skills. Equally important may be that as students are learning interrelated content, they are also learning how to learn and learning that they are capable of learning things for themselves.

Learning to read is of little value unless students eventually read either for pleasure or for information. Knowing math facts is also of little value unless this knowledge can be put to use, as in calculating amounts of rainfall, differences in rainfall, and possibly percentage of days that it typically rains. Learning continents, oceans, and geographic locations is of little value unless it provides useful information about these things that students can use to solve problems that interest them. Science can easily become the learning of lists of plants and animals unless the learning is accomplished through themes that integrate science with other content areas. Finally, when academic skills are integrated, students begin to understand how knowing about almost anything requires one to consider all the aspects of what is to be learned. In the developmentally appropriate classroom, all subjects are integrated throughout the day. This integration of subject areas and domains contributes to the goal of helping children become lifelong learners.

"In the developmentally appropriate program, it's assumed that mastery in *all* areas of living, using *all* kinds of intelligences (musical intelligence, aesthetic intelligence, interpersonal intelligence, etc.) is valid and worthwhile" (Greenberg, 1990, p. 78). The actual content of this learning is whatever **schemes** children are constructing. Schemes are our understandings and they guide what we take from any new experience. "From a developmental perspective, knowledge is always a construction, inevitably reflecting the joint contributions of the subject and the object" (Elkind, 1989, p. 114). The subject is the learner. The learner brings a wealth of experiences that are understood in terms of other experiences and in terms of where the learner is developmentally. The object is the current experience for the learner. In this respect, developmentalism is much like humanism and constructivism.

The subject and the object are considered within the context of two types of knowledge—**fundamental knowledge** and **derived knowledge** (Elkind, 1989). Fundamental knowledge is what we construct for ourselves while derived knowledge is knowledge that has been constructed by others and is given to us second hand. Derived knowledge can be right or wrong, for example $2 + 2 = 4$ and not 5. However, fundamental knowledge cannot be wrong. It is always "right" in terms of where the learner is developmentally and what the learner is currently experiencing (Elkind, 1989).

An example of fundamental knowledge occurs when a five year old's grandparents visit and grandpa says to daddy "How are you, son?" The five year old will often argue saying "He's my daddy." The relationships may be clearly explained in words the five year old is familiar with in an attempt to pass on derived knowledge. However, in the end, the five year old may not believe or understand the relationships. To this five year old, daddy can only be daddy. It is the child's fundamental knowledge of this man he calls daddy and it is correct for the five year old's level of development. The developmentally appropriate approach does not deny the need for derived knowledge or the need to know facts; it only cautions that the derived knowledge should follow the fundamental knowledge. If in our teaching we can maintain curious active learners who are encouraged to use their fundamental knowledge, then through their active learning they can learn facts and ultimately become thinkers who are creative and critical.

"From a developmental perspective, the important task for educators is *matching curricula* to the level of children's emerging mental abilities" (Elkind, 1989, p. 114). Somewhere between the ages of 6 and 9 children move from the preoperational to the concrete operational stage of development. This move, like all developmental moves, brings with it new mental abilities. A major new ability is the mental manipulation of what exists in reality. In the preoperational stage, children can mentally represent what they experience, that is, they have words and pictures for things they have experienced. They can identify specific symbols as numbers and write the symbols if someone says the numbers. They cannot, however, mentally manipulate these numbers and their symbols. Therefore, one would not expect them to be able to do addition that requires them to carry a ten from the ones place to the tens place. In the concrete operational stage, children can mentally manipulate what exists in reality, and so it is only at this point that we should begin to provide problems that require borrowing and carrying in subtraction and addition. Even though they can mentally manipulate what exists in reality, they cannot yet mentally manipulate in the abstract. This ability is found in the formal operations stage when students can be expected to solve for an unknown.

"Curriculum materials should be introduced only after a child has attained the level of mental ability needed to master them" (Elkind, 1989, p. 114). When implementing a developmentally appropriate curriculum, it is likely that students will be successful because the curriculum is being matched to their developing mental abilities and current schemes. Students' success has far reaching implications not just for their present learning, but also for their future success and well-being. "A major cause of negative self-image for children this age is failure to succeed in school, for instance failing to learn to read 'on schedule' or being assigned to the lowest ability math group" (NAEYC, 1988, p. 67). In the developmentally appropriate classroom students do not face the possibility of being assigned to the lowest ability math group because there are no math groups. Similarly, it is not possible for them to fail to learn to read on schedule as there is not a predetermined schedule for learning to read. It is expected that all students will learn to read when they are ready. Rather than providing reading and math groups, children learn to read and to compute through their natural interactions in the environment. This is an environment that is rich in print materials, offers many hands-on opportunities to experience math, and eliminates the opportunity for failure.

Eliminating the opportunity for failure and providing an environment in which it does not matter *when* students are ready because what students need will be provided when they need it, allows children to develop a sense of competence.

Achieving these competencies leads to the development of self-esteem, which correlates with school success. "Self-esteem is generated in children in large part through the process of frequently meeting and mastering meaningful new challenges" (Greenberg, 1990, p. 76). Students easily meet and master meaningful new challenges when those challenges are developmentally appropriate.

However, what is developmentally appropriate is not consistent across a group of students the same age. In the developmentally appropriate classroom, consideration is also given to the individual. While there are chronological age ranges during which children enter new stages of development and develop specific mental abilities, individual children vary in the timing of their development. To be developmentally appropriate one must consider individual differences among children (Bredekamp, 1991). "A major premise of developmentally appropriate practice is that each child is unique and has an individual pattern and timing of growth, as well as individual personality, learning style, and family background" (NAEYC, 1988, p. 67). It is important that these differences are not seen as differences in ability but as differences in "*rates* of intellectual growth" (Elkind, 1989, p. 114). That being the case, we can assume that all children can learn and that all children will succeed if we present them with a curriculum that is appropriate for their developing mental abilities. Further, if they are not succeeding, it is because of a mismatch between students' developmental level and the level of development necessary for the experiences currently being offered in the classroom.

Developmentally appropriate instruction is not concerned just with what children *can* do or learn at a particular point in their development, but also with what is most appropriate for them to be doing at that time. "The developmental question is what is it that young children should do that best serves their development in the long term" (Katz, 1988, pp. 29-30). What best serves their development in the long run is that which feeds and does not weaken their disposition for learning. Children are developing dispositions at the same time they are developing skills. The concern is that in their learning of subjects such as reading, we do not destroy their desire to read. Being a competent reader who does not choose to read does a disservice to children in the long run. Children need skills and dispositions. The concern from a developmental perspective is that if we teach the skills too young, children will lose the dispositions. You can instruct young children in academics, such as phonics and counting, but that may not be reason enough for requiring it of them. "Just because children can do something when they are young does not mean they should do it" (Katz, 1988, p. 29).

It would be nice to end this section with an evaluation of developmentalism. Unfortunately, it would have to be speculation on our part as we could find no empirical evidence of the effectiveness or ineffectiveness of educational practices based on developmentalism. Without empirical evidence to the contrary, one might be wise to consider Stone's (1994) caution. "Educators who limit their interventions to those deemed developmentally appropriate are like physicians who forgo medications and surgery. They may do no harm, but neither do they confront any real educational challenges" (p. 58).

A Developmentalist School?

Is developmentalism the theory you will use as a guide for your school? Will you try to hire teachers who are well grounded in developmentalism? If students are not succeeding, will you assume that developmentally they are not ready for the instruction being offered? How will you help teachers and students make appropriate adjustments? Will you combine developmentalism with constructivism in your classrooms? If so, how will you integrate the two? Will you be guided by developmentalism in the early grades and then by constructivism in the intermediate grades? Do you expect any problems with such an arrangement?

Behaviorism

"Let's recognize the incredible potential for being intelligent and creative possessed by even the least impressive children, and with unyielding passion, let's pursue the goal of assuring that this potential becomes reality" (Engelmann & Carnine, 1982, p. 376). While this is the last sentence in their book *Theory of Instruction: Principles and Applications*, it is the starting point for behaviorism in the classroom. A basic assumption of behavioral education is that all children *can* learn and if they are not learning, there is something wrong with the instruction, not with the learner. "Mistakes the learner makes are perfectly lawful and are caused by the communication, not by aberrations of the learner" (Engelmann & Carnine, 1982, p. 370). These communications, of course, are outside of the learner, in the learner's environment.

From this view, what the learner learns is determined by the environment. The teacher's responsibility is to arrange the environment in such a way that students learn what they need to learn from it. What students need to learn is clearly decided in advance as the behavior analyst begins with a set of learning objectives for the students. Based on these objectives, the environment is arranged in a way that it will communicate concepts and skills to the students. Therefore, how teachers arrange the environment is the key to effective instruction.

Actually, the environment is the key to all learning whether inside or outside the classroom and whether the behavior is appropriate or not. Let's look at an example of learning by looking at a typical behavior of some preadolescent boys. These boys can often be seen with their friends making the most offensive noises imaginable. When they do this they often slap each other on the back, laugh, and generally behave as if they are all pretty "cool." Now let's imagine any of these boys at home eating dinner with his family and emitting any one of the offensive noises. What is likely to happen? Are parents likely to slap him on the back and laugh with him? Probably not, rather they are likely to at least ignore the sounds and possibly scold their son for making such noises at the table.

Technically, for the behavior analyst, what happens is the boys learn to make their offensive noises in some situations and not in others. That is, being around peers is a sign to engage in these behaviors, and being around parents is a sign that says "better not do that now." Learning in the classroom occurs in the same way. We teach students signs for certain responses and when they make those responses in the presence of the signs, we send other signs that let the students know that this response is the correct response in this situation. Behaviorism explains effective educational environments through the use of Skinner's **three-term contingency**. The three-term contingency includes a sign (peers) that prompts a response (making offensive noises), and a consequence contingent upon that response (approval from peers). The consequences can be either reinforcing (approval from peers) or punishing (reprimand from parents). If the consequences are reinforcing, they strengthen or maintain the response they are contingent upon (making offensive noises) and if they are punishing, they weaken the response (making offensive noises) they are contingent upon.

In the presence of a particular sign, the learner makes a response and there are consequences. If the consequences are reinforcing, the learner is likely to make the same response in the presence of the same or similar sign in the future. If the consequences are punishing, the learner is not likely to make the same response in the presence of that sign in the future. The students learn to discriminate between signs (peers and parents) so that they make some responses in the presence of some signs and different responses in the presence of other signs. Therefore, the signs that prompt responses are called **discriminative stimuli** and the stimuli that reinforce or punish responses are called **consequating stimuli**.

Discriminative stimuli and consequating stimuli are both found in the environment and, to a large extent, they are things that the teacher can control. At its most basic level, if the student responds incorrectly—does not give the "correct" answer—it is not because there is something wrong with the student but because the appropriate discriminating and consequating stimuli have not been provided. Providing those correct stimuli become the key to providing effective education in the behavioral classroom. With this philosophy, "when students encounter difficulties, the locus of blame is placed on current instructional procedures or histories of instruction, not on the students or parents" (Greer, 1992, p. 66). It is an approach that holds teachers accountable to students and to their parents.

In the behavioral classroom one can expect to find clearly specified **learning objectives**. Learning objectives specify what students will be able to do and how well they will be able to do it given a particular set of circumstances. For example, an early learning objective may be for students to read a 16-word story at a pace of two seconds per word with no more than one error. Once learning objectives are specified, the teacher assesses prerequisite skills the learners bring to the learning environment. The focus is on assessing those skills that indicate a preparedness for the new objectives. With this information, teachers provide structured instructional activities that require a high degree of active responding. Their responding receives feedback in a timely manner and is continually assessed to guide instruction and eventually to assess for mastery of the objective (Heward, 1994). If students demonstrate mastery, they continue on with the next lesson. If when assessed, students do not demonstrate mastery, they engage in additional instruction and are reassessed until they demonstrate mastery.

It is not surprising that in an approach that holds the teacher accountable for student learning, the teacher has a great deal of control—teachers cannot be held responsible without being given control. Teachers can take both the responsibility for and the control of learning. Teachers do not control the environment students come from, the knowledge they bring with them, whether they had breakfast before school, or whether they will go home to an empty house after school. However, they do control the learning environment in the classroom.

> A learning environment is composed of (1) teachers and the repertoires they
> bring to the environment, (2) learners and the repertoires they bring to the
> environment, (3) curricular materials and instructional formats available to
> the environment; and (4) the physical structures and furnishings in the
> environment. Instructional conditions created by various arrangements of
> the parts of the learning environment either establish, strengthen, maintain,
> or weaken the learners' repertoires. (Tucci & Hursh, 1994, p. 260)

Behavioral educators arrange their learning environments so that students are likely to respond correctly and to have that response reinforced. If it happens that students respond incorrectly, there is no reinforcement. When there is reinforcement for a response, that response eventually diminishes.

The only way to know if responses are maintained or diminished is to keep accurate measures of performance. Keeping such measures is a fundamental feature of the behavioral classroom. Collecting and being guided by the data serve several functions. Possibly the most important function is to let teachers evaluate the effectiveness of the instruction. If the data indicate that students are not mastering the material, then clearly there is something wrong with the instruction. Maybe the step from what students know to what is being taught is too big with some important subskills missing. Once diagnosed, teachers can change the instruction to teach the subskills first. Another reason students may not be succeeding is because the instruction is not clear—there may not be enough examples, the examples may not clearly distinguish between positive and negative instances of the concept being taught, or there may not be enough practice. Each of these problems can be corrected by teachers because they understand the students are responding correctly based on their present repertoires and on what they are receiving from the environment. However, if the data indicate that students are mastering the material, teachers are fairly confident they have an effective strategy for these students and should continue using that strategy.

Another important reason for collecting data is to be able to communicate clearly with parents. This can be in a conference or in a written communication sent home. With data, teachers can show parents what students have been working on, what they have mastered, and what they may be having trouble mastering. When students are having trouble, the teacher should have plans to remedy this trouble and communicate that to the parents as well. Finally, when teachers make a regular practice of measuring behavior, those measures can be posted in the form of charts and/or graphs. Public posting can prompt students to work hard, and can reinforce their accomplishments.

The teacher's role in a behavioral classroom is clearly a challenging one, but it in no way diminishes the role of the students. The behavior component of the three-term contingency requires that students behave in ways that are observable and measurable. Students in the behavioral classroom engage in a great deal of **active responding**—responding that can be observed and measured.

When compared to teaching methods in which students passively attend and actively participate by infrequent responses, teaching strategies that increase the frequency with which each student makes academic responses during instruction have (1) consistently produced better performance on same-day, next-day, and follow-up tests of the content taught; (2) resulted in higher levels of on-task behavior (or conversely, reduced levels of off-task, disruptive, and "looking bored" behavior); and (3) been preferred by the vast majority of students over traditional methods of classroom participation. (Heward, 1994, pp. 315-316)

Active responding is often accomplished through **choral responding** or the use of **response cards**. When students engage in choral responding they are responding orally as a group so that if the teacher points to the word rabbit and says "read it the fast way," all students respond "rabbit." Response cards are cards that students write on. They are often made by laminating white poster board cut into 5 by 7 inch rectangles. When the teacher asks "what is 5+3" all students write the response on their response card and hold it up for the teacher to see.

Using choral responding and response cards, all students can respond each time. This results in a great deal of active responding from each student during instruction and "generates more learning" (Heward, 1994, p. 290). Additionally, active student responding allows the teacher to assess *during* the teaching rather than finding out at test time, *after* the teaching, that some students did not understand the material. It is not enough to ask students if they understand. Many students will simply nod because they really do understand it, or because they *think* they understand it although they really do not—they just do not realize yet that they do not understand it. Other students will nod because they do not understand it but they are not willing to make that public information. That is, they are sitting there assuming everyone else understands it so they will not admit they do not.

Teachers in a behavioral classroom do regular assessments of learning partly because they hold themselves accountable for student learning and because they know that if students are not learning with the current methods there are other effective methods available. Lindsley (1992) contends "effective educational methods are available. They have been available for a long time. They are mostly behavioral, structured, fast paced, and require a high proportion of regular daily practice" (p. 21). To many, that does not sound like much fun. There is a common belief today among many educators that learning should be "easy and fun. They do not realize that it is fluent performance–the result of learning–that is fun. The process of learning, of changing performance, is most often stressful and painful" (Lindsley, 1992, p. 23). While some students begin reading with little formal instruction in reading, they are the exception, not the rule. For most students reading needs to be taught carefully and systematically. There are also some people who, without formal instruction, after hearing music can play that music on the piano. However, most people who wish to learn to play the piano must be carefully and systematically taught. For most, "reading comes with a lot of reading practice" (Lindsley, 1992, p. 25) just as playing the piano comes with a lot of piano practicing.

It is common practice when teaching someone to play the piano to have the student practice scales over and over again. It is also common practice to teach the student the note-key associations. Much like different letters and different combinations of letters represent different sounds, different notes represent different keys that need to be played on the piano. There are only seven key names, A through G. However, which A or B or D is played depends on where the symbol is written on which staff. In the beginning, it is a note-key association that is being learned just as in beginning reading it is a letter-sound association that is being learned. In piano as in reading, learning is slow and controlled in the beginning until initial skills are practiced enough to make playing and reading automatic and efficient. Learning the notes is only the beginning of learning to play the piano, but it is an essential beginning. Learning the sounds to make when looking at written symbols in text is only the beginning of learning to read, but it is an essential beginning. This, of course, is not the only way to teach piano, just as teaching phonics is not the only way to teach reading. Regardless of the instructional approach, however, in both reading and piano it is practice that produces the fluent performer, which is the result of the learning and which is the part that is fun.

In a behavioral classroom one can expect to find a great deal of practice. Practice is often criticized as boring and ineffective in getting to more advanced learning, like problem solving and critical thinking. Lindsley (1992) points out however, that while educators may be opposed to practice in academics, they readily "accept the need for disciplined regular daily practice in the performing arts and in athletics" (p. 23). It is with much drill and practice that athletes and artists are eventually able to perform creatively and to solve the problem of the performance or the game. Lindsley (1992) goes on to suggest that the difference is often that teachers are not held as accountable as coaches. That is, we keep score in athletics and we do not in teaching. If the team does not perform well–win, the coach is readily replaced. If the students do not perform well–learn, the teacher is rarely replaced.

The teacher's responsibilities for arranging an environment that communicates content and skills, means not only setting up an environment that prompts frequent active responding from the students, but also one that responds to the students' responses. That is, what happens after the students respond is equally important in the behavioral classroom. Initially, teachers provide feedback for every response to avoid practicing of incorrect responses. Later, however, teachers require several responses before feedback. During this kind of practice, learners are trying to develop fluency (Heward, 1994).

Similarly, teachers begin with frequent **extrinsic reinforcement** that is gradually presented less frequently and ultimately replaced by **natural reinforcement**. Extrinsic reinforcement is often provided in the form of praise. For example, after reading correctly, the teacher may say "yes, good for you" or "correct, good job." Extrinsic reinforcement is typically controlled by another person, in this case, the teacher. Natural reinforcement is the reinforcement naturally available for a behavior. It is not controlled by another person, but is controlled by the behavior itself. It is often called intrinsic reinforcement or motivation. For example, natural or intrinsic reinforcement for reading is the information it makes available or the pleasure it provides. Unfortunately, these natural or intrinsic reinforcers for reading usually are not available until the student becomes a competent reader. In order to get the student to that point of competency, extrinsic reinforcement is provided.

It is important that this extrinsic reinforcement be provided in a way that does not decrease the intrinsic or natural reinforcement students are likely to experience from the behavior. Several studies have suggested that when extrinsic reinforcement is provided for a behavior, the natural or intrinsic reinforcement for engaging in the behavior is lost once the extrinsic reinforcement is removed. For example, if students frequently choose to read during free time, we believe there is something intrinsically reinforcing about reading. If we design a program in which we reward these students for reading and later remove the reward, the students are less likely to read. This suggests a serious concern for using extrinsic reinforcement.

While it is true that extrinsic rewards *may* reduce intrinsic motivation, Dickinson (1989) and Eisenberger and Cameron (1996) clarify conditions under which this is likely to occur and conditions under which this is not likely to occur. Extrinsic rewards are likely to reduce intrinsic motivation when those rewards are provided simply for engaging in an activity or for completing an activity regardless of the quality or quantity of the student's performance. Intrinsic motivation is also reduced when the rewards are not reinforcing to the child. By definition, reinforcers are stimuli that increase the probability of the behavior they are contingent upon. Rewards may or may not increase the probability of the behavior they are contingent upon. When rewards that are not reinforcing are used as extrinsic reinforcement, one can expect a decrease in intrinsic motivation in the future. However, when the rewards are reinforcing, one does not find a decrease in intrinsic motivation after extrinsic reinforcement.

When extrinsic reinforcement is implemented the way it was designed to be implemented by behavior analysts, one does not find a reduction in intrinsic motivation after extrinsic reinforcement. When students' performance is reinforced, not just rewarded, contingent upon a particular standard or quality of performance that students are able to achieve, there is no decrease in the intrinsic value of the behavior. For example, if extrinsic reinforcement is provided for reading at a predetermined rate with a predetermined limited number of errors within the students' competency level, the students will increase the frequency with which they read because reading is being reinforced. They will become better readers as a result of increased reading practice. The intrinsic or natural reinforcement for reading will not be diminished when the extrinsic reinforcers are no longer available. Behaviorism recommends the use of rewards that are "noncompetitive, reinforcing, and contingent upon performance standards rather than task engagement" (Dickinson, 1989, p. 13).

Behaviorism also supports and encourages the use of natural reinforcers as they are necessary to maintain the behavior in environments outside of the classroom. When arranging the environment for effective instruction, then, teachers must consider the natural reinforcers that will ultimately control the behavior and the discriminative stimuli (signs) that are likely to be in the natural environment to prompt the behavior. These stimuli are then made available in the learning environment.

Producing competent learners allows individuals to function effectively and efficiently in their everyday environments (i.e., without contrived educational contingencies). They can *observe* their circumstances, *listen* to input from others, *talk* to others as needed, *read* and find out what to do, *write* and keep track of what has happened or prompt what to do next, *problem-solve* as necessary, and *participate* until they accomplish what they set out to do. (Tucci & Hursh, 1994, p. 258)

The difference between the competent learner and the incompetent learner is that the competent learner has better observational, listening, speaking, reading, writing, and problem solving skills. Therefore, a behavioral approach calls for the teaching and development of these skills. This teaching begins with high levels of content knowledge and skills that are practiced to proficiency and moves on to learning from professionals in the field. As with early learning of specific content, the more advanced skills learned from professionals in the field are also practiced until the learners are not only capable of saying and doing what the professionals do, but are able to do so proficiently and in a variety of settings. Johnson (1981) suggests:

Experienced learners should learn a variety of concepts and skills derived from observations of what professionals say and do. Further, while many individuals may be able to successfully engage in these behaviors given enough time and in a narrow range of circumstances, that behavior does not make them proficient at what they do. *Proficient performance is accurate, extended or generalized, and fluent, and instruction for experienced learners should terminate only when proficient, real-world performance is achieved.* (p. 104)

Behaviorism in the classroom is guided by Skinner's three-term contingency. Teachers begin with clearly stated objectives of what students will learn. They then assess students' current understandings to the extent they are relevant to the objectives. Beginning at the students' current level of expertise, teachers arrange a learning environment in which students are capable of responding correctly as they carefully progress through skills that will bring them to mastery of the objectives. Students' responding is active and frequent with sufficient practice to reach a point of fluency so that ultimately students become independent learners. This is accomplished in the behavioral classroom by ensuring that students learn the skills necessary to be independent learners in any environment.

A Behavioral School?

Will you choose a behavioral school in which the teacher decides the learning objectives for the students and is then held accountable for all students learning those objectives? Do you want the teachers deciding what the students will learn and how they will accomplish that learning? Maybe like other orientations you see both advantages and disadvantages to a behavioral orientation and would like a combination of orientations in your school. Do you think there is enough compatibility across philosophical orientations to accomplish that? Possibly, you are not willing to choose a philosophical orientation for your school until you have had an opportunity to examine the empirical evidence. We think that is a wise decision and will oblige you throughout this book as we carefully examine behavior analysis in education and the empirical evidence to support it.

Comparing the Philosophical Orientations

This brief chapter was not intended to teach the full extent of any of the philosophical orientations to education. Rather, its purpose was to introduce you to four philosophical orientations currently found in education. It should be noted that humanism is currently not as popular as it once was and is more likely to be a focus in high schools and colleges than in elementary schools. In contrast, developmentalism and constructivism are currently very popular with developmentalism concerned primarily with elementary education, especially in the primary grades, and constructivism found throughout all levels of education. Behaviorism is also found throughout all levels of education, but like humanism it is not as popular as it once was.

Each philosophical orientation was presented as a different approach to education rather than as an aspect of *one* effective approach to education. This is because there is little, if any, integration of philosophical orientations in today's classrooms. Educators are typically well grounded in only one of these orientations and as a result believe that their orientation provides the most effective approach. The philosophical orientation educators become well grounded in is often a result of *where, when, and with whom* they studied. An unfortunate effect is that we rarely stop to examine the similarities and differences among these philosophical orientations.

Therefore, we conclude this chapter with an examination of similarities and differences among humanism, constructivism, developmentalism, and behaviorism. It is likely that if representatives from each of these philosophical orientations were gathered for a meeting, all would agree that all children can learn. Then each would set out to assure that all children learn, but would do so with different beliefs about children and how they learn. The humanist would be sure all children would learn by letting students choose their own problems to solve and then helping them to read, question, and reflect to solve their own problems. The constructivist would assure that all children would learn by first determining students' current understandings and then presenting experiences that are a little past the students' current understandings. If there is a good match—that is, the new experience is in the zone of proximal development, it will push students to a new level of understanding. The developmentalist would be sure all children would learn by assessing their current level of development and then presenting learning experiences that match the mental abilities of children in that level of development. The behavior analyst would assure all children would learn by designing learning objectives, assessing children's current knowledge and skills relevant to those objectives, and then carefully sequencing instruction with mastery requirements along the way until the objectives were mastered.

Suppose, however, students are not successful—some of them do not learn. This is not hard to imagine as we are constantly reminded by the media that students are not learning what they should. One can look to the different philosophical orientations to see where the burden of responsibility lies. For the humanist, it is not possible for the student to not succeed. The problems are student selected and student solved. Any way that the student solves them is acceptable and the student is successful. For the constructivist, students construct whatever fits their way of knowing and so they cannot be unsuccessful. Similarly, the developmentalist believes the students understand from their own level of mental development. If that understanding is currently different from the way others understand, the developmentalist assumes the understanding will change with development and more experiences.

Assessment is difficult in humanism, constructivism, and developmentalism because these theories typically provide no specific objectives for students to master. What students learn is guided by their own problems, by the way they understand the world, and by their level of development. The teacher has some control in helping students identify their problems and work through the solutions to those problems, in assessing current understandings and presenting experiences just a little past those understandings, and in assessing the level of development and matching the curriculum to that level of development. Beyond that, the student is responsible. This is a point of departure for the behavior analyst. Students in the behavioral classroom have a set of learning objectives that they are expected to master. The burden of responsibility for mastery of these objectives falls on the teacher. The teacher has not properly arranged the learning environment or the students would have learned. Yes, all children can learn, but the teacher's responsibility for that learning is different from one philosophical orientation to the next.

What students are expected to learn also varies with the different philosophical orientations. In a classroom guided by humanism, children choose their own problems to solve, while in the constructivist classroom what students are expected to learn is a function of what students already know. What they learn will be driven by what they bring to the learning experience and therefore cannot be predetermined by the teacher. Similarly, in a classroom guided by developmentalism, what students learn will be a direct result of their developmental level and the students' exposure to units prepared by the teacher. Again, even though the teacher prepares the units, what students learn from these units varies as students are encouraged to study what interests them and to study in a way that meets their developmental needs. Only in the behavioral classroom is one likely to find predetermined learning objectives written by the teacher who knows exactly what the students are to master.

Yet, there are similarities found in all the philosophical orientations. All do some assessment of entering students to determine what students already know, how they know it, and what their needs are. They just all do different things with this information. Humanists do this assessment so that they can respond to students' needs—help them solve their own important problems. Constructivists assess so they can provide educational experiences that are within the zone of proximal development. Developmentalists assess so they can match curriculum to the students' level of development. Behaviorists assess to be sure students have the necessary prerequisite skills for the learning objectives they are expected to master. If students do not have these prerequisite skills the skills are taught to mastery before continuing on with the learning objectives. Educators within each of the orientations are driven to some extent by the initial assessment of entering students.

Similarly, each addresses the importance of active learning, but each accomplishes it in a different way. For the humanist, active learning is a matter of reading, reasoning, and problem solving either independently or in small groups. In the constructivist classroom, active learning occurs when students solve problems often by working in small groups and sharing their experiences so they can try out their understandings and so they can learn from each other. The developmentalist utilizes active learning by having students engage in hands-on experiences and the behavior analyst accomplishes active learning by having students respond frequently at high rates to stimuli presented by the teacher. The students' responses in the behavioral classroom are often choral responses or responses made with response cards so that all students can respond each time. Clearly, all philosophical orientations represented here support the use of active learning, even if each accomplishes it in a different way.

What is happening as students are actively responding depends on the philosophical orientation guiding the explanation. In the humanist classroom, students are generating knowledge from within themselves as a result of active responding. In the constructivist classroom, students are constructing mental models of knowledge, and in the developmentalist classroom, students are constructing schemes. In the humanist, the constructivist, and the developmentalist classrooms, what is learned is guided by what the learner brings to the learning environment and what the learner is currently experiencing in this environment. In the behavioral classroom, students are learning to discriminate among different stimuli and to respond appropriately to those stimuli based on what research tells us students need to know.

Equally important in all philosophical orientations is the development of a healthy self-concept, although the means to developing a healthy self-concept vary across the different orientations. Humanism works from the basic premise that humans are good by nature; therefore students learn good values. Students also find teachers addressing students' needs and realize that their needs are considered important. In these two ways, the humanist works to develop a healthy self-concept in students. Both constructivists and developmentalists help students to develop a healthy self-concept by valuing and accepting what students construct in their learning. Whatever is constructed is correct given the students' current mental models and the students' current level of development. It is easy to see how, if whatever is constructed is correct and accepted, students begin to feel good about themselves. The developmentalist addresses the importance of a healthy self-concept for future success in school. Behavior analysts are not likely to discuss healthy self-concept as something to be taught; however, they work to assure mastery of predetermined knowledge and skills and then find that with such mastery comes a healthy self-concept.

While humanists, constructivists, and developmentalists may actively seek to develop a healthy self-concept and the behavior analyst does not, the behavior analyst actively seeks to motivate the learner and the others do not. According to humanists, constructivists, and developmentalists, motivation is internal. For the humanist, the reward for learning is the learning itself. Students start school with a natural need to make sense out of their experiences and when allowed to do so, the sense they make of their experiences is the reward for the work; therefore, external motivation is not necessary. What motivates students in the constructivist classroom is the same thing that motivates students in the developmentalist classroom; that is, a desire to incorporate what the students are experiencing now with their current mental models so that they come to new levels of understanding. In both perspectives, teachers take advantage of students' natural interests, their need to know, and their enthusiasm for learning. With this internal motivation, extrinsic motivation is not necessary.

Behavior analysts readily use extrinsic motivation to begin the learning process. Possibly because behavior analysts believe learning is not always easy or fun, they use extrinsic motivation in the way of reinforcement. Initially this reinforcement may be contrived. There is not much intrinsically reinforcing about the drill and practice behavior analysts use to teach reading, for example, so external reinforcement is used. This is only used, however, until the natural reinforcers take control of the behavior. The natural reinforcers begin to take over as students begin to learn to blend sounds together and find themselves reading. Eventually they become competent readers. This is when reading is its own reward—for the pleasure it brings or the information it provides. While behavior analysts readily use extrinsic reinforcers (motivation) early in instruction, part of the instructional plan involves gradually reducing the amount of extrinsic reinforcement and planning for the natural reinforcers to take control of the behavior. Behavior analysts realize the only way the behavior will be maintained in the real world is if it is maintained by the natural reinforcers. When this happens, the reward for learning is the learning itself just as it is for the humanist.

The importance of social interaction is also not consistent across the different philosophical orientations. The methods of inquiry espoused by the humanists suggest that social interaction would facilitate this process, but may not be essential to it. For the constructivists and the developmentalists, however, social interaction is crucial to an effective learning experience. In the constructivist classroom, tasks are often completed in small groups, allowing students to learn from each other. In the developmentalist classroom, students learn from each other in much the same way. Additionally, the development of social skills is one of the broad objectives of the developmentally appropriate classroom. These skills are seen as important for future success in school and in life and are therefore consciously taught.

For the behavior analyst, social interaction in the classroom is incorporated into the learning environment, which includes the people present in the classroom, both teachers and other students. Each is continually providing discriminative stimuli and consequating stimuli; therefore, each is contributing to what students learn. What is contributed by the teachers is carefully controlled in an attempt to make it functional to the students' learning. Teachers do not have quite as much control over the social contributions made by the students in the classroom, but arrange an environment in which those social contributions will facilitate learning.

Regardless of their points of agreement and disagreement, supporters of all the philosophical orientations are working to help students become lifelong learners. Their approaches to accomplishing this goal vary, but each is sincere in the attempt to do so. Each is also supportive of a learning environment that accepts all students and provides a nurturing supportive environment. The only ones sometimes accused of not supporting such an environment are the behavior analysts. However, some have made the argument that the behavioral approach may be the most humane of the approaches because it begins with the premise that all children are capable of learning. Then it designs a learning environment in which students are engaged and academically successful in mastering the skills that will allow them to have important career options. If the students are struggling, the instruction is faulty and revised accordingly (Engelmann & Carnine, 1982). Behavior analysts believe "students are entitled to attend schools in which they are treated with care and individual attention, comparable to the attention they would receive as members of a caring family" (Barrett et al., 1991, p. 81).

In this chapter, we have presented philosophical orientations and the educational practices they support without evaluating them. Given the title of this book, it is clear we believe the most effective educational practices come from behaviorism. It will be our job in the remainder of this book to demonstrate to you, via

Table 2.1. Themes Across Conceptual Orientations

	HUMANISM	CONSTRUCTIVISM	DEVELOPMENTALISM	BEHAVIORISM
Typically found:	in high school and college	at all levels of education	in the primary grades	at all levels of education
Student failure is:	not possible, given the philosophy of humanism	not possible, given the philosophy of constructivism	not possible, given the philosophy of developmentalism	found when students don't master the objectives, the teacher is held accountable for this failure
What students are expected to learn is:	chosen by the students	a function of what students already know	determined by students' current level of development and what students extract from the units	determined by the teacher with the writing of learning objectives
Assessment of entering students allows teachers to:	respond to students' needs	work within students' zone of proximal development	match curriculum to students' level of development	determine mastery of prerequisite skills
Active learning occurs when students are:	reading, reasoning, and problem solving	solving authentic problems through cooperative experiences	engaging in hands-on experiences to explore units	responding frequently at high rates to teacher presented stimuli
The effect of active learning is seen when students:	generate knowledge from within themselves	construct mental models	construct schemes	discriminate among different stimuli to respond correctly
A healthy self-concept is developed by:	teaching students that their values are good values	valuing and accepting the mental models students construct	valuing and accepting the schemes students construct	mastering the content
Motivation is:	intrinsic	intrinsic	intrinsic	first extrinsic and later intrinsic
Social interaction:	facilitates but is not essential for learning	is essential for learning	is essential for learning	is a natural part of the learning environment that facilitates learning
The ultimate goal of education is to:	help students become life-long learners	help students become life-long learners	help students become life-long learners	help students become life-long learners
The learning environment is:	nurturing and supportive of all students	nurturing and supportive of all students	nurturing and supportive of all students	nurturing and supportive of all students

empirical evidence, that these practices will result in safe schools where all students learn and develop a healthy self-concept. If in the end you agree and choose these practices for your school, you will not have to call yourself a behavior analyst. We are working from the premise that we are all first and foremost educators choosing the most effective educational practices for the populations of students we serve.

Summary

In this chapter we examined four conceptual approaches–humanism, constructivism, developmentalism, and behaviorism–that characterize current educational theory. Several themes were addressed in each orientation and later compared across orientations (see Table 2.1). We focused on the approach offered by each orientation without evaluating the approach and suggested instead that you evaluate the approach when you answered the questions at the end of each orientation.

The approach offered by the humanist begins with what the students see as their own needs. These are addressed by having students study primary sources to read, reflect, and think critically about their needs. What is learned is from within the student and can only be facilitated by the teacher, not taught. This is an approach that is most likely to be found in high schools and colleges.

The constructivists offer an approach that begins with what students bring to the learning situation. Anything students experience in the learning situation is guided by what they bring to that situation. A strong emphasis is placed on social interaction as a form of learning in which students solve problems cooperatively and then must come to some consensus about the solution. In working this way, students are frequently being pushed into their zone of proximal development where they realize shortcomings in their understandings and are forced to move to some new, more advanced understanding. Realizing that students must always begin with their current mental models, the goal is to facilitate the construction of new, more sophisticated mental models.

An approach geared toward the primary grades (K-3) is offered by developmentalism. A central theme of this approach is to determine students' current level of development and offer educational experiences that are appropriate for that level. Students learn quickly and easily when they are developmentally ready for the new experience. They may be able to learn from those experiences for which they are not developmentally ready, but in doing so they may lose their desire to learn. The outcome of these experiences is the revision of and development of schemes that are similar to the constructivist's mental models.

The behavior analyst does not talk of schemes or mental models because no one knows what is going on inside students' heads. An approach based on behaviorism looks at how the student responds to questions and assignments offered in the learning situation and what happens after the student responds. Through carefully sequenced educational experiences students come to respond in ways that are predetermined to be correct and functional for more advanced learning. What students already know is assessed as a means of determining where to begin in the educational sequence.

Ultimately, we suggest that each orientation attempts to provide effective education for all students. The responsibility then rests on educators to take from these orientations what is most effective and implement it in their schools. This is what you have been asked to consider throughout the chapter. However, we asked you to do this based only on what sounds good or promising or effective because we provided no empirical evidence of the effectiveness of these approaches. In the remainder of this book we offer a behavioral approach to education along with the empirical evidence of the effectiveness of such an approach.

Annotated Bibliography

Humanism

Davis, C. G. (1993). Humanism and anti-humanism: The contest for education. *Improving College and University Teaching, 31,* 155-159.

    Argues for keeping humanism in higher education by delineating what can be accomplished with humanism that is lost with a more direct teacher-centered approach to education.

Jackard, C. (1983). Humanism: An answer to problems facing education. *The Humanist, 43* (3), 20-23.

    Describes a program based on humanism that focuses on teaching values to address the common problems of absenteeism, tardiness, drug usage, and lack of motivation and discipline commonly found in schools.

Kramlinger, T., & Huberty, T. (1990). Behaviorism versus humanism. *Training and Development Journal, 44* (12), 41-45.

    Presents what behaviorism, humanism, and cognitivism have to offer to training in the workplace, but can readily be applied to high school and college education.

Mills, R. K. (1985). Let's keep humanism in the classroom. *The Social Studies, 76,* 108-110.

    Presents the principles of humanism that are significant for today's education as a response to the critics of humanism who would have humanism removed from the classroom.

Constructivism

Cunningham, D. J. (1991). Assessing constructions and constructing assessments: A dialogue. *Educational Technology, 3* (5), 13-17.

    Uses a dialogue to address constructivist views compared to objectivist views in order to make a case for a constructivist approach to education.

Poplin, M. S. (1988). Holistic/constructivist principles of the teaching/learning process: Implications for the field of learning disabilities. *Journal of Learning Disabilities, 21,* 401-416.

> Provides principles of constructivism that can be readily applied to any field of education.

Prawat, R. S. (1992). Teacher's beliefs about teaching and learning: A constructivist perspective. *American Journal of Education, 100,* 354-395.

> Presents current teacher thinking that may interfere with adopting a constructivist approach and in so doing clearly delineates many central features of constructivism.

Resnick, L. B. (Ed.). (1989). *Knowing, learning, and instruction: Essays in honor of Robert Glaser.* Hillsdale, NJ: Lawrence Erlbaum.

> Provides a collection of chapters addressing innovative research on cognition and instruction which relies heavily on constructing mental models across various content areas while also addressing the importance of social interaction in learning.

Wheatley, G. H. (1991). Constructivist perspectives in science and mathematics learning. *Science Education, 75,* 9-21.

> Presents instructional practices compatible with constructivism while providing many good explanations of what is meant by constructivism in education.

Developmentalism

Elkind, D. (1989). Developmentally appropriate practice: Philosophical and practical implications. *Phi Delta Kappan, 71,* 113-117.

> Presents a developmentally appropriate approach to education by contrasting it with psychometric educational practices.

Katz, L. G. (1988). What should young children be doing? *American Educator, 12* (2), 28-45.

> Discusses what is developmentally appropriate in kindergarten and the importance of not imposing academic requirements just because children can achieve them, if in fact, children are not developmentally ready for those requirements.

Liben, L. S. (Ed.). (1987). *Development and learning: Conflict or congruence?* Hillsdale, NJ: Lawrence Erlbaum.

> Presents a series of chapters addressing developmentalism in the schools from the notion of constructing knowledge to the implementation of developmentalism across curriculum areas.

NAEYC. (1988, January). NAEYC position statement on developmentally appropriate practice in the primary grades, serving 5- through 8-year olds. *Young Children, 43* (2), 64-84.

Carefully delineates a developmentalist approach to education in the primary grades including a contrasting of appropriate with inappropriate practices as determined by the National Association of Education of Young Children.

Wortham, S. C. (1994). *Early childhood curriculum: Developmental bases for learning and teaching.* New York: Macmillan.

Presents a thorough description of developmental characteristics of young children along with appropriate educational practices based on developmentalism.

Behaviorism

Axelrod, S. (1992). Disseminating an effective educational technology. *Journal of Applied Behavior Analysis, 25,* 31-35.

Discusses reasons why educators have not adopted behavioral approaches to education and what might be done to change the situation.

Grander III, R., Sainato, D. M., Cooper, J. O., Heron, T. E., Heward, W. L., Eshleman, J. W., Grossi, T. A. (Eds.). (1994). *Behavior analysis in education.* Belmont, CA: Wadsworth.

Presents behavioral approaches to education for early childhood, school age, and adult learners with an emphasis on using strategies that are measurably superior.

Horcones, C. L. (1992). Natural reinforcement: A way to improve education. *Journal of Applied Behavior Analysis, 25,* 71-75.

Addresses the issue of intrinsic versus extrinsic reinforcement focusing on the importance of gradually moving to the reinforcers that will maintain the behavior in the natural environment.

Lindsley, O. R. (1992). Why aren't effective teaching tools widely adopted? *Journal of Applied Behavior Analysis, 25,* 21-26.

Suggests the data are in and we have effective teaching strategies which we are not using then discusses why we are not using these strategies by drawing analogies to other situations in which we would never allow the profession not to use the most effective strategies available.

Chapter 3

Schools and Schooling

In this chapter we will provide a brief overview of schools and schooling from the one room schoolhouse typical of 19th and early 20th Century American education to the larger, more comprehensive schools of today. We will describe some current and future issues relating to the goals of education at the national, state, and local levels, and we will discuss several of the criticisms levied at today's schools along with some of the suggestions posed for changing schools and schooling in America. Where appropriate, we will cite research findings that suggest "better" ways to conduct learning and note whether the data gathered in these studies are used by policy makers and administrators to make substantive changes in educational practices.

This chapter differs from the other chapters in this book since we are attempting to provide you with an overview of schools and schooling from a perspective that goes beyond behavior analysis. Often educators or administrators suggest methods for improving schools in the general vernacular of our culture. Behavior analysis, since it is the science of behavior, employs many terms that have precise meanings. Frequently, behavior analysts and other educators are "saying the same thing," they are just using different terminology. Where appropriate, we will attempt to translate these statements into terminology or concepts used by behavior analysts.

While not everyone agrees, Huitt (1995) defines education as "a process that indoctrinates new members into society such that they have the opportunity to be successful" (p. 3). What he is saying in behavioral terms is that education is the process that changes students in such a way that various academic and social repertoires of behavior are developed through the complex process known as contingencies of reinforcement—the arrangement of antecedent and consequent events with behavior. If contingencies of reinforcement are arranged in such a manner that students can solve novel or creative problems, then their "success" will be greatly enhanced. However, if educational contingencies are established that do not support such conceptual issues as creativity or problem solving, then students will be unable to "respond" correctly to novel situations. If a student cannot respond appropriately to new or novel situations, the probability of being successful is greatly diminished.

Educational Change

There is almost universal agreement that our country is in the midst of massive change. Over the last 200 years we have made the transition from an agricultural to an industrial based society and are currently in the midst of a transition to an information based society. Will schools and schooling be ready, willing, and able to meet the challenges required of the information age? This is a question that has been bandied about for years in educational circles and, at present, no general consensus appears to be on the horizon.

Although elected and appointed individuals tend to set educational goals prescribed by society, educators possess a certain degree of power with respect to what students are exposed to in the classroom. Along with this power is the attendant burden and responsibility to insure that students achieve their potential in order to be successful, contributing members of society. School systems are charged with teaching students the skills and knowledge deemed important to society. Although the global outcomes of education are set by others, professional educators are charged with implementing procedures to reach these outcomes on a daily basis. Educational administrators determine the content students must master and the methods employed for mastery in order to meet society's goals, and classroom teachers are charged with assuring that students reach these goals. This general system of education has been in place for over 100 years in this country.

Educational change tends to be evolutionary in nature rather than revolutionary. Numerous modifications or even dramatically different methods of conducting instruction have been proposed and articulated by behavior analysts and others over the years (e.g., Programmed Instruction, Computer Assisted Instruction, Direct Instruction). Each of these techniques has been tried in various schools or school systems but the general education community has either ignored these methods or been slow to adopt them. One revolutionary change in education that cannot be ignored, however, will involve the Internet. This tool will dramatically alter the way in which learning is conducted. Hardin and Ziebarth (1996) suggest that the Internet has impacted the K-12 educational atmosphere to the point that an educational revolution will take place that cannot be ignored by educators or administrators.

For most of the 20th Century, educational practices in this country tended to discourage collaboration between students or teachers. Traditional education practices and course content were delivered in a "top down" manner by local, state, and national education administrators. Teachers had limited freedom to modify the mandates "sent down from above" and usually spent most of their day confined to a classroom with little time available for interaction with other teachers or students. Students were usually rewarded for keeping quiet and working independently, and communication between teachers and parents was typically limited to once or twice during the school year.

Yet, beyond the K-12 atmosphere, collaboration is central to success. Learning, as a successful lifelong process, mandates collaboration. Whether you are a college student, business person, professional, or craftsperson, collaboration is essential. Once K-12 educational leaders begin to realize this (and many already have), the revolution will spread through the educational community. The Internet will be the vehicle that will facilitate this revolution since it has the potential to create previously unavailable collaborative possibilities between students and teachers in the same classroom or school, as well as among students, teachers, and other sources anywhere on the planet. With this tool and the ability to collaborate with others, learning should become a "self-reinforcing" activity.

Although behavior analysts did not create the Internet, their knowledge of the interaction among antecedent events, behavior, and consequences can be used to ensure that the information learned and the methods used via the Internet will develop, sustain, and increase all sorts of educational activities. We are not suggesting that the Internet is the panacea for the ills of 20th Century education. We are, however, suggesting that this tool will bring about significant changes to the educational process. Schools and schooling have come a long way from the one room schoolhouse to the large centralized school systems of today. It is likely that the next step in the evolution of schools and schooling, at least for some content and learning processes, will be the virtual schoolhouse.

Define Education

How will you define education for your school? How will this definition reflect a changing society? Will it include the teaching of social behaviors as well as academic behaviors? Who will be responsible for teaching the different behaviors? Will your school take full responsibility for teaching all behaviors? How might you share this responsibility with the community?

Nineteenth & Early Twentieth Century Schools

Even if you have never seen one, merely mentioning the one room schoolhouse probably evokes several images. If you've ever watched the television show *Little House on the Prairie,* you might recall boys and girls of differing ages, abilities, backgrounds, and grade levels sharing all available educational resources in a small wooden school. The desks were arranged in neat rows facing the teacher and chalkboard; the student body co-mingled in no particular order. Younger students often learned what was expected of them by observing the behavior and attendant consequences of older children in the school. This type of learning is often referred to as **vicarious** or **observational** learning by behavior analysts, and has been empirically verified to be an effective means of changing behavior (Kazdin, 1973; Lancioni, 1982; Ollendick, Dailey, & Shapiro, 1983; Weisberg & Clements, 1977).

As the older children mastered some topical area, they were often called on to aid the younger students in various content areas. The effectiveness of such peer tutoring is well documented in the behavioral literature (Bell, Young, Salzberg, & West, 1991; Dineen, Clark, & Risley, 1977; Greenwood et al., 1987; Kamps, Barbetta, Leonard, & Delquadri, 1994) and is a critical component of the Personalized System of Instruction (PSI) developed by Keller.

These types of environments made it possible for the teacher to individualize lessons and spend more time with each student on a daily basis. According to Barker

(1986), one room schools were the catalyst of many of today's educational innovations.

Notions such as non-graded classrooms, individualized instruction, low student/teacher ratios, cross-age grouping, peer tutoring, using the community as resources, "mainstreaming" mildly handicapped pupils, and emphasizing the basics all have their roots in the small school of the past. (p. 1)

As appealing or idyllic as this picture may seem, however, the purpose of schools during this era was quite different from today's schools. During the 19th and early 20th Century, the United States was primarily an agricultural society. The main purpose of schools was to instill the "basics" in each student with little thought or aspiration for education beyond basic literacy. According to Brown (1993), in the 19th Century, learning to read and cipher constituted literacy. Few schools or school systems provided training beyond the elementary level and high schools were virtually nonexistent.

The goal of basic literacy originated in legislation passed in 1642 in colonial Massachusetts. According to Cubberly (1920), the 1642 law required:

. . . certain chosen men of each town to ascertain from time to time, if parents and masters were attending to their educational duties; if the children were being trained in learning and labor and other employments . . . profitable to the state; and if children were being taught to read and understand the principles of religion and the capital laws of the country. (p. 364)

Interestingly, this law represented the first time any English-speaking country's legislative body enacted a requirement that children be taught to read. However, this law did not mandate the establishment of schools.

It was not until 1647 that the Massachusetts legislature enacted the *ye olde deluder law* that brought about the development of schools. At the time, it was generally agreed that one of the chief goals of *ye olde deluder Satan* was to keep people ignorant of the Scriptures. "The obvious way to defeat Satan's purpose was to teach the people to read and write" (Alexander & Salmon, 1995, p.7). According to Alexander and Salmon (1995), the 1647 law required

1.   that every town having fifty households shall at once appoint a teacher of reading and writing, and provide for his wages in such a manner as the town might determine; and

2.   that every town having one hundred householders must provide a grammar school to fit youths for the university, under a penalty of 5 pounds for failure to do so. (p. 7)

By 1840, only a dozen high schools had been established in Massachusetts with an equal number in all the other states combined. It wasn't until the Supreme Court of the state of Michigan rendered its famous Kalamazoo decision in 1875 that the development of high schools began to be accepted in most states. However, this acceptance came very slowly. By 1900, only 8% of children ages 14-17 were enrolled in grades 9 through 12, and high schools did not become generally available in rural American communities until after the end of World War I. This period marked the transition from the one room schoolhouse to the more modern and contemporary schools and school systems to which we have grown accustomed.

Will There be Remnants of the One Room Schoolhouse in Your School?

What aspects of the one room schoolhouse will you keep in your school? Will you have multi-age classrooms with students learning from each other and with individualized instruction? If you have multi-age classrooms, how will you decide what ages to put together? How will you design the instruction in these classrooms and how will student learning be evaluated? Will you look for empirical evidence of the effectiveness of such strategies in current schools before making such decisions? Will you make the same or different decisions for your elementary, middle, and high school students?

The Modern Era of Schools and Schooling

Schools have acquired many responsibilities beyond the basic skills of reading, writing, and arithmetic that predominated the previous era of American education. Today, public schools are not only charged with teaching students basic skills but also other academic and social repertoires needed to successfully meet the challenges of post secondary training, employment, and productive citizenship. As complex as today's schools have become, the mission of schools in the future is likely to change even further as they take over responsibility previously provided by the family, church, and community.

What are the characteristics of today's schools? The answer to this question is important because it provides a reference point against which we can begin to predict the nature of tomorrow's schools. In many communities, public schools fit into three categories: **elementary, middle**, and **high schools**. In general, elementary schools begin with pre-kindergarten or kindergarten and continue through fourth or fifth grade. Among the key characteristics of elementary schools are the following. First, elementary schools are more likely to be smaller (serving 300 or fewer students) than middle or high schools. Second, the student/teacher ratio is lower in the elementary schools than in the middle or secondary schools. A ratio of 18:1 (often with a paraprofessional in addition to a certified teacher) is not uncommon, although a ratio of 22:1 would not be unusual. Third, students in elementary school classrooms tend to remain together with the same teacher throughout the school day. Most elementary school teachers are trained as generalists so they have some expertise in teaching a variety of academic subjects.

Middle schools (generally sixth through eighth grade) are usually larger than elementary schools with class size averaging about 24 students for each teacher.

Additionally, middle school teachers often specialize in two of the four basic academic areas (i.e., mathematics, science, social studies, and language arts). Students in the middle grades have more than one teacher during the day.

Often, several elementary schools "feed" into a centrally located middle school that might serve 500 or more students. Although most middle schools tend to serve a student body of this size, an increasing trend toward mega-middle schools has been emerging in recent years. For example, the Gwinnett County School System in Georgia opened the Creekland Middle School in the Fall of 1996. Creekland was designed to serve 2400 students and is one of the largest middle schools in the United States.

High schools are different from both elementary and middle schools. Typically, the instructional focus in both elementary and middle schools is primarily on academic skills. High schools place a strong emphasis on both academic preparation (basic and college preparatory) and vocational training. Additionally, each of these options provides students with increased levels of specialization. According to the National Center for Education Statistics (U.S. Department of Education, 1995), the overall student/teacher ratio for high schools in 1993 was 14.8:1. However, it is often meaningless to describe a single student/teacher ratio because upper level electives (e.g., chemistry, calculus) may have very low ratios while classes required of all students (e.g., freshmen English) may have a ratio of 30:1 or higher.

While several elementary schools tend to feed into a single middle school, several middle schools tend to feed into a single high school. Thus, enrollments in some high schools are quite large; more than 4100 high schools in the United States have enrollments that exceed 1000 students. Although few, if any, behavior analysts have focused their research on the effect of school size on student academic achievement, an abundance of data are available in this area. For example, a substantial body of research suggests a negative relationship between school size and student achievement: the larger the school population, the worse the academic performance of students (Fetler, 1989; Friedkin & Necochea, 1988; Huang & Howley, 1993; Plecki, 1991; Walberg, 1989). Yet, school systems continue to build large schools.

This move towards large, centralized schools is based on the notion of **economies of scale**, an economic principle that supports the notion that "big is better because it is more cost effective." For example, the fixed expenses associated with running a school (all other factors being the same) are similar whether the school has 1000 students or 2500. Thus, from an economic perspective, it makes sense to have one large high school instead of three smaller ones. In the era of budget cuts, fiscal restraint, and facility planning, the concept of economies of scale has merit from the viewpoint of the superintendency or local school board. However, from the perspective of educational research in the area of school size, economies of scale seems to be at odds with sound pedagogy.

To overcome this inconsistency between economies of scale and the research findings on school size and student achievement, some educational administrators are looking to a concept known as **schools-within-schools**. The purpose of schools-within-schools is to create a site within the framework of the larger school building that provides an autonomous setting for students–typically 200 or fewer–and teachers who share similar interests or career orientations. Little research is available on this matter; hence, it is too early to determine if this outlook will overcome some of the problems noted in the area of student achievement.

How Big Will Your School Be?

Will you have separate elementary, middle, and high schools? How big will you allow each school to be before building another school? What student/teacher ratio will you try to maintain? Will it be different in your elementary, middle, and high school? How might you design schools within your middle or high school?

Indices of Student Performance and the Parent's Paradox

In 1969, the combined average score on the Scholastic Aptitude Test (SAT) was 956; in 1995, it was 910. Student performance on the 1994 administration of the National Assessment of Education Progress (NAEP) showed a serious decline in scores compared to the 1992 administration of it. Performance on the NAEP is classified into four categories: below basic (i.e., illiterate), basic, proficient, and advanced. According to Kondracke (1995), the reading scores of high school seniors on the NAEP showed that only 4% scored at the advanced level while 30% placed below the basic level.

Summaries of evaluation data based on how well students performed on standardized achievement tests tell us that our students, thus our schools, are not doing a very good job. This conclusion is neither surprising nor shocking.

We have become inured to educational crisis. Daily, it seems, television reports another embarrassment of the American public school system. Newspapers discuss the latest dismal performance of U.S. students on a new international achievement test–a discussion that, as few commentators rarely fail to point out, is written in prose that vast numbers of students cannot decode or comprehend. (Loveless, 1996, p. 1)

A recurring criticism of American education is that no uniform standards of student performance exist in the more than 15,000 school districts in the U.S. Lack of national standards is one of the glaring distinctions between how our country governs its educational programs compared to those of other countries. In a recent issue of *Academe*, Albert Shanker, the president of the American Federation of Teachers, stated his support for a national standard "that closely ties academic achievement to measurable goals, such as job attainment. In other industrialized nations, 'How well you do is directly linked to getting what you want'" (American Association of University Professors, 1995, p. 53).

Paradoxically, many parents feel that their neighborhood schools are doing a good job educating our young people. McDowell (1995), reporting on the findings of the *Phi Delta Kappan* 27th annual Gallup Poll on education, indicated that 65% of American parents believed the school their children attend is doing a good to excellent job, but only 20% would assign grades of A or B to schools across the country. Eighty-seven percent of the people polled believed schools should have high standards, 64% felt that the influence of the Federal Government over state and local schools should be decreased, and 69% of the respondents felt that they should be able to choose which public school their children attend. Sixty-five percent of the respondents believed that public school funds should not be used as "vouchers" to support students attending private schools.

With the repeated criticisms of American education and the numerous calls for school reform, it seems likely that school reform will remain at "center stage" on the political and social agenda for years to come. The concern of most behavior analysts and other professional educators steeped in "data based decision making processes" is that whatever reforms emerge do so after careful research and evaluation of data. An axiom commonly heard in behavior analytic circles goes something like this: Past behavior is a good predictor of future behavior. Unfortunately, based upon previous attempts in the area of school reform, the likelihood that changes will occur based upon the evaluation of collected data is not encouraging.

Effective planning for educational reform should include parents, teachers, community members, and professional educators. Most likely, educational reform will involve several different areas including what is taught, how information is presented (technology issues), who is taught, and who is teaching. In *Projections of Education Statistics to 2005* (U.S. Department of Education, 1995), the National Center for Educational Statistics (NCES) provided information that is used for making predictions relating to several expected growth patterns schools and schooling are likely to experience over the next decade. Three levels of projections are included—low, medium, and high—with each alternative reflecting what could happen under different conditions. What follows is based on medium level projections.

Both public school (K-12) and college enrollments are expected to grow annually between now and 2005. For example, in 1971, enrollment levels in grades K-12 where approximately 51.3 million students. By the year 2005, K-12 enrollment is projected to be 55.9 million students. The greatest increase is projected to occur at the secondary level, with high school graduation rates increasing from approximately 2.5 million students per year in 1993 to more than 3 million students by the year 2005. These projected enrollments will vary regionally with enrollments rising most rapidly in the West and South. Obviously, as the number of students in schools increases, our need for additional teachers will also rise. NCES projects that the number of teachers will increase to 3.37 million by the year 2005.

As the total number of students and teachers increases during the next decade, we can also expect school expenditures to rise. The projected increase in educational funding is expected to grow from approximately 234.5 billion dollars per year in

1995 to 301.9 billion dollars by 2005. In terms of the annual expenditure per student, by 2005 schools will spend an average of $6576 (compared to $5712 in 1995). Teacher salaries also are expected to rise about 12% between 1993 and 2005.

According to critics, increased educational spending has not previously improved student performance. Osier (1994) cited a study conducted by the American Legislative Exchange in which no significant relationship between student performance and educational expenditures was found. It would not be surprising if findings such as this provide an impetus to attempt to reduce educational budgets in many school systems.

Any approach to reforming schools that requires educators to do more or as much with less is not, in our viewpoint, an appropriate response to the crisis in education. Even Lewis J. Perelman (1992), perhaps the most vocal critic of traditional education programs in the U.S., has noted that the country needs to maintain its current funding levels rather than decrease them, although he feels the monies should be spent in vastly different ways than is now done.

The NCES suggests healthy growth for the educational enterprise. However, this expected growth may not occur in schools and school settings as we know them today. People from all walks of life have regularly pointed out many weaknesses in our educational system. For example, some people feel that American schools and students have been inferior to those of other countries for at least 30 years, but employment for most high school graduates was still available even if on-the-job-training was requisite. However, the situation has changed so much that current students, in order to be employable in the global marketplace, must acquire work skills and basics during their formal school years.

> With all of education's problems today, on balance our system is doing a better job educating all children. Unfortunately, our competition isn't standing still and resting on its laurels. The bar seems to be set higher all the time just as the number of challenges before educators seems to increase. (J. Varner, personal communication, May 12, 1995)

Supporting Varner's position, a member of the California Commission on Teacher Credentialing, cited the work of Peter Drucker who stated that over the last 100 years the primary sources of American employment have changed from domestic service and farming, to manufacturing, to one of service delivery and information.

> The point is that the educational requirements for competing successfully for jobs have increased steadily. The question is not so much whether K-12 has improved, but whether it has kept up. In this context literacy is defined not in absolute terms, but in relation to the demands of the economy. The evidence from the National Adult Literacy Survey suggests that the system has not kept up, and that large segments of the population are falling behind. (M. E. Fetler, Personal Communication, May 12, 1995)

How Will You Evaluate Your School?

What indices of student performance will you use in your school? What level of performance will you consider appropriate? If you do not reach that level, what modifications will you make? How will you keep your parents informed of students' performance? Will you tie teacher salary to student performance? How will you make your school financially accountable?

Schools Must Change

Just as the one room school of the 19th and early 20th Century was transformed to meet the educational needs of a more urban and industrialized society, so must the schools of today change to meet the needs of tomorrow's society. As we shall see, great diversity exists regarding the direction in which schools and schooling must move. However, there is almost unanimous consent that substantive changes must occur, and occur soon, if we, as a nation, are to avoid dire consequences.

In a provocative article on the issue of how schools and schooling need to change, Deborah Meir (1992) argued that without a "new" type of teacher, any reform movement in education will fail. Meir believes that one reason reform movements have yet to be successful is that teachers, before they even step into their own classroom, have at least 16 years of direct experiences that have shaped and molded their perceptions of what teaching is and how teachers do it.

> Aside from our many years of direct experience as students, we have books, movies, television shows, advertisements, and myriad other activities, games and symbols that reinforce our view of what school is "supposed" to be. Our everyday language and metaphors are built on a kind of prototype of schoolhouse and classroom, with all its authoritarian, filling-up-the-empty-vessel, rote-learning assumptions. (Meir, 1992, p. 596)

At first glance, Meir's position may seem contradictory to the views on learning associated with behavior analysis, but it really is not. What one has already learned (prerequisite skills) and how that learning occurred (behavioral history) dramatically influence how new information will be learned, how easily it will be acquired, and the extent to which it can be applied. A person's current behavioral repertoire and/ or behavioral history are important components of contingencies of reinforcement.

For example, Bryceland (1995) conducted research on the effects that instructions have on a complex sequencing task. Some participants were instructed on the sequence necessary to complete the task while the remaining participants were required to figure out the sequence on their own. Once the first sequence was correctly completed, a new sequence was instituted without the participants' knowledge (i.e., the previously correct sequence was no longer valid). Participants instructed on solving the first sequence required significantly more trials to complete the new sequence than did the participants who figured out the first sequence on their own. Weiner (1969, 1970) found similar history effects with schedules of reinforcement. Participants who initially responded under various schedules of reinforcement responded differently when later exposed to identical schedules of reinforcement.

Meir's (1992) view of why a "new" teacher will be required if educational reform is to be successful melds with the precepts of behavior analysis in terms of history and repertoire. This position also holds for student behavior. Obviously, John Locke's view of the mind as a *tabula rasa* (i.e., the mind as a blank slate that our experiences "write" on) does not apply, but educational administrators or theorists are in error if they assume that each new school year, academic topic, or lesson stands alone. Nothing could be further from the truth. The content of each new year's curriculum, academic topic, or lesson should be built upon the content of previous topics. This view of complex behavior built upon prior or requisite behaviors has been advocated by educational behavior analysts for years. As obvious as this may sound, without certain requisite skills, many academic topics simply cannot be learned. Imagine trying to learn algebra with no prior foundation of basic math facts.

To their credit, many educators and educational organizations (e.g., Anderson et al., 1995; Kagan, 1992; Meir, 1992; National Center for Research on Teacher Education, 1991) stress that today's successful teacher (and program) must build on the information and experiences that students bring to the learning setting. From this perspective, it cannot be assumed that student outcomes will be similar unless one insures that all learners share common background skills and experiences (a feature built into some curricular programs such as Direct Instruction). For Meir (1992) and the prominent task forces that have called for radical change in the educational system, the failure of today's schools is not a function of students lacking certain requisite skills. Rather, it is simply that the educators have little, if any, training in understanding and changing human behavior.

To perform effectively, schools and schooling must engage in several major transformations. First, teachers must begin to perceive learning and teaching differently (i.e., not returning just to basics, or learning/teaching as filling-the-empty-vessel). Second, instructional episodes or activities must begin where previous ones, including non-school activities, left off, and they must be collaborative in nature. Third, educators will have to develop new teaching repertoires that complement their reformed understanding of the teaching/learning process, and these new repertoires must be subject to public, collegial, and professional scrutiny.

Traditionally, the classroom has been an exemplar of feudalism in which "things" passed on to students were inviolate. As such, what teachers did in their own classrooms (e.g., how they organized lessons, how they presented content, how they assessed learning) was generally left up to themselves. Even in situations where central authority mandated certain pedagogies, teachers tended to enjoy a much wider latitude than other professionals. This territoriality enjoyed by teachers has long been recognized. In a clever play on the television character "The Lone Ranger," Bijou (1970) referred to public school teachers as the "lone arranger" because each individual teacher was solely responsible for establishing the contingencies in the classroom designed to promote and support students' acquiring and using academic and social skills. What Meir (1992) and others propose is a massive reversal of the "lone arranger" mentality, which will be difficult, but not impossible, to implement.

To achieve the type of school or classroom advocated by Meir (1992), teachers would meet regularly to share with each other and the public (e.g., parents, district officials, etc.). Teachers would discuss what they are doing in their lessons, and why they are doing it. Then they would solicit feedback from those in attendance so that they could incorporate this feedback into their lessons. This will, at least initially, be difficult to implement because it has the potential for making each educational practitioner vulnerable to criticism and possibly censure. For this reason, Meir advocates that teachers must be more "in charge" of schools than is currently the case.

As Meir (1992) points out, the process of reinventing schools will likely require that certain principles be followed. First, schools will have to be small enough so that it is possible for faculty to regularly share with one another what they are doing (see also Klonsky & Ford, 1994). Second, students would remain with the same teachers for at least two years. During a typical academic day in Meir's school, students spend more time (about 2 hours) in each subject than occurs in traditional schools. This approach, depth over breadth, has gained educational popularity and research support, and is commonly called fluency in the literature (Johnson & Layng, 1992).

Recognizing, as most educational models do, that no single lesson plan or activity perfectly "reaches" or teaches every student, the reinvented school emphasizes both cooperative learning strategies and individualized instructional methods that build on student interests and on their background experiences. Rounding out this principle, each teacher teaches an interdisciplinary class in a collaborative setting (i.e., the same 4 or 5 teachers have the same set of students), and they teach only the subjects in which they are certified, and desire, to teach. (By itself, having teachers teach only those subjects they are formally trained in is a type of "best practice" that many schools regularly violate.)

To offset the potentially high levels of perceived vulnerability, criticism, or censure associated with the level of professional disclosure that such a school requires, the faculty of the school must be actively involved in all aspects of decision making. The role of administrators in such schools would likely be that of a facilitator and procurer of resources rather than one of evaluator and overseer of faculty. Lastly, formal evaluation of students and faculty performance would be conducted by external groups. For example, student promotion to the next level (not necessarily the next grade because age-based grades probably would not be a component of most reinvented schools) is based on student performance on standardized tests in conjunction with blind reviews of student portfolios conducted by a board that consists of parents, politicians, business leaders, professors, and educators from other schools. As a result of the "systemic" changes incorporated into her school, Meir's (1992) students, "succeed in far greater measure than their socio-economic, ethnic, and racial background and prior academic skills would predict" (p. 607).

Although claiming some success, Meir (1992) does not offer what works at her schools as a panacea for other schools:

> If we want schools for the twenty-first century to resemble schools of the twentieth century, we can afford to tinker a little and leave the structure pretty much intact. Then teacher-training institutions need only follow suit, tinkering too. But if we want the least of our citizens to know and be able to do the kinds of things that only those lucky few at the top of the ladder have ever achieved before, then we need to begin a slow and steady revolution in how and what teachers must know and know how to do. To do this means we have to learn how to drive while changing not only the tire but the whole mechanism! Impossible? No, but very, very hard. The place it will happen is in the schools themselves—not the schools as we now know them, but reinvented schools created by school people and their communities. And it does not come with guarantees. (Meir, 1992, p. 609)

Will There Be Schools of Tomorrow?

As we have already stated, there appears to be almost universal agreement that schools must and will change. However, not everyone accepts Meir's (1992) analysis that schools as we currently know them can (or even should) change sufficiently to pass tomorrow's muster. One of the most outspoken critics of our public schools is Lewis J. Perelman. In his book, *School's Out: Hyperlearning, the New Technology, and the End of Education*, Perelman (1992) advocates that with (a) the current poor state of schools, and (b) a powerful technology that is available and waiting to be introduced, traditional schools really have no place in the future (recall the "virtual schoolhouse"). In fact, to continue efforts to reform or reinvent them is not a productive or proper use of our public resources. Metaphorically, Perelman is applying the Queen of Hearts command ("Off with their heads!"), from *Alice in Wonderland*, to the entire educational establishment.

According to Huitt (1995), Perelman does not see education of the future occurring in the supposed computer-rich classrooms of today's school building. Instead, learners will learn at home, at work, in shopping centers, in fact, just about anywhere except in schools. To accomplish this radical transformation, Perelman advocates the development of a concept called **micro-vouchers**. A voucher, ostensibly, allows parents to take the money normally given to the school district to educate their child and use it to pay for enrollment in any school they desire. A micro-voucher would provide parents with the same amount of money, but they could spend it on any educational product or service they choose. For example, if parents wanted to buy a computer for educational purposes, they could use part of the micro-voucher. If they wanted to buy a curriculum package, hire a tutor, or purchase the latest CD-ROM on human anatomy, they could.

One problem inherent in the use of micro-vouchers is that they convey to parents the impression that the methods and topics used to educate their children are their choice alone. We contend that the education of children has serious social implications that will affect the stability of current and future members of society.

The American education system, even if flawed, still produces many capable students who mature into competent adults.

Perelman's view appears to be excessively radical viz-a-viz most contemporary views of school reform and a number of critics of his position have spoken out. For example, Osier (1994), like Huitt (1995), disagrees with Perelman's (1992) assessment that today's schools are anachronisms that will not figure into tomorrow's educational equations. "What will the classroom of the 21st Century look like? One possibility is that, strangely enough, it may be more like the classrooms of the 19th Century, the era of the one-room schoolhouse, when every student worked at his own pace" (Osier, 1994, p. 42).

What Direction Will Your School Take?

Will your school be the result of minor tinkering with the current state of schools? If so, what type of tinkering will you do? Will your school follow Meir's advice and be a reinvention of schools? If so, how will you accomplish collaboration, in-depth study of content, and students working with the same teachers for two years? In what other ways might your school be a reinvention of schools? Will you instead, follow the advice of Perelman? Could you establish a "school" that is simply a home base for computer rich education that occurs throughout the community? How would you incorporate the use of micro-vouchers?

Some Thoughts on School Reform

Among the various educational changes to which Huitt (1995) alludes are such things as how schools are financed, options for parents to choose the school to which students are sent, the expansion of the charter school movement, increased emphasis in the curriculum on the roles of women and minorities, alteration of the school year, implementing new technologies such as distance learning, local (LAN) and wide area networks (WAN), and more cooperation between businesses and school in order to produce graduates who are employable.

Employment Related Issues

According to Bean (1994), simply being literate in the 3 R's will not be enough for students to be successful members of society. Such literacy is critical, of course, since it is prerequisite for most academic areas, but it is not sufficient. Besides being literate, tomorrow's students must be collaborative, analytical, and competent users of technology.

While schools will never be businesses, they can learn some important lessons from the private sector. Schools need to be held accountable for their work, just as private sector managers are. At the same time, school administrators need to have the freedom to innovate and devise creative strategies for dealing with their problems. (Bean, 1994, p. 6)

As schools grapple with the complex problems of preparing students for employment, the link between schools and business is likely to become more collaborative.

This theme of dovetailing the common interests shared by both business and school has been further developed by Clendenin (1994). As Chairman of Bell South Corporation, Clendenin believes that one of the reasons our schools are not helping students develop the academic and verbal skills needed for career success is due to the private sector's failure to state clearly what skills students should possess upon graduation.

Once these skills are identified, behavior analysis can provide educators with a certain degree of expertise. Educational behavior analysts have a long history of developing behavioral objectives designed to specify and measure performance. Additionally, behavior analysis stresses the use of **task analysis**. That is, behavior analysts break a complex task into its constituent parts and use this outcome to develop training methods designed to ensure mastery of the skill at each step. Providing assistance to both educators and their business counterparts in specifying and defining these skills is an area in which behavior analysis can provide extensive support.

Clendenin (1994) also feels that the second class status of students who receive vocational training in public schools must change. Only about a third of all high school graduates enroll in college. The vast majority of high school students seek immediate employment or enroll in trade and technical programs. To recognize this reality and facilitate these students' opportunities, schools need to develop and expand programs such as distributive education (DE). In DE, students spend part of each school day engaged in academics and part employed in the community. Distributive education programs offer obvious benefits to students. Unfortunately, too often the work experiences afforded DE students (e.g., fast food jobs) do not provide them with the potential for career growth.

In order for DE to be effective, students must possess a discrete set of skills (Clendenin, 1994) including a high level of reading comprehension, the ability to accurately and swiftly compute using basic algebra and geometry, training in how to "think through" a problem (i.e., analytical skills), and well developed oral and written communication skills. In addition, Tucker (1994) believes that tomorrow's workers increasingly will have to be able to communicate in at least a second language in order to maintain a high level of employability as the marketplace becomes more global, and as other languages become more commonplace among various segments of the U.S. population.

There should be at least three positive outcomes produced by every good school-to-work program. First, the teachers in such programs are likely to stay current with technological changes being implemented in the non-school world. This type of "real world" awareness should help decrease the lag time between the use of information age tools in the work setting and their adoption in the classroom. Second, school to work programs should prompt the development of new, and revision of existing, high school core courses that are more directly geared to helping students acquire the academic, technical, and work-specific skills needed for career success. Third, this approach should facilitate the transition from high school to employment in ways that are similar to the transition from high school to college found with students following that track (Clendenin, 1994).

Technology Related Issues

The increased emphasis on technology in our schools is a pervasive theme that connects virtually all of the literature on school change or reform. Shaw (1994) states that for schools to be considered "good" in the future, they will have to be wired literally and figuratively. Literally in the sense of being physically capable of using and accessing modern technology. Figuratively, schools will need to be connected to community support such as local businesses and state and local agencies.

Another interesting observation that Shaw (1994) makes concerns whether the textual materials used in tomorrow's schools will be similar to the books used today. He thinks that students, instead of using textbooks as we currently know them, will access materials electronically through the Internet or various CD ROM software titles. It may be difficult for many of us to accept that within a few years paper-based textbooks might not be widely used in our schools, but analogous change has already taken place. For example, Huitt (1995) points out that although he has an extensive collection of phonograph records, his children have none. Instead, they have tapes and CDs and machines that play them.

One of the main concerns that computer-based technology raises is centered on its effectiveness. For example, will the use of computers in classrooms help students learn more efficiently and will students in electronic classrooms manage their learning better than students in traditional classes? According to Pogue (1994), early studies suggest that answers to questions such as these are incomplete for at least two reasons. First, there are not enough "electronic classrooms" to date. Second, those classrooms currently in use haven't been around long enough to evaluate fairly. Nevertheless, "computers are expected to change students' study habits, engage them in self-directed learning, encourage their curiosity, and promote their acquisition of critical thinking skills" (Warren, 1995, p. 2).

There are data available that suggest computerized instruction is an efficient and effective mode for learning. Orlansky and String (1979), for example, found that military trainees who used Computer Assisted Instruction reached similar levels of achievement in 30 percent less time, when compared to peers exposed to more traditional modes of training. Similarly, in a review of more than 130 academic studies on the use of technology, Bailo and Sivin-Kachla (1995) found that technology, as a support to instruction, raised students' performance in language arts, math, social studies, and science. Perhaps the most impressive results of computer-based technology can be found with students with disabilities. For example, the U.S. Department of Commerce, National Telecommunications and Information Administration (1995) found that the use of computer-assisted learning techniques allowed almost 75 percent of school-age children with disabilities to remain in classrooms. Furthermore, approximately 45 percent of these students were able to minimize the use of school related services traditionally provided for their handicapping condition because of the availability of this technology.

Although computer based technology is expensive to buy and maintain–today's state-of-the-art equipment quickly becomes obsolete as seemingly daily advances are announced–and the use of this technology requires constant training, its advantages far outweigh its cost. By using telephone lines, fiber optic cable, or satellite hookups, schools of the future will be able to access information in unprecedented fashion. Warren (1995) emphasized that technology increases the types of learning opportunities and experiences students have available, and can decrease any educational inequities that exist between poor and rich schools.

Already, familiarity with such technology is a near requirement for academic and career success, and the graduates of schools that promote technological literacy will be in higher demand than those who are technologically illiterate. As Tucker (1994) stated, "whether the collar is white or blue, the worker must be able to use computers, think independently, produce quality results with little or no supervision, and function highly effectively in teams" (p. 34).

Behavior analysis can help to meet the changing requirements brought about by the inclusion of technology in classrooms. Many behavior analysts have used computers as a research tool for years and the transition to using computers in classrooms has been relatively easy. Helping teachers use various computer technologies has become increasingly more important and behavior analysts have been steadily making advances in this area. For example, Kritch and Bartow (as cited in Bostow, 1995) developed a computer tutorial that teaches users to make instructional and assessment materials for use on personal computers. Their tutorial requires little previous knowledge of behavioral or computer principles, yet within a relatively short period of time, users can create behaviorally sound tutorials.

Additionally, Appleman (1995) advocates a shaping approach to learning both how to use and to teach students various aspects of technology. Shaping requires that each successive performance more closely resembles a final desired outcome in order to be reinforced. "As you become expert with one tool, the less mysterious other tools will become. You'll begin to recognize strategies common to all interface designers, and tools you've never used before will be more intuitive right from the start" (Appleman, 1995, p. 6). Behavior analysts would state that Appleman's position promotes response generalization. As the behavior of teachers and students becomes more fluent with respect to various software packages or software commands, those skills and fluencies will generalize to other similar software products.

Choosing One's School

Until the late 1960's, most children attended their neighborhood schools. This changed dramatically when a number of desegregation cases were brought before the courts. The outcome of these cases resulted in the pervasive school busing programs that began in the 1970's. At best, school busing produced mixed results and angered almost all parents whose children were required to attend schools outside their neighborhood, particularly when that school was a considerable distance away. Busing is still an active and costly component of most school systems and the issue of where kids go to school is very much alive and well. However, rather than bus children to distant schools solely to achieve racial balance, some parents want to bus their children to schools that will provide them with a better education than the school they currently attend. And, as often as not, these parents want to send their children to private rather than public schools. The problem is that many of these parents want to be able to use the money allocated to the local school system to help pay the tuition.

Basically there are two approaches to the school choice issue that politicians and educational administrators will be grappling with for the next several years. In the first approach, public schools would "charge" tuition. The parents of each child would be provided with a voucher or chit that would probably be a bit less than the per pupil annual allocation the state makes available to the public school district in which the parents live. Parents would then select the school they want their child to attend and use the voucher to cover the cost of tuition. A controversial variation would allow the voucher to also be used at private schools. The Georgia Public Policy Foundation, a conservative think tank, contends vouchers are a way to inject competition into public education in a way that is similar to what is done at the college and university level. Furthermore, the Georgia Public Policy Foundation argues that vouchers will allow children from low socio-economic areas a means to avoid substandard inner city or rural schools (Trends and Ideas, 1994).

The other approach to the issue of school choice involves the idea of charter schools. The charter schools movement is an attempt to improve the quality of public schools by exempting them from certain state and local regulations governing more traditional schools and by making them compete for students. Typically, parents and teachers of a charter school agree to meet certain performance goals, and the local and state school boards free the school from bureaucratic regulations. The school is then able to develop innovative curricula so that it can then "compete with private schools for top, deserving students" (Trends and Ideas, 1994, p. 9). Echoing this sentiment, L. M. Studness (Personal communication, May 19, 1995) stated that charter schools are important to reform efforts because they can dramatically impact not only where students go to school, but also teacher autonomy, competition, and accountability.

Charter school proponents argue that the laws and regulations governing public schools force schools to take an academically homogeneous view toward students, thus, failing to provide the best education possible for each individual student. Each child learns very differently, hence, he or she may require different teaching styles, curricula, and so on. Many see charter schools as laboratories for innovation. For example, the goal of the Foothills Academy, a private school that gained charter school status in the Fall of 1996, is to provide an alternative to gifted students who may need a different kind of educational environment. Many of the students at the Foothills Academy come from schools where students were frustrated by the slower pace. Alternatively, many consider charter schools to be the best remedy for chronically low-performing schools. Some charter schools target students who are at risk of failing or dropping out. For example, Colorado's Charter Schools Act allows up to 50 charter schools with thirteen reserved as schools that serve at-risk children.

Charter schools give teachers a stronger voice and more input into new teaching methods in classrooms. Teacher unions (e.g., National Education Association) have noticed how the charter idea can be used to give teachers authority over the learning program and more control over professional issues. Additionally, charter schools can more easily cut through the rules and red tape required by most state and local districts. However, leaders of some state teacher organizations are concerned that people could teach in charter schools without having to meet the certification requirements of other public school teachers. But this increased flexibility has positive effects as well. For example, charter schools can hire retirees who specialized in certain fields, such as chemistry, to teach or assist students without requiring them to obtain the more traditional teacher certifications or licenses.

Naturally, some problems will arise as the charter school movement unfolds. For example, many organizers of charter schools do not realize that they are setting up a business enterprise and, as such, they might have to struggle before the school becomes profitable enough to sustain itself. Furthermore, many charter laws are unclear, creating a number of challenges and roadblocks for proponents. Still, many successes have been reported. For example, one charter school in the San Fernando Valley area of California reported a $1.2 million surplus in its first year budget, which it used to hire more teachers and expand and improve its facilities.

Will Your School Meet the Demands of School Reform?

How will you prepare high school students for employment after high school? What types of collaborative efforts will you try to establish with the business community? What place will technology play in your school? How will you keep your faculty well versed in technology so that they can use and share this expertise with students? How will you assess the effectiveness of the school to work programs, and of your use of technology? If parents have the option of choosing a school for their children, why would they want to choose your school? Are you confident enough in this school that you are designing that you would be willing to establish it as a charter school?

Summary

Substantial educational reform is needed to raise academic standards, enhance student skills, and increase parental involvement. While many of the ideas presented in this chapter have yet to take hold in education circles, we, as a culture, still have to deal with many vexing problems that affect schools and schooling. One encroaching problem that has begun to receive considerable attention concerns the amount of time our students spend in school. For parents, the concerns about year-round schooling center on possible scheduling problems that may occur if children at one school are on break while other children are not (O'Neil & Adamson, 1993; Sardo-Brown & Rooney, 1992). With planning, these and other issues associated with year round schooling can certainly be overcome or substantially minimized.

Longer school days and year-round schooling have the potential to both improve students' academic performance and simultaneously help schools better address some of the social deficits students bring to school. For example, Knox (1994) found that decreasing the length of summer break substantially reduces the amount of information students forget and minimizes the amount of time teachers must spend in review at the beginning of each new term. Gandara and Fish (1994) suggest that year-round schooling will be especially helpful for at-risk and educationally disadvantaged students while Alcorn (1992) indicated that students in year-round classes achieved at higher levels than students in traditional programs.

The business of today's schools is much different than in previous eras and the new challenges schools and schooling face have, in part, produced some of the problems we now see. Fantuzzo and Atkins (1992) emphasize the new social demands schools must address because of the massive societal changes that have occurred. In years past, schools and schooling were primarily charged with insuring that students graduated as literate citizens. Socialization skills were left to the family or church. During the past thirty years, however, family structure and communities have changed significantly. Because of the diversity found in the current student body, the demands placed on schools in terms of meeting the educational and psychological needs of students have exceeded the resources of schools. Extending the school day and year might allow us to better address students' unmet academic and social needs. After-school programs could provide safe environments for play, enrichment and remedial programs, or other supervised extracurricular activities that many children need.

Annotated Bibliography

Brown, R. (1993). *Schools of thought: How politics of literacy shape thinking in the classroom.* New York: Basic Books.

Presents the different types of literacy (reading, math, cultural, computer) that compete for attention and resources in American schools, and the multiple agencies (school boards, courts, state departments, legislatures, federal government) that influence schools' policy and practices, suggesting that with so many demands on American schools and so many different philosophies and definitions of what education should be, educational reform lacks clear direction.

Bean, E. (Ed.). (1994). Special education edition. *Georgia Trend.*

Focuses on several important educational issues such as vouchers, job skills needed for the next century, technology in public schools, previous reform efforts, and the role of values in schools.

Friedkin, N. E., & Necochea, J. (1988). School system size and performance: A contingency perspective. *Educational Evaluation and Policy Analysis, 10,* 237-249.

Using data from the California Assessment Program, the authors report an interaction between school size and students' socio-economic-status (SES) with high SES students performing better in larger schools and lower SES students performing better in smaller schools.

Perelman, L. J. (1992). *School's out: Hyperleraning, the new technology, and the end of education.* New York: William Morrow.

Calls for the elimination of schools, and suggests students learn at home, at work, in shopping centers—anywhere except schools. This learning would be supported by micro-vouchers parents could use to purchase educational services from a variety of vendors.

Chapter 4

Instructional Strategies

In this chapter we present six behavior-analytic instructional strategies or systems. Each strategy is introduced with a brief discussion of its history, a presentation of its guiding principles, a description of how the strategy is implemented in the classroom, and the empirical evidence of its effectiveness. As we recommended in Chapter One, we are only offering instructional strategies which research has shown to be *effective*. The six instructional strategies included are Precision Teaching, Personalized System of Instruction, Direct Instruction, Programmed Instruction, Peer Tutoring, and Computer Assisted Instruction. Five recurring themes in these instructional strategies that make them effective are frequent active responding, mastery, teacher accountability, student centered learning, and reinforcement.

Precision Teaching

Precision Teaching (PT) is presented first since it is a method that can facilitate the other instructional strategies. The principles of PT can be effectively combined with any of the instructional strategies presented in this chapter. Ogden Lindsley, who is credited with being the founder of the principles of PT, was a student of B. F. Skinner at Harvard University where he learned about and committed himself to operant conditioning (Lindsley, 1990). Much of what Lindsley learned from working in the laboratory with Skinner is reflected in Precision Teaching. However, he credits regular classroom teachers for fully developing PT into an effective system for students.

In order to meet students' educational needs, teachers must analyze students' behavior and determine how it changes with an instructional strategy. Any strategy found to be effective should be continued; strategies found to be ineffective should be changed immediately so that valuable instructional time is not wasted. Precision Teaching allows teachers to determine the effectiveness of their instruction by following these guiding principles: (a) trust that the student is always right, (b) use continuous direct measurement of behavior, (c) work with observable and repeatable behaviors, (d) use rate of response to measure behavior, (e) record performance on a semi-logarithmic chart and analyze by visual inspection, and (f) use a positive approach to learning (West & Young, 1992; White, 1986).

Lindsley learned from Skinner in their work with laboratory animals that "the rat is always right." Lindsley recounts an amusing exchange with Skinner in which Lindsley, after implementing an extinction procedure, told Skinner that the rat did not respond the way it was supposed to according to Skinner's book. Skinner replied, "In this case the book is wrong! The rat knows best! That's why we still have him in the experiment!" (Lindsley, 1990, p. 12). For Lindsley, in the classroom, *the student is always right*. Student performance is an accurate measure of the effectiveness of the instruction the student is receiving. The student's performance, then, is used to make informed decisions about which strategies to continue and which to change (West & Young, 1992). Precision teachers are to "assume that learners respond in lawful ways to environmental variables and that if learners behave in an undesirable way it is the responsibility of teachers to alter those variables until they produce the desired result" (Binder & Watkins, 1990, p. 78).

Because teachers are trying to produce learning, it is important to *measure behavior continuously rather than periodically*. Teachers typically measure learning by testing periodically, usually at the end of a chapter or unit of study. When testing is conducted at the end of a chapter or unit of study, the teacher may know who learned the material and who did not learn the material. Unfortunately this information is usually only used to record a grade in a grade book so that at report card time, the teacher can assign a grade. Students for whom the instruction was effective, learned the material. Those for whom the instruction was not effective, will not have the opportunity to learn that material because the class will move on to new material.

The alternative to measuring learning periodically is to measure learning continuously. It is best if the learning is measured daily (Binder & Watkins, 1990; West & Young, 1992; West, Young, & Spooner, 1990; White, 1986). When learning is measured daily, changes in instructional strategies can be made in a timely manner so that all students have the opportunity to learn the material. Changes in performance indicate learning. If, after three measures of the behavior, there is no change in performance, learning is not occurring and appropriate adaptations should be made in the instruction. This means, of course, adaptations may have to be made for some students, and not for other students.

An additional advantage to daily measures of behavior is that each measure is an opportunity to practice what is being learned. A direct positive correlation exists between opportunity to practice and academic gains. That is, higher academic gains are found with increased opportunities to respond (Greenwood & Carta, 1988; West et al., 1990). Lindsley (1990) reports research showing the importance of daily practice in locating and abbreviating state names on a blank map. Practicing for one minute a day produced more progress than practicing for two minutes every other day. Students practiced the same number of minutes in both learning situations, yet learned more when those minutes occurred daily.

The behavior that is to be measured daily must be **observable** and **repeatable**. To be observable, it must be public behavior rather than a private behavior. Writing or saying multiplication facts is an observable, overt behavior. However, studying multiplication facts may not be observable. That is, students may study multiplication facts by looking at them and repeating the facts to themselves. This behavior is not observable and therefore not measurable. To consider the behavior observable, it must pass Lindsley's "Dead Man Test." That is, "*if a dead man can do it or look like he's doing it, then it's not behavior*" (White, 1986, p. 526). The behavior must also be one that can be repeated many times during an instructional session or measurement opportunity. Students may write answers to math problems, read orally, write the weights associated with each element in the periodic table, or complete analogies. For each assessment, teachers need a representative sample of the behavior. This representative sample has been found to be a minimum of 20 responses. It may be solving 20 math problems, reading 20 words, writing the weights for 20 elements in the periodic table, or completing 20 analogies (West & Young, 1992).

Observable and repeatable behaviors are continuously measured and then reported as a **rate of response**. Rate of response is an average number of responses per minute. It is more important than percent correct because it provides information about **fluency**. Fluency tells us not only that the student knows the correct answer, but that the student can generate the answer quickly. The more fluently students can respond, the better they know the material. Fluency provides information that is not available when teachers measure only percent correct. "Fluency is 'second nature' knowledge, near-automatic performance, the ability to perform without hesitation. In short, fluency is true mastery" (Binder, 1988, p. 12).

If Shalisa, a third grade student, is learning the six times table and correctly writes answers to all twelve in 10 minutes she may be said to know the six times table. Her performance is 100% correct. It is quite likely, however, that if there was some distraction in the classroom at the time she was writing the answers to these problems that she would either not be 100% correct, or that she would not finish in 10 minutes. Now, with practice—daily practice and measures of performance, Shalisa can soon write all 12 answers to the six times table in 30 seconds. She is still 100% correct, however, now she is also fluent and if there is some distraction while she is writing the answers it is likely that she still will get them all correct in close to 30 seconds. Learning clearly occurred between when Shalisa needed 10 minutes to write the 12 answers to the six times table and when she performed the same task in 30 seconds. The change is in rate of response and we can now be sure she is more fluent.

Teachers trained in Precision Teaching understand the importance of students being fluent in what are called **tool skills**. "Tool skills are the most basic elements of more complex skills" (Johnson & Layng, 1992, p. 1479). Writing digits and math facts quickly, and saying sounds and words quickly are tool skills for math computation, and problem solving and for reading comprehension. The more fluent students are in tool skills the more prepared they are for more complex learning. When students "do not achieve sufficient levels of basic arithmetic computation (e.g., 50 to 70 problems per minute), students usually experience difficulty learning long division, algebra and other advanced math skills" (Binder, 1988, p. 13). Knowing the importance of fluency allows the teacher to be sensitive to fluency in tool skills before moving on to more complex learning tasks. Additionally, when students are not progressing in complex skills, teachers can examine fluency of tool skills to identify the dysfluent tool skills that are inhibiting progress and then work with those skills to build fluency.

The more proficient students are in the tool skills, the faster they will learn the more complex skills that build on the tool skills. "Students proficient at analysis, synthesis, and evaluation are very fluent at the tool and component skills necessary for these complex recombinations" (McDade & Goggans, 1993, p. 299). Maybe even more surprising and exciting is the realization that becoming fluent in tool skills can lead to success in higher level tasks without instruction in the higher level tasks. Johnson and Layng (1992) report that teaching whole number problem solving and fraction calculation to fluency was sufficient for students to solve word problems involving fractions successfully. That is, while lack of fluency in tool skills is likely to interfere with learning more complex skills, fluency of tool skills may result in more complex learning even *without additional instruction.*

As in earlier chapters, we see a close analogy between athletics, where drill and practice are common, accepted, and encouraged, and what works in academics. The soccer coach teaches her team how to do a throw-in and then practices that skill— a tool skill—until a correct throw-in is done automatically without having to think about all the requirements (keeping the back foot on the ground, bringing the ball directly over the head, etc.). Rather than thinking about the mechanics of the throw-in, the player can be focusing on the field of play so that she can direct the ball to a teammate who will take the ball in the direction of the goal. When six-year-old children play soccer, a throw-in can take a full minute or more to execute. Once executed, the player is happy it was an acceptable throw-in regardless of where the ball lands on the field, or in whose possession. In a college soccer game, the throw-in is executed in seconds without the player even thinking about the mechanics of what she is doing. Instead, her thinking is focused on the position of the players on the field.

When students read and write letters, numbers, words, and math facts effortlessly, they are likely to understand what they read, communicate their ideas clearly, and accurately perform advanced math. These are obvious tool skills for the primary grades, but they are not the only tool skills. With each new content area there are tool skills to be mastered. If you are to debate the different philosophical orientations to education, you must be fluent in those orientations. That is, you must practice the vocabulary associated with each orientation. When you can use the vocabulary effortlessly, you are better able to debate the different orientations. Fortunately, "the rate of a student's response is very sensitive to changes in instruction, so the effects of a new teaching strategy will be immediately obvious" (West & Young, 1992, p. 140). If the instructional strategy being used is not producing fluency in tool skills, the strategy should be changed as soon as possible because without fluency in tool skills students will not be prepared for higher level skills such as analysis, synthesis, and evaluation.

Precision Teaching requires daily measures of observable, repeatable behaviors to monitor for fluency. These measures are then charted on a semi-logarithmic chart. The chart is called a standard celeration chart since it "always depicts rate of change or progress in a standard manner, regardless of the initial frequency of the behavior" (White, 1986, p. 525). On the chart, the X and Y axes are always the same; that is, assessments (days) are found on the X axis and number of responses per minute are found on the Y axis (see Chapter 6). The lines of the Y axis are spaced so that changes in the rate of response are easily detected. That is, if a student's rate of response doubles, a line through the points on the graph will be at the same angle whether the doubling in rate is from a rate of 2 to a rate of 4 per minute or from a rate of 100 to a rate of 200 per minute. Once teachers learn how to read the line that connects the points on the graph, they can easily see if students are making progress regardless of the student's level of functioning at the start of instruction. Because the chart is a standard chart, it can be used to display both academic and social behavior. With academic behavior we look for an acceleration in rate of correct responding and deceleration in rate of incorrect responding. With social behaviors we look for accelerations and decelerations in rates of appropriate and inappropriate behaviors—all on the same charts.

The measures for the daily assessments are charted as soon as they are completed so that teachers and students can continually evaluate progress by visual inspection of the chart using two decision rules. "*If the pupil is progressing in the right direction, leave the program alone; if the pupil is essentially 'flat' or going the wrong way, then change the program*"(White, 1986, p. 528). Students as young as five can learn to chart their own behavior (Lindsley, 1990). Together, students and teacher can make decisions about which strategies to keep and which to change. In addition, a public display of performance can function to accelerate performance (Lindsley, 1990) and to increase self-esteem (Beck & Clement, 1991). When a parent calls to inquire about a student, the teacher can quickly check the chart and tell the parent what skills the student is working on and how well the student is progressing. Maybe what is most effective is that the charts are a constant reminder to the teachers that they are responsible for utilizing instructional strategies that result in changes in behavior, both social and academic, and if the changes are not occurring teachers need to take the responsibility for implementing alternative instructional strategies.

The Precision Teaching classroom, with all its practice, measurement, charting, and analyzing, may suggest a very dreary place to learn. However, that is not the case. It is an approach that focuses on positive methods to strengthen behavior. Helping students become fluent helps them succeed and enjoy school (West & Young, 1992). Remember, the final guiding principle of Precision Teaching, is to *use a positive approach to learning.*

When students succeed, they are happy. Precision Teaching facilitates success through the use of positive rather than punitive procedures. In the PT classroom students do not work to avoid failure, they work to succeed. If they are not succeeding, *they* are not failing, the *instruction* is failing and it is changed. The best we can do for students is to allow them to succeed. We allow them to succeed by helping them master the skills they need to progress. Precision Teaching provides a way for us to monitor our instruction to be sure we are providing strategies that allow students to succeed. With early success comes the competency to succeed in more advanced classes and with success in these classes comes the opportunity to enter the best colleges and universities, and ultimately to enter the professions of their choice. Along with competency, success provides confidence, which students need to meet the challenges that will result in the best opportunities later.

A classroom in which Precision Teaching is being used is a classroom in which students are engaged in a great deal of active responding throughout the day. There are usually semi-logarithmic charts posted around the room or readily available in students' folders so that students can chart their behavior. The instructional strategies being implemented are limited only to the extent that they result in efficient learning for the students. That is, if the data on the semi-logarithmic charts show that the instruction is effective it does not matter what the strategy is. If, however, the data on the chart show that the instruction is not effective, a new strategy is implemented.

Different students may be utilizing different strategies. Some students may move quickly from one strategy to the next until they find one that is effective while other students may find the first strategy they use is effective and they stay with that strategy. For brief periods of time throughout the day there will be assessments of performance that are then recorded as rate of response on semi-logarithmic charts. These assessments can be done by students working in pairs (one assesses the other), they can be done with the entire class simultaneously as students complete a fact sheet, they can be done by a paraprofessional, an aide, a volunteer, or a teacher working with individual students, or they can be done independently by a student who times himself while he writes responses on a paper and then gets an answer key to check his work. There will also be frequent inspection of the data on the charts as students and teachers make decisions about instruction. The students in the Precision Teaching classroom are active learners in a very student-centered classroom. Students' individual daily performances determine their individual instruction.

It is not surprising, then, that teachers have demonstrated the effectiveness of PT with a wide range of students across various disciplines. Precision Teaching has been implemented in Great Falls Public Schools in Montana for 15 years and has been found to be effective in grades K-12 for both special education and regular education programs (Beck & Clement, 1991). In a well controlled study reported by White (1986), two carefully matched schools were compared. In one school, Precision Teaching was implemented throughout the school, while in the matched school PT was not used. In the PT school, the average performance of the students "was raised to the 95th percentile in reading and the 86th percentile in math on standardized measures" (p. 530). On the same measures in the matched school the average performance was only the "71st and the 54th percentiles in math and reading" (p. 530). At the university level, Precision Teaching has been used to improve performance in anthropology, biology, geography, and psychology (McDade & Goggans, 1993). Precision Teaching has also been successfully used to facilitate the reduction of disruptive behavior (Schoen & James, 1991).

Possibly, this is your first glimpse of Precision Teaching and you are wondering why, if there is something so effective available to educators, you have not been in a classroom in which PT has been used. It is quite likely that you have not used

Precision Teaching because much, if not most, of what we do in classrooms is not guided by the research that empirically demonstrates the effectiveness of different instructional strategies. In the case of PT, however, it is not entirely the fault of the local academic community, as Precision Teaching has not been widely published or publicized. That is, those involved in the development of Precision Teaching often chose to share the information among themselves rather than to publish it. Further, you are not likely to read about Precision Teaching in an education textbook. In checking five undergraduate educational psychology textbooks by five different authors, published by five different publishers between 1994 and 1995, we found that none list Precision Teaching in the index. Maybe it's meant to be a secret—we hope not!

Did you know you could use Precision Teaching yourself to improve your performance in your current college classes? Begin by identifying any terms, formulas, names, theories, etc. and making study cards for each. Then simply quiz yourself every day and see how many you can recite orally in one minute—it is important that you say the responses aloud. By test time you should be quite fluent in the basic vocabulary of the content you are studying and this will facilitate your comprehension, analysis, and synthesis of the larger concepts.

This is a requirement in an educational psychology course taught by one of the authors. During the first class meeting of the term or the first class meeting after a test, students receive a review sheet with important terms and concepts to be mastered before the next test. As soon as terms and concepts are introduced in class or in the readings, students make flash cards for them. At the start of each class period, students spend four minutes quizzing themselves on terms and concepts that have been introduced. This is followed by a one minute timed quiz so students can track their progress—how many they said correctly in one minute each class period. The number of flash cards increases each class period, but students are just adding a few at a time. It is important to emphasize that this method is only effective when practice begins early and continues regularly. It simply is not effective the night before the test.

Will You Use Precision Teaching in Your School?

Now that you know a little about Precision Teaching, is it something you would like to know more about? Would you like to incorporate Precision Teaching in your school? What types of tool skills would you assess using Precision Teaching? What instructional strategies would you pair with Precision Teaching? What follows are five strategies you might find appropriate.

Personalized System of Instruction

The Personalized System of Instruction (PSI) is also called The Keller Plan, named after its designer, Fred S. Keller. Just as we associate Ogden Lindsley's name with Precision Teaching, we associate Fred Keller's name with PSI. Both Lindsley and Keller drew heavily from Skinner's work in designing their instructional strategies. However, while Lindsley was one of Skinner's students, Keller was one of Skinner's peers at Harvard. Keller was a graduate student at Harvard when Skinner arrived in 1928 (Bjork, 1993) and soon became a friend of Skinner's as well as a supporter of the new behaviorism Skinner was developing. Skinner's new branch of behaviorism was carefully described in *The Behavior of Organisms* published in 1938. "Keller, then teaching at Columbia University, surprised Skinner by incorporating the book into his lectures" (Bjork, 1993, p. 109). It comes as no surprise, then, that almost 40 years later when Keller and Sherman wrote *The Keller Plan Handbook* they dedicated it to B.F. Skinner (Keller & Sherman, 1974). Keller credits Skinner with being the architect of reinforcement theory and the leader in the search for effective education (Keller & Sherman, 1974).

The Personalized System of Instruction is based on reinforcement theory. "The designers of the system had the goal of maximizing the rewards for educational behavior, minimizing chances for extinction and frustration, eliminating punishment and fear, and facilitating the development of precise discriminations" (Keller & Sherman, 1974, p. 52). The original design began in March, 1963 in Keller's home when he, Gilmour Sherman, Rodolpho Azzi, and Caroline Martuscelli Bori brainstormed in front of the fireplace (Keller & Sherman, 1974). The four colleagues had been invited to begin a Department of Psychology at the University of Brasilia. Now was their opportunity to put together what they thought would be the most effective way to teach psychology. With all four well trained in reinforcement theory, it is not surprising that what developed was an instructional strategy based on reinforcement.

While delays in Brasilia kept Keller and Sherman from being present for the actual implementation of the first PSI course, it was successfully implemented by Azzi and Bori. In the meantime, Keller and Sherman had both taken positions at Arizona State University where they first introduced PSI in an introductory psychology course (Keller & Sherman, 1974). Out of these beginnings grew the five defining features of PSI. A Personalized System of Instruction requires mastery, allows self-pacing, relies on written materials, utilizes proctors, and provides lectures as reinforcement (Keller & Sherman, 1974).

The **mastery** requirement means that students may not continue until they have demonstrated mastery—typically 90% correct with a predetermined level of fluency on a test of the content they are studying. Unlike the traditional classroom in which content is studied for a period of time, a test is given, a grade recorded, and the class moves on to the next content, students in the PSI classroom only move on when they have mastered the current content. In the traditional classroom, many students only master small amounts of the content "taught." In the PSI classroom all students master all the content "taught." Notice that the mastery we are concerned with is the mastery of the content thought to be important for a particular course. That is, mastery is not meant to imply that after the course the student knows all there is to know about the subject area being presented in that course. Rather, if it is second grade math, it means the student has mastered what the student is expected to learn about math in the second grade. Whatever the instructor determines students should know as a result of taking the course is what is mastered. It allows the next instructor to assume correctly that the students are entering the new course with a particular content base.

Students may demonstrate mastery by responding orally or by responding on a computer. However, they typically demonstrate mastery on written tests. These tests are short and can usually be completed in about 20 minutes (Buskist, Cush, & DeGrandpre, 1991). Students take these tests when they determine they are ready. Once completed, tests are graded immediately by a proctor, who then discusses the test with the student. If, from this test the student has demonstrated mastery of the content, the student is allowed to begin work on the next unit of study. However, if the student has not demonstrated mastery of the content, the proctor offers clarification on misunderstood concepts and tries to help the student in any way possible–this is the personalized aspect of PSI. The student then studies the materials again and takes another form of the test for the same content. This continues until the student demonstrates mastery of the entire content.

Whenever mastery is required, it is essential to allow for **self-pacing**. One does not expect all students to master the same content in the same amount of time or in some lock-step fashion. Allowing self-pacing benefits both the advanced and the slower students without penalty to either. Advanced students may move as quickly through the units as they like without waiting for their classmates. Similarly, slower students may take as long as they need to master the content without being left behind as they often are in the traditional classroom. Further, as is often the case in any course, there will be portions of the course that are entirely new for some students and a review for other students. What is a new or review portion of the course will vary for different students. That is, reinforcement theory may be a review for the student who has had a previous psychology course, especially one taught by a behavior analyst, while it may be either new or still confusing for another student who either has not had a previous psychology course or has had such a course, but with very little emphasis on reinforcement theory. The students who already know reinforcement theory quickly demonstrate mastery of the concept and move on to another unit, while the students who are struggling with reinforcement theory for the first time are allowed all the time and assistance they need, without penalty, before moving on to the next unit.

Just as the mastery component necessitates the self-pacing component, the self-pacing component necessitates a **reliance on written materials**. If course content is provided via written materials, students can spend as much time as they need with those materials in order to learn the content. When the bulk of the information is provided in lecture form, once the lecture is delivered the information is no longer available to learn from except for the notes students have taken, which vary greatly in their accuracy and completeness. Typically, the more background students have in a subject area, the more accurate and complete their notes are from the lecture, which once again leaves those students with less background information at a serious disadvantage when trying to learn from lectures. Relying on written materials allows students to return as often as necessary to the content they are trying to master.

As students rely on written materials to master content at their own pace, one quickly sees the need for the instructor to have help. This help comes by way of the **proctors**. Proctors are usually either students who have already completed the course or students who are currently enrolled in the course and are further along than their classmates. In either case, it is essential that the proctor has a firm grasp of the content to be mastered. While an answer key is provided for scoring the tests, the proctor's job involves more than just marking items correct and incorrect. If an answer appears incorrect based on the key, the proctor asks the student to clarify the answer. Sometimes with clarification it is apparent that the student actually knows the answer and credit is given for the answer. Also, for the content students have not grasped on the test, the proctor provides clarification—mini-teaching to help students through difficult concepts. This makes the PSI classroom very individual-ized. Whatever content students are struggling with in their studies is individually analyzed and support is provided.

What's missing in the PSI classroom that is so prevalent in more traditional classrooms is the lecture, although the lecture is not always completely abandoned. Instead, **lectures are offered as reinforcers**. Reinforcers are events that serve to strengthen the behavior upon which they are contingent. That is, students must behave in particular ways in order to be eligible to attend a lecture (the reinforcer for behaving in particular ways). Only if a certain number of units have been mastered may students attend the lecture.

Now you may be thinking, I've never heard a lecture that would function to reinforce my working hard. However, haven't there been some (however few) lectures that you found exciting or stimulating—that you actually enjoyed attending? Hopefully, the answer is yes. Well, those are the types of lectures that have to be offered in PSI classes. These are lectures and/or demonstrations that supplement or expand the required course content. They are often motivational in nature (Buskist et al., 1991). They may be ideas for further investigation or presentations of current research based on the course topics. An advantage of these lectures is that they are interesting and students can simply enjoy them. That is, there is no requirement to master the content of the lecture or even to attend. Students do not need to bother taking notes, they can just listen and become absorbed in what is being offered knowing full well that no one is going to hold them accountable for the content at some later time. This is truly the way to spark interest in a discipline.

Two common modifications to PSI as presented here are seen in the lecture feature and in the self-pacing feature. It is not uncommon for lectures in today's PSI classes to provide clarification of the content from various units. Aspects of the unit that may be particularly difficult for students to grasp can be offered through lectures. In addition, because of the frequent administrative problem of open-ended self-pacing, it is common practice to set a date by which a certain number of units must be mastered or the student is dropped from the course. Students in these college PSI course tend to enjoy the courses, attend only those lectures they feel they need for clarification, and work at a brisk enough pace to finish the course in one semester.

Let's look at how a classroom might operate if PSI is being used. As you will see from the research that follows later in this section, PSI has been successfully implemented across all ages of students in many different content areas. For the sake of our description of a PSI classroom, we have chosen the college classroom for two reasons. Personalized System of Instruction was first implemented in the college classroom and in the previous section we used an elementary school in the description of our classroom. It should be noted, however, that PSI can be effectively implemented at any grade level once students are competent readers. Personalized System of Instruction relies heavily on written materials and therefore would not be an effective strategy for students who could not read and comprehend well. As we develop this example in a college classroom consider an elementary or middle school classroom in which students don't have the option of not attending, but they may be working on a unit in any one of many different content areas at any one time. Instead of carrying their units with them, they would file them in the classroom and retrieve them when they were ready to work on that unit. From there they would proceed just as our college students in this example proceed.

Long before the students gather for the first class of the semester, the instructor has done a great deal of work. Based on the course being taught, the instructor has identified appropriate objectives for that course. That is, at the end of this course the students should be able to do the things specified in the objectives. Based on these objectives, the instructor must identify written materials (book chapters, published articles) that will provide the information necessary for students to master the objectives. Whenever written materials are not available to teach those objectives, the instructor must write the materials. These objectives along with the written materials that will allow students to master the objectives are then combined into units of study. The final number of units is determined by the length of the course. "For a fifteen-week semester, eighteen units has proved to be a popular choice. Any number of units between fifteen and twenty seems to work equally well and describes what we might think of as the normal range" (Keller & Sherman, 1974, p. 27). For each unit, the instructor provides not only written materials and objectives, but often some practice test items. These units are compiled into packets, one for each unit. After a course has been taught several times so that it is in a form the instructor has found effective, these packets may be copied at the bookstore where students may purchase them. Next, the instructor meets with the proctors who will be working in this PSI class. These proctors are students who completed this PSI class during a previous semester. At this meeting, the instructor reviews proctor duties and content to be learned in the class, and provides answer keys to the mastery tests.

On the first day of the class you can expect the instructor to explain how a PSI class is run and what will be expected of you as a student in this class. You will be introduced to the proctors. Sometimes there are individual proctors assigned to individual students for the duration of the semester and other times proctors are available to all students so that as students are ready to take a test or have a test scored, they can approach any available proctor. You go to the bookstore to purchase your packets for the course. You open Unit One to find objectives, reading materials, and practice test questions. You may read these materials anywhere you like. Some students will choose to do their reading in the classroom while others will only come to the classroom to take mastery tests. Some students will form study groups to help each other learn the materials while others will choose to study alone. Those decisions are left up to the students.

Students learn the content using whatever strategies work best for them. Some students will simply read the material and know it while others will have to read the material and write down the important points in order to know it. Still others will read and explain to someone else what they think they learned in order to clarify it for themselves. Some students may make study cards to quiz themselves on the objectives before they attempt the first test and a few may even use Precision Teaching strategies to work towards fluency. The instructor is very comfortable allowing students to use the methods they find most effective.

When you believe you have mastered the objectives for Unit One, you seek out the proctor and report that you would like to take the test for Unit One. The proctor gives you the test, which you complete at an open desk in a designated area. When you complete the test you return to the proctor, who grades it while you wait. Any incorrect answer will cue the proctor to ask you for clarification—possibly the answer really is correct. If based on your clarification, the proctor thinks you know that content, the proctor will mark the answer correct. Sometimes, the proctor will also question you on an answer that is correct just to determine that you really understand the content. Any items you missed will be explained by the proctor who will then offer any necessary learning assistance.

Mastery is typically set at a minimum of 90% accuracy with some additional criterion for fluency. If you score at least 90% correct within a designated time limit, the proctor will record that you have mastered Unit One and you will be ready to start working on Unit Two. If you score lower than 90% or do not complete enough responses within the designated time limit, the proctor will record which form of the test you took, and that you did not demonstrate mastery. You will then study the materials again, usually there is a required wait period (about 30 minutes) before retesting is allowed. When you are ready to retest, you return to the proctor, who checks your records and sees that you have already taken Form A of the test and gives you either Form B or C. As before, you complete the test that the proctor scores immediately, providing the same type of feedback as before. If this time you score 90% or higher within the designated time, the proctor will record that you have mastered Unit One and you will be ready to start working on Unit Two. If your score is lower than 90% or you did not complete enough responses in the designated time you will repeat the procedure above.

On the rare occasion that a student fails to demonstrate mastery of a unit on three attempts, the student meets with the instructor who can provide additional help as needed by the student. Also, if at any time along the process—before failing to demonstrate mastery—the student requests help or clarification the proctor cannot provide, the student meets with the instructor. This system allows the instructor to provide the assistance that students need when they need it.

The course continues along this format until students have demonstrated mastery of all the units. Typically, there is also a cumulative final exam that may be offered early for those students who mastered all the units before the end of the semester. When students finish they need not return. Some will finish early while others will take more than a semester. This requires flexibility on the part of the administration to allow incompletes to be reported for those courses until they are completed. Many students start strong and then back off as mid-term approaches as this is typically a very busy time with exams and papers due in their more traditional courses.

Maybe you find such an approach to learning appealing and would like the opportunity to take such a course; however, maybe you would first like to know if such an approach is effective. That is, how likely is a student to be successful in such a course? According to Buskist et al. (1991), a meta-analysis conducted by Kulik, Kulik, and Cohen (1979) "showed that, despite aptitude, students taking PSI courses scored higher final examination scores than those taking traditional courses. PSI students with high aptitudes outperformed their counterparts in traditional courses by about 5 points, and PSI students with low aptitudes outperformed their respective counterparts by about 7 points" (p. 223). PSI has been used effectively to teach a broad range of college courses including: astronomy, biology, chemistry, computer science, engineering, English composition, English literature, French, geography, mathematics, music, philosophy, physics, political science, psychology, sociology, Spanish, and statistics (Boylan, 1980).

In a meta-analysis that examined five types of technology frequently used in the college classroom, Kulik (1983) found PSI was the most effective in raising "the final examination score of a typical student in a typical class from the 50th to the 70th percentile" (p. 958). Canelos and Ozbeki (1983) found PSI to "improve problem-solving learning for engineering problems over the traditional lecture/recitation strategy." In addition, with PSI, students performed equally well on average and more difficult problems while "the lecture/recitation group had a significant decrease in problem-solving ability on the more difficult problems" (p. 68). Not only do students perform better in a PSI course as compared to the traditional lecture course, they also report very positive attitudes towards the PSI approach (Davies, 1981). We also learned from Reboy and Semb (1991) that "PSI has successfully been used to teach complex subject matter at levels of achievement that exceed those attained by a lecture-discussion format" (p. 214) and that the strategies and skills students learn in PSI courses transfer to later courses and new situations.

Unlike Precision Teaching, PSI is not a strategy you can implement for yourself. However, if you were planning to take a course and two instructors were offering the course, one using traditional teaching methods and the other using PSI, which would you choose? It may be helpful to know that the best predictor of final exam scores in a PSI course is reading comprehension (Roberts, Suderman, Suderman, & Semb, 1990). With the heavy reliance on written materials, students who are good readers tend to succeed quite easily while poor readers may struggle some although they still tend to perform better in the PSI course than in a traditional course. If students like PSI courses, perform better in PSI courses, learn higher order cognitive skills in PSI courses, and are able to transfer skills and strategies learned in PSI courses it is expected that students would choose PSI courses if they were available.

Will You Use PSI in Your School?

Does the idea of a PSI course intrigue you? Would you like to design and implement PSI courses for your school? Remember, PSI places a heavy demand on reading. Will this affect the grade levels in which you implement PSI? If you are considering using PSI, how will you make sure the students entering these classes are competent readers? You may want to consider the next instructional strategy which has an excellent reputation for developing competent readers.

Direct Instruction

Direct Instruction (DI) is "a systematic approach to the design and delivery of a range of procedures for building and maintaining basic cognitive skills" (Becker, 1992, p. 71). If there is one name to associate with DI it is Siegfried Engelmann. Unlike Lindsley and Keller, however, Engelmann was not a student or a colleague of Skinner. He is not even a psychologist or formally trained in education. Rather he became involved in education when he and his wife felt they needed to teach some cognitive skills to their own children. While Engelmann is not a behavior analyst, he understands the importance of dealing with observable events in the learning environment and views the teacher "as a behavioral engineer" (Becker, 1992, p. 89).

In 1964, Engelmann joined Carl Bereiter and with financial support from the Carnegie Foundation developed a preschool. After two years of three hour days, the 12 low income children in this preschool "averaged a 26 point gain in Binet IQ (from 95-121) and performed at mid-second grade in reading and math" (Becker, 1992, p. 91). It was primarily because of the success of this preschool that in 1967 Engelmann was asked to participate in Project Follow Through. Project Follow Through was a national experiment in teaching economically disadvantaged, kindergarten through third grade children to "see what works." For this project Engelmann was joined by Wesley Becker and Douglas Carnine. Together they developed the Direct Instruction Model for the Follow Through Project.

Over the years several DI programs have been developed, revised, and implemented with outstanding success for economically disadvantaged children as well as for children who are not economically disadvantaged. The guiding rule for DI is to "teach more in less time" (Becker, 1992, p. 72). This was clearly a necessity when teaching disadvantaged children if they were ever to catch up with their middle class peers. To not catch them up in the early years is to deny them the educational and economic opportunities available to their peers. To teach more in less time, instruction moves at a fast pace, keeping the students focused at all times so that their engaged academic time is increased. The more instructional time students spend actually engaged in academics, the more they learn.

A basic assumption of DI is that all children can learn. This means that when children do not learn we cannot place the blame on the children. Direct Instruction arranges a learning environment in which "faultless communication" allows all children to learn. This learning begins with the tool skills discussed in Precision Teaching. The tool skills for reading include identifying sounds of letters, blending letter sounds, and reading orally. These are all skills that are taught through faultless communication and then practiced until students become fluent in them. If it becomes apparent that children are not learning or reaching fluency it is because the instruction is not effective and it is the instruction that is changed so that the children can learn. This makes the teacher accountable for the students' learning. However, once trained in DI, it is not difficult for teachers to be accountable because they are provided with a script and directions that are known to be effective.

There are five components of DI: "carefully-designed curriculum, increased teaching time, efficient teaching techniques, thorough implementation procedures, [and] increased teacher expectations" (Engelmann, Becker, Carnine, & Gersten, 1988, p. 304). The **carefully-designed curriculum** begins with basic skills and their application in higher-order skills such as comprehension and problem solving. In order to achieve higher-order skills students must first master basic skills and see how these skills are used in the higher-order skills. This is accomplished through careful task analyses of objectives to determine necessary skills and the best sequence for teaching these skills. Reading, for example, begins with letter sounds and skill in blending these sounds. This strong emphasis on phonics is followed by comprehension skills, following instructions, and remembering what is said. By the third grade, students learn to read for information and learn how to use the information they gain from reading.

The second component of DI, **increased teaching time**, is especially important when working with children who come to school with few school skills, or are in any way behind other students. Students who are behind in kindergarten or first grade can still catch up if educational time is used well. In the primary grades, kindergarten through third, students can expect a 30 minute lesson in each of the DI programs being implemented. If the teacher were using DI programs to teach reading, math, spelling, and language, students would have two hours of intense instruction each day. The DI programs also allow for increased teaching time because teacher aides can readily implement these programs with training.

To use **efficient teaching techniques**, teachers simply follow the program provided. That is, the program tells teachers exactly what to say and do. It is a scripted text. "The scripts provide teachers with directions, sequences of examples, and sequences of subskills and wordings that already have been tested for effectiveness" (Engelmann et al., 1988, p. 306). Even with effective teaching scripts, students may make errors; therefore, efficient teaching techniques include correction procedures. All errors are corrected and just as there is a script for teaching, there is a format for corrections. Basically, the teacher models the correct response, or reviews the rules, then has all the students respond correctly, and ends with an individual check of student responses to be sure students have learned it. Efficient teaching techniques also include the effective use of reinforcement. Training procedures in the use of DI include instruction and practice in systematically reinforcing students' responses to increase their motivation.

A frequent immediate reaction to teaching from scripts is often negative. That is, it is too stilted; teachers need to be allowed some creativity in their teaching; good teachers know how to present material and should not have to follow a script; teachers reading from a script is boring for the teachers and for the students; and students only accomplish rote memorization that is useless when they try to apply it. On the surface, these seem like legitimate concerns, but let's look more closely. The scripts need not be presented in a stilted way. When teaching from a script, teachers and students are interacting at a very lively pace with opportunity for the teacher's creativity in the fine tuning of the presentation. Think of the actor who has memorized a script to be presented on stage night after night for months or more. He says the same words each time, but rarely is the presentation exactly the same. Few would argue that he lacks creativity in his nightly presentation of the same script.

Similarly, teachers have a script to follow, but they present it with their own personalities and passion for teaching. The reason for following the script is because the faultless communication has been carefully researched and presented in a script that will be the most effective in teaching the concept. When individual teachers decide for themselves the best way to present new material sometimes it works and sometimes it doesn't, or sometimes it works for some students and not for others. The scripts are not at all boring when presented properly. One of the advantages of the scripts is that students are readily successful. That is, the teacher is reading a script that provides a signal for students to respond and most of the time *all* the students respond correctly. There is little opportunity for boredom when students are all responding approximately six times a minute for a twenty minute lesson. Compare this to the potential for boredom in a more traditional twenty minute lesson in which most of the students have an opportunity to respond once or twice during the entire lesson. Finally, what may appear to be rote memorization is the mastery and fluency of tool skills which allow students to advance to higher level skills. It is also worth mentioning that most teachers who use Direct Instruction are very happy with the scripts after using the program for a year or so because they see the success their students are experiencing (Gersten, Carnine, Zoref, & Cronin, 1986). After all, student learning is the real reinforcer for teaching.

As with any program, **implementation** is a key component. An excellent program not properly implemented is usually worthless. Therefore, training is necessary to implement DI programs. The teacher does not have to consider what to teach and how best to teach it, the program provides that. However, the teacher must learn how to deliver the program. Typically, this training occurs just before the start of school so that teachers are then ready to start when the students begin the school year. If the training is completed too far in advance, teachers may forget much of what they have learned before they have an opportunity to implement it.

Training includes an introduction to the program and how the program came to be what it is. It is important that teachers realize that they should not adapt the wording or add their own examples—all wordings and examples have been carefully researched for maximum effectiveness. Instead, teachers learn the formats used in presenting the lessons. While the lessons are scripted and tell teachers what to do and say, teachers initially find these presentations very awkward and need to practice presenting them. They also need to learn how to signal students to respond and how to reinforce and provide correction procedures. As teachers begin to implement DI they need supervision. That is, someone trained in the program needs to visit the classroom frequently while the teachers are teaching DI programs and offer any needed assistance. Typically, this includes confirming what the teachers are doing well (especially since it often feels uncomfortable and possibly incorrect in the beginning), making some suggestions for needed changes, and modeling correct formats. It helps if teachers realize that it will probably only take a couple months to master the scripted text, but a year or more to get comfortable with correction procedures and maintaining high levels of student accuracy. Eventually, the goal is to identify local teachers who will serve as supervisors for the other teachers.

One final aspect of implementation is to monitor student progress. The highest performing students will typically complete 1.2 to 1.5 lessons a day while the lowest performing students will typically only complete .7 of a lesson a day (Engelmann et al., 1988). It is not enough simply to complete lessons; students must be demonstrating mastery of the skills they are learning. Therefore, there are frequent mastery tests included in the daily lessons. The early reading programs assess mastery every five lessons. If necessary, remediation is provided. If students continually need remediation, they may be misplaced and need to be moved to a lower level. Conversely, if all students always earn perfect scores on the mastery tests, maybe they need to move more quickly. Possibly these students will be able to skip lessons and still attain mastery of the skills.

The final component of DI is **increased teacher expectations**. Expectations alone, however, are not likely to improve student performance. Students need skills that allow them to succeed. As students begin to succeed, teacher expectations are likely to rise. Prior to DI, many teachers have little or no experience with academic gains with their at-risk children. However, when teachers see students succeed, especially those who have a history of not succeeding, their expectations for those children usually increase. According to Engelmann et al., (1988)

> Cronin (1980) reported that most of the teachers initially disliked several features of Direct Instruction—the scripts, in-class supervision, prescribed teaching techniques. After six months, however, the teachers reported that their students were reading at a level they had thought unimaginable for inner-city minority students; the teachers' attitudes toward Direct Instruction changed dramatically. (p. 308)

We have looked at a guiding rule of DI—teach more in less time, we have looked at a basic assumption of DI—all children can learn, and we have examined five components of DI. What is it about DI, however, that makes it so different from other instructional programs and so effective? Possibly it is the designers' understanding that students need clarity, especially when they are presented with new and challenging material (Gersten, 1992). With this in mind, the goal of DI is to provide faultless communication. If the communication is faultless, the students will learn. If the students do not learn, the communication is flawed and must be changed. Not surprisingly, "logical analyses of what is to be taught and how to teach it guide the development of lesson scripts, which are then tested on students to see if they are effective" (Binder & Watkins, 1990, p. 91). Once designed, programs are systematically field tested and revisions are made based on the data from the field tests.

When teaching a problem solving strategy, the sequence of instruction begins with explicit teaching of each step in the sequence (Gersten, Woodward, & Darch, 1986). Initially, the teacher models the steps and then students go through the same steps orally. This allows the teacher to hear students' descriptions of the steps to be sure the students are following them so that the students can learn the steps. Eventually that which is done orally becomes subvocal. That is, the students may still be saying the steps to themselves as they solve the problem, but the teacher cannot hear them. Finally, with enough practice, students can solve the problem without stating the steps even subvocally. At this point, a new skill has reached the level of automaticity.

Regardless of whether the DI program is teaching a concept, a problem solving skill, or basic phonics, the objective is always to teach the general case rather than an independent member set. This is nicely illustrated in the teaching of reading. Teaching sight words is teaching an independent member set while teaching letter sounds and blending of those sounds is teaching the general case. If students are taught 40 reading sounds and blending skills "they can read any of more than 10,000 regular-sound words. In the same time as it might take to teach basic phonic skills, one might be able to teach 80 to 100 sight words" (Becker, 1992, p. 81). Because there are so many irregular words in English, DI provides "a temporary world of only phonetically regular words." Students can then be "taught rules *that work all the time*....By the time irregular words are introduced, the students are firm, confident decoders" (Gersten et al., 1986, p. 29). After becoming competent readers it is not difficult for students to read the less highly structured instructional materials.

Let's take a look at a DI classroom. For the description of this classroom, we are returning to the elementary school, specifically the primary grades, as that is where DI was first implemented and where is it still most often used, although the programs have been expanded to include middle school. You are looking into a second grade classroom in which DI programs are being used to teach math, reading, language, and spelling. At the beginning of the year the teacher completed placement tests for all the children so that they are all working at an appropriate level in the different content areas. It is reading time and you notice that some students are working independently at their seats. They may be completing take-home pages from their reading program, writing stories, or completing other independent work the teacher has assigned.

Gathered at a small table in the back of the room are 8 students and the teacher. The teacher has arranged this table so that the students at the table are facing her with their backs to the other students in the room while the teacher is facing both the students at the table and the students in their seats. The teacher is holding a presentation book for all the students in the reading group to see. She is very careful to have them focused on the book, which she points to and reads from to present the scripted lesson. Each time the students are to respond the teacher gives a clear signal—the signal varies with the type of material being presented, but all the students have learned the signal and respond as soon as it is presented. During most of the lesson the students are responding orally and in unison. This is called **choral responding**. Choral responding allows all students to respond each time, providing many more opportunities to respond than are frequently available during a traditional lesson. It also keeps the students focused as they all must be ready to respond at all times. Finally, it allows the teacher to check constantly to see if students are responding correctly. Often throughout the lesson, however, the teacher asks each student to respond individually. This is so the teacher can check each student's grasp of the lesson. Periodically, but not very often, students will make an error. When this happens, the teacher corrects the error immediately by following the error correction procedure provided in the presentation book. Before the end of the lesson, the teacher will distribute the students' story books and students will have an opportunity to read from their books. Once again, this is oral reading with all students following along and ready to take a turn when asked to do so by the teacher. Before the end of the lesson, the teacher distributes the appropriate page from the take-home book. This page is started in the group and usually finished independently by the students. The teacher checks the page and it is sent home so that students can share with their parents what they are learning in school.

One thing that will be very obvious in your observation is that the lesson moves along at a very quick pace. This helps to keep students focused and it allows teachers to teach more in less time. If it was a high functioning group you just observed, it is likely they completed more than one full lesson during this 30-minute small group instruction. When they are finished, they return to their seats to begin the independent work that has been assigned and the next group moves quickly and quietly to the reading table. You are not likely to find any wasted time in this DI classroom.

It may surprise you to know that DI "programs are taught to at least five million children in regular and remedial programs around the English speaking world" (Becker, 1992, p. 106). However, when you see the empirical evidence that follows you may be surprised that it isn't provided for even more children. What is not surprising is that DI is effective for teaching both basic and higher order skills (Kinder & Carnine, 1991) because it "is a research-based approach to instructional design and implementation based on over 25 years of development" (Binder & Watkins, 1990, p. 84).

As mentioned earlier, DI was one of the model programs for Project Follow Through. The initial evidence of the effectiveness of DI came from the research conducted for Follow Through. This was a "large scale longitudinal study of 13 different major approaches to teaching economically disadvantaged students in kindergarten through third grade" (Engelmann et al., 1988, p. 309). Measures were taken in total reading, total math, spelling, and language. Of all the approaches, DI was the only one to show consistently positive effects on all measures. The low income children who started in the DI program in kindergarten finished third grade with reading skills measured at the 5.2 grade level (Becker, 1992). Students in the DI program also scored high in self-concept supporting the idea that when students perform well they feel good about themselves. DI provides the means to allow students to be successful and to feel good about themselves.

The best performance on measures of higher cognitive processes were also found with the students from the DI model (Engelmann et al., 1988). Follow-up studies indicate a continued impact of DI as seen in fifth and sixth grade reading, spelling, and math problem solving, and in ninth grade reading and math. In addition there was a decreased retention rate, and an increased graduation and college acceptance rate for students who initially experienced the DI model in kindergarten through third grade than for similar students who did not receive the DI programs (Gersten, Keating, & Becker, 1988).

Perkins and Cullinan (1984) demonstrated the effectiveness of the DI program called Fractions I. Over a two month period they taught three third grade students, two from a high-achieving class and one from a low-achieving class, to solve fraction problems. Instruction began sequentially with one student at a time. Each student made more correct responses and fewer incorrect responses only after beginning the Fractions I Program. At the end of the two month period, "the students' correct and incorrect rates on basic fraction problems were considerably better than those of students one grade higher in school who had been exposed to a standard fractions curriculum for several months" (Perkins & Cullinan, 1984, p. 116).

A nationally-based report, *Becoming a Nation of Readers,* supports the practices of DI as summarized by Becker (1988). The report emphasizes the importance of fluency in decoding to facilitate comprehension scores. Direct Instruction places a heavy emphasis in decoding early in the program. Learning to read is hard work for most students and might be avoided if teachers do not provide the motivation.

Direct Instruction does this with its fast paced instruction, choral responding, and success. Basically, we cannot expect students to learn to read on their own by just exposing them to reading and/or reading to them. There is no substitute for direct instruction in learning to read. Further, to develop vocabulary students need independent reading time. The more they read the more they develop their vocabularies. The easiest way to get students to read more is to teach them to read so that reading is something they do well. If they do it well, they are likely to do it more.

A recent implementation study conducted in a large urban city, demonstrated the effectiveness of Reading Mastery, a DI program (Fredrick & Keel, 1996). This study compared students' rate of academic gain prior to the implementation of Reading Mastery to their rate of academic gain during the implementation of Reading Mastery. Students' performance was analyzed on the Woodcock Reading Mastery Test before the implementation of Reading Mastery and after nine months of Reading Mastery implementation. Before the implementation of Reading Mastery, students in two of the first grade classes were averaging .7 of a month academic gain for each month of instruction. The students in the other first grade class in this study were averaging one month of academic gain for each month of instruction. During the months of implementation of the Reading Mastery Program, all classes showed higher rates of academic gain than they demonstrated prior to the implementation of the program. The two classes that were averaging .7 of a month gain for each month of instruction *prior* to the program averaged 1.0 month and 1.2 months gain per month of instruction *during* the implementation of Reading Mastery. This indicates that students would be either on grade level or above grade level with Reading Mastery instead of being three to six months behind. In the class in which students were already averaging one month academic gain for each month of instruction prior to the program, students averaged 1.5 months gain for each month of instruction during implementation of the program. That is, rather than being on grade level, these students would be expected to complete a year and a half of reading for each year of instruction.

The success of DI was recently publicized on *20/20* when John Stossel (1995) showed DI reading and math being implemented in several different classrooms. The students were eager for their lessons and successful. The teachers were happy to have effective instructional materials available to them, and the children's parents were "thrilled" with the progress their children were making. One Mississippi school raised their test scores from among the lowest in the state to the second highest. Every place DI has been tried, children have learned to read. Direct Instruction is simple and effective; in 30 to 40 minutes of DI instruction each day, students learn to read in a year.

Clearly DI works, but it does not accomplish the same level of gain in all classrooms. Concerned about this discrepancy in gain, Gersten et al. (1986) analyzed teacher implementation of DI. They found that in order to be most effective, teachers must place students in the appropriate group, assure a success rate of at least 80%, and maintain a brisk pace with enough enthusiasm to hold students' attention. They concluded that "all the studies indicate consistent relationships between measured level of implementation and gains in student reading" (p. 264). They also found that while teachers are often reluctant to implement DI, once they see the dramatic effects of the program, they change their reaction to the program and become strong supporters of DI.

Will You Use Direct Instruction in Your School?

It is time once again to consider another option for your school–DI. It is true that if you are designing a high school, DI is not an option unless you have students who are in need of remediation. What about for your elementary school, however? Would you consider a DI school in which students became competent readers and mathematicians by about fourth grade? If so, will you include Precision Teaching strategies along with your DI programs? The two are very compatible.

Programmed Instruction

Programmed Instruction (PI) presents small amounts of information to be read by the student followed by questions about what they just read. Students provide answers to the questions, receive immediate feedback on their answers, and if they are correct, they receive the next bit of information. If they are incorrect they receive additional information followed by questions. Programmed Instruction began in 1953 after B. F. Skinner visited his daughter's fourth grade class as part of Father's Day at her school. During this visit Skinner identified two problems with the math instruction. Feedback was too slow–the teacher collected the papers and would be returning them with feedback the next day–and students were not working at their own pace–students waited for all to finish before continuing. Some students quickly finished and were left with no academic activities to do while waiting for their classmates. Other students struggled and possibly never finished the problem (Vargas & Vargas, 1992).

Skinner saw a need and responded immediately by developing a teaching machine. His first teaching machine allowed drill and practice while requiring students to generate answers rather than choosing them from a set of possible answers. The machine also gave immediate feedback and allowed students to move at their own rate. One student may practice 50 math problems in the time it takes another to practice 20 (Vargas & Vargas, 1992). It was not long after this first teaching machine that Skinner brought us PI. Programmed Instruction includes the components of the first teaching machine (generating the answers, receiving immediate feedback, and moving at the student's own rate) as well as a careful sequence of instruction that allows students to learn new academic skills gradually rather than just practicing skills already learned. This is the shaping feature of PI.

What followed was the development of many kinds of Programmed Instruction formats to teach a variety of subjects. These programs could be presented to the student on simple machines or in books. Instructional material is divided into "frames." In each frame was information to shape the student's learning and a question to test the grasp of that information. In evaluating the effectiveness of such frames, the standard practice was to rewrite any frame or break it into smaller steps if more than 5% of the students missed it (Vargas & Vargas, 1992).

Eventually two basic types of programs were developed, **linear programs** and **branching programs**. Basically, the difference is that linear programs present small bits of information that require student generated responses through a sequence of frames that is tightly designed to avoid errors. In contrast, branching programs typically present larger amounts of information along with multiple choice items. When students choose a response to the multiple choice item, the choice they make determines the information they receive next. For each incorrect choice the reason it is incorrect is presented to the student and the student is then returned to the original frame to try to answer the question again. When the student chooses the correct response, the student receives confirmation of the accuracy of the response and is given the next frame in the sequence (Vargas & Vargas, 1992). The linear programs are designed according to "Skinner's philosophy that the program should bear the burden of teaching so that mistakes would not be made" (Vargas & Vargas, 1992, p. 46). Linear programs are the ones that support the behavioral approach to instruction.

A behavioral approach to instruction is seen in the components of PI: behavioral objectives, immediate feedback, high rates of active responding, shaping, and mastery (Vargas & Vargas, 1991). **Behavioral objectives** state what the learner will be able to do once the objective is mastered. What the learner will be able to do is stated as an observable and measurable behavior. An example of a behaviorally stated objective is "the learner will be able to solve long division problems that have two digit divisors and answers with remainders." Once we know what we want students to be able to do we can conduct a careful task analysis to identify all the tasks that need to be mastered to achieve that objective. These tasks are then taught by individual frames that initially provide the responses for the students and then gradually remove this help as students continue to respond correctly. With careful pacing through these frames, students learn the tasks that ultimately allow them to master the objective.

As they complete the frames, they receive **immediate feedback**. The feedback occurs before students have the opportunity to make another response. When this feedback also functions as reinforcement, that is, it is enough to keep students interested and working, that is all that is provided. When feedback alone is not sufficient to function as reinforcement, a reinforcer is delivered immediately, just as the feedback is. This may be in the form of points the students can see accumulating as they respond correctly, it may be in the counting off of items that are left to be completed, it can be anything that can be delivered immediately after the response and that functions to increase the likelihood that the student will continue to work.

The work that is required is a **high rate of active responding**. This is one of the ways the linear programs support the philosophy of behavior analysis. The act of generating the response rather than recognizing it from a list of possible responses facilitates the learning process. When responding occurs at a high rate, it builds fluency, which we addressed as an important component in learning when we examined Precision Teaching.

When students are actively responding their behavior is being **shaped**. When we identify objectives for students to master, we stipulate behaviors students cannot yet do. Therefore, we must shape these behaviors. Shaping occurs as we gradually go from what students can do now to what they are to be able to do to master the objective. If they can already do long division with single digit divisors, we start from there and carefully add the remaining steps through frames with sufficient practice at each step before moving to the next step.

When teaching through PI, all students **master** the objectives. Programmed Instruction programs are designed so that few if any errors occur, and students are continually responding and moving in a carefully designed sequence that only allows for mastery. Mastery is achieved only when students are both accurate and fluent.

As with other behavioral approaches, if the student using PI is not successful, the student is not blamed, the instructional material is revised. "The student interacts with materials designed by an instructional designer, and the student's success, or failure, at each step of the instructional process shapes the teacher's revision of materials or design of future ones" (Vargas & Vargas, 1991, p. 238). This suggests a learning environment in which students are undoubtedly happy and successful.

Let's look at that learning environment. For this classroom example we chose a middle school grade—seventh grade. Please note, however, that PI can be effectively implemented at all age levels through college and into training programs in business and industry. In our seventh grade classroom you can expect to see both paper and pencil PI and computer-presented PI. Students may be working individually or possibly with the teacher. They are all working at their own pace so that while one student may be mastering pre-algebra objectives, another may be mastering long division. The teacher may be implementing PI for several content areas, or just for one or two. The programs may be programs that are purchased from a publisher or programs designed by the classroom teacher.

In all cases, students are presented with individual frames of the programs to which they generate a response, either by writing the answer on a piece of paper, or in a space in the programmed textbook they are using, or on a computer screen. All students are actively engaged in academics the entire time they are working with the programmed materials. The teacher is helping individual students who may need help, guiding students to their next program, and writing revisions to frames that students are answering incorrectly. Typically, there are many charts, often in individual folders to keep students on task with the sequence of programs they are completing in the different subject areas.

By middle school, it is quite common for schools to be departmentalized, that is, students have different teachers for different subjects. Therefore, if PI is in place in the middle school, it may be that the math teacher or the social studies teacher is using PI while teachers who teach other subjects are using other instructional strategies. If the math teacher is using PI the students would progress in their math as far as they were able in a school year. That is, there is no predetermined end to seventh grade math; students simply follow along in the designated sequence. This means that some students may complete algebra I by the end of seventh grade. Other students may start algebra I during seventh grade, but not finish it until eighth grade, and still others may not finish pre-algebra by the end of seventh grade. Students begin the next school year wherever they left off the previous year.

Programmed Instruction, with its self pacing feature, its high rate of student success on daily lessons, and its philosophy of fixing the program when students are having difficulty sounds wonderful, but does it work? It turns out that answering this question for PI is more difficult than it was for the strategies discussed previously in this chapter. Programmed Instruction has been used to label many instructional programs that do not incorporate the important elements of PI as identified by behavior analysis. That is, you are likely to find instructional packages labeled PI that do nothing more than provide drill and practice after the concept is taught. They do not shape new learning–an important feature of the PI we are discussing here.

"By the mid-sixties, Programmed Instruction was well established as a specialized field of instructional technology" (Vargas & Vargas, 1992, p. 49). However, by the late sixties it had reached its peak and in many classrooms all that remains of PI is behavioral objectives and immediate feedback, which is rarely immediate as defined by PI (Vargas & Vargas, 1992). Kulik, Schwelb, and Kulik (1982) conducted a meta-analysis of studies on PI in secondary education and reported "that in general Programmed Instruction did not improve the effectiveness of secondary school teaching" (p. 137). However, the guidelines they used to choose the PI research do not address the defining features of PI as presented here. That is, with so many programs labeled PI it is quite possible that many of the research studies included in this meta-analysis are not true PI programs as defined by behavior analysis.

Some interesting additional findings reported by Kulik et al., (1982) are that PI of the 1970s showed more positive student achievement than PI in the 1960s. During that time, a great deal of PI research was conducted to identify the necessary and sufficient elements of PI. It is possible that the more recent (1970s) PI programs included more of the defining features of PI than the earlier PI programs, but we have no way of knowing that. In addition, they found that PI "added more to student learning in social science than in science and mathematics classes" (Kulik et al.,

1982, p. 137). Again, however, we have no information about the quality of the programs in the different content areas.

In an introductory psychology class, Fernald and Jordan (1991) compared the effectiveness of PI and standard text. While they found the two approaches to be equally effective in terms of quiz scores, they also found that PI required less time to achieve the same effects as the standard text, which suggests that PI is a more efficient approach. Given that there is more and more we would like students to learn, it seems reasonable that if an approach can teach well and do it in less time than other approaches, it is an appealing alternative. Fernald and Jordan offer several reasons why they believe PI is superior to textbooks and lecture. With PI, students are active rather than passive learners, they get immediate rather than delayed feedback, they get continuous rather than periodic evaluation of their learning, and they get individualized rather than group instruction–that is, each is met at his or her current level of understanding and moved along at his or her own pace. Would you rather be completing this course with excellent PI or by reading and discussing this book in class? By excellent PI we mean that the frames would be written, field tested, and revised until they produced the shaping and learning of the objective. The objective in this case would be for students to choose the most efficient teaching strategies for the different subjects to be taught across the different age levels of students.

Will You Use Programmed Instruction in Your School?

It is time once again to make some decisions about your school. Are you interested in utilizing PI in your school? Will you shop for PI that incorporates all the defining features as presented here? Or, will you try to write some of your own PI following the principles of behavior analysis necessary for effective PI? If you have any interest in PI, will it be across the curriculum or just in particular subject areas? Will you want it at all age levels or only in some?

Peer Tutoring

Peer Tutoring had its beginnings at the Juniper Gardens Children's project in Kansas City in the mid-1970s. It was originally designed to meet the needs of minority, disadvantaged, and learning disabled students. However, its success with these populations has since lead to its use in regular education classes. Although it is not an evaluation strategy as Precision Teaching is, it is a strategy that can be used for brief periods along with other teaching strategies.

The defining principles of classwide Peer Tutoring are an "opportunity to respond, functionality of key academic skill areas, and behavioral principles that facilitate responding" (Delquadri, Greenwood, Whorton, Carta, & Hall, 1986, p.

536). **Opportunity to respond** is directly related to academic achievement. The problem is usually that with only one teacher and 25-30 students it is difficult for the teacher to provide many opportunities for any one child to respond. As a result, while the teacher tries to allow some responding for most students during the lesson, many students may respond as little as once in a 30 minute lesson. In contrast, Peer Tutoring creates an opportunity for frequent academic responding as pairs of students take turns asking and answering questions.

This responding is done in **key academic skill areas**. That is, students practice what is functional to practice—they practice the skills they will be expected to demonstrate. These are skills that match the teacher's outcome criteria and often include practicing math facts, vocabulary, spelling, oral reading, and reading workbook assignments (Delquadri et al., 1986).

To implement Peer Tutoring, the teacher divides the class into different teams each week. This provides all students with the opportunity to be on winning teams. After the teams are assigned, the teacher designates pairs of students within each team. Within this pair, each student has an opportunity to be the tutor and the tutee. A typical Peer Tutoring lesson lasts approximately 30 minutes and may be conducted across any number of content areas including math, reading, spelling, and vocabulary. For the first ten minutes of the lesson, Student One in each pair is the tutor and Student Two is the tutee. Students then switch roles for another ten minutes, leaving approximately ten minutes to tally their points and report them to the teacher who posts the points by teams to identify the winning team.

Reinforcement, to facilitate responding, is provided throughout the Peer Tutoring lesson. It is provided immediately for each correct response and for correcting errors. It is provided a second time for team scores and a third time as scores are posted. Compared to our other strategies, the defining features of Peer Tutoring are minimal. Students receive lots of practice performing key academic skills with ample reinforcement to maintain their responding at high rates.

Students need to be taught how to play the "game" as it is often called. Teachers accomplish this by modeling the role of tutor and explaining the procedure. One pair of students then imitates what the teacher has modeled while the teacher clarifies and corrects as needed. This is usually sufficient training for third grade students and older. However, first and second grade students are likely to need more than one session to learn the procedures (Delquadri et al., 1986).

The first thing you might notice in a classroom where Peer Tutoring is being implemented is that the noise level is higher than in more traditional classrooms. This is because about half the students in the class are responding at any one time, and they are *not* doing it in unison. Each student is responding to his or her tutor's questions. In the class we are presenting here, Danielle and Christine are partners on the Green Team. There are seven pairs of students on the Green Team and seven pairs of students on the Orange Team. The lesson is spelling. For the first ten minutes Danielle is the tutor and Christine is the tutee. During this time, Danielle reads a word to Christine and Christine repeats the word and writes it. Danielle checks Christine's spelling of the word. If it is correct, Christine earns two points. If it is incorrect, Danielle corrects it for Christine who then practices writing the word correctly three times. This practice earns Christine one point. This continues for ten minutes with Christine earning as many points as she can. At the end of this time, Christine becomes the tutor and Danielle the tutee. They continue in the same manner for another ten minutes. At the end of the second ten minutes Christine and Danielle add up their points. They then report their individual points to the teacher who adds them to the Green Team points for the lesson.

While tutors and tutees are working, the teacher is walking around the room answering questions, observing that students are following the procedures, and awarding points for tutor's behaviors (Greenwood et al., 1984). Tutors can earn points for asking questions clearly, for using the designated correction procedure, for delivering points accurately, and for offering praise and support to the tutee. In addition to the daily practice, students take quizzes at least once a week on the skills being practiced. These quizzes are taken individually to provide careful monitoring of the progress students are making with the strategy.

It appears this increased opportunity to make key academic responses with reinforcement for that responding is a very effective teaching strategy. However, before describing the empirical evidence of its effectiveness, it is important to note that the *key* responses must be made for optimal effectiveness. For example, Greenwood et al., (1984) found that when tutees spelled words orally rather than writing those words their performance on weekly spelling tests was not as good as when they wrote the words during Peer Tutoring. This is a good example of the importance of having students actually practice the outcome skills you will expect them to demonstrate.

Working with both regular education and learning disabled third grade students, Delquadri, Greenwood, Stretton, and Hall (1983) implemented Peer Tutoring in the form of a spelling game. Peer Tutoring utilized 15 minutes of the 30 minute spelling lesson. During this time students practiced the 18 words they would be tested on on Friday. The learning disabled students went from averaging 9 errors before tutoring to averaging 2.5 errors with Peer Tutoring. The regular education students went from averaging 3 errors to averaging .5 errors.

Greenwood et al. (1984) found that across three content areas (spelling, vocabulary, and math) students performed better under Peer Tutoring conditions than under more traditional teacher procedures as demonstrated on weekly tests. Additionally, the low-performing students in the group "often performed as well as" other students when all students were receiving Peer Tutoring. Their data also suggest that the largest academic gains occur in the content areas that receive the longest exposure to Peer Tutoring.

In a 1987 field replication of the above study, Greenwood et al. compared classwide Peer Tutoring in spelling to teacher instructional procedures with 211 inner-city first and second grade students. Once again, Peer Tutoring was found to be superior in producing academic gains. This was the case for both low achieving and high achieving students.

Maheady and Harper report spelling gains that average 12 percentage points when students are using Peer Tutoring while Cook, Heron, and Heward report effective implementation of Peer Tutoring to teach sight words and math facts (as cited in Delquadri et al., 1986). More recently, Muirhead and McLaughlin (1990) implemented Peer Tutoring with four fifth-grade students identified as the poorest spellers in the class. Even with only two days of Peer Tutoring each week before the weekly Friday spelling test, these students improved their performance. Their weekly test scores increased from an average of 74.4% to an average of 89.6%.

Peer Tutoring has also been successfully implemented in a less traditional course—driver education. Bell, Young, Salzberg, and West (1991) combined Peer Tutoring with Direct Instruction and Precision Teaching to facilitate mastery of driver education. In this study tutors used Direct Instruction and Precision Teaching in their tutoring. Of the four participants in this study, three of them passed the written test and obtained a driver's license.

Will You Use Peer Tutoring in Your School?

We hope by now your identification of instructional strategies is becoming clearer to you as this is the last true instructional strategy we have to offer. Will you use Peer Tutoring in your school to teach spelling or vocabulary? If you decide to use Direct Instruction to teach reading and math, will you consider also implementing Peer Tutoring to provide additional opportunity to practice oral reading and computation?

Computer Assisted Instruction

"In the 1980s, no single medium of instruction or object of instructional attention produced as much excitement in the conduct of elementary and secondary education as did the computer" (Becker, 1991, p. 385). This excitement does not appear to be diminishing, but rather building. Between 1985 and 1990 there was a consistent increase in the number of computers in schools (Becker, 1991) and there is reason to believe those numbers will continue to grow. In Georgia, for example, there is a state-wide goal of having a computer for every student.

Along with the increased availability of computers in the classroom, advances in technology have brought increased educational capacity. In 1985, computers were not used regularly to provide instruction. Instead they "were used primarily as enrichment to provide variety to the classroom routine" (Becker, 1991, p. 386). In high school they were often used to teach about computers rather than as a teaching tool for other subjects. Between 1985 and 1990, there was an increase in computer use in the elementary schools to practice basic skills and in middle and high schools to write papers and to analyze information. Word processing became a major focus of computer instruction in our schools (Becker, 1991).

Computers can be used in many ways–**drill and practice, simulations,** and **tutorials**. Drill and practice is an opportunity for students to practice what they are have learned how to do so that they can do it more fluently. Students may practice math facts on a computer using a drill and practice program. Simulations are educational experiences that put the student in a situation much like those that the student may encounter when trying to apply what is being learned. Flight simulations are a common example of teaching with simulations. They allow pilots to practice flying skills on a computer, which is less expensive than actually flying and much safer during the early learning process. Tutorials are designed to teach new concepts and skills to students. A math tutorial can teach students how to add and subtract fractions rather than just provide practice in the skill after it is already learned. Tutorials are behavioral if they incorporate the components of PI as presented here, but they often do not. We are hopeful that after this chapter you will know enough of the principles found in good behavioral instruction to analyze available Computer Assisted Instruction (CAI) programs.

However, the new generation of educational computers and software is beginning to change how computers are used in schools. The future direction of computers in education will be greatly enhanced by the increased availability of CD-ROM. CD-ROM (compact disc read-only-memory) and multimedia can be used for everything from reference materials, such as the Encarte Encyclopedia, to interactive learning tutorials, such as The Oregon Trail. Critical thinking activities, problem-solving, decision making, and exploration can now be enhanced by using computers in schools. These activities can be incorporated into various curricula and used as classroom practice activities.

As computers find their way into more and more classrooms, they are moving beyond drill-and-practice or word processing and beginning to take on two very different roles. One role is to allow students to access vast amounts of information. Because of this capability, some are arguing that schools should not be teaching as much information in the classroom. That is, the amount of information available and the changing nature of information makes it impractical, some would argue, to teach information. Rather, students need to learn only how to access and use information.

It is difficult, if not impossible, to argue against students learning how to access and use information. However, easily accessible information requires students to be very competent readers. Competent reading will be more important than ever as more information becomes available to students. If we teach students how to access the information on the computer, and they cannot comprehend what they are reading, the information will be of little use to them. We would suggest, therefore, that you look at the available research on reading and choose an approach to reading that is most likely to teach all students to read efficiently. When students become competent readers, this role of the computer will serve them well for a lifetime. In addition, information available on the Internet or CD-ROM is highly sophisticated. Students need to know information at a simpler level in order to understand more complicated information.

The second role the computer is likely to take is that of instruction. The computer has the capability of teaching subject matter at all levels of complexity to students (if it has been properly programmed to do so). In this case, the computer is the medium through which instruction is delivered. The only truly unique defining feature of CAI, then, is that the instruction is delivered via a computer. The instruction delivered may or may not be behavioral in nature; the instruction may or may not be effective. That is, while effective DI is likely to be available on CD-ROM in the near future, many other programs that are much less effective will also be available. Computers can provide an excellent opportunity to advance PI, provided we write excellent PI (PI that incorporates the components described earlier in this chapter). In the Precision Teaching classroom the computer can be used to chart progress; fluency is a very simple process when children are working on a computer. In the Peer Tutoring classroom, a computer could probably take the place of the peer. Finally, in the PSI classroom, computers can be used to provide the units of information and to administer and score the unit tests. No matter what instructional strategy is programmed into the computer, it will always be the responsibility of the teacher to determine if the program is effective. We must never assume that just because a computer is being used the instruction is any better than it is without the computer.

Given the vast number of possibilities for the computer in the classroom, a look inside a classroom using CAI is limited only by the reader's imagination. Possibly the teacher will be conducting Direct Instruction in a corner of the classroom and students who are not in the group will be doing seatwork, but it will be very different from what we typically imagine when students are doing seatwork. That is, they may all have computers on their desks that they may be using for drill and practice (until fluency is achieved), for tutorials, for accessing information for reports they are preparing, or for writing their reports.

Imagine each student accessing his or her file on a computer that lists the day's individualized learning activities for that student. Some of these learning activities may be completed on a computer while others are not. Elizabeth may access her file to learn that she is to begin the next unit in social studies. This is a PSI unit with the written material and the quiz provided on the computer. She may also find that she is to pair up with Mark to complete a session of Peer Tutoring for their spelling words. Quite possibly, however, the Peer Tutoring would be done with the computer as the tutor and Elizabeth as the tutee. At some point during the day, Elizabeth may be expected to complete the math tutorial on fractions that happens to be PI presented on the computer. There may also be a scheduled time in the day's activities to conduct a science experiment with classmates and the teacher. This experiment may or may not be facilitated by the computer. Finally, Elizabeth may find she has time to read her novel and begin designing a computerized summary of her novel to share it with classmates.

Will You Use Computer Assisted Instruction in Your School?

Will you put computers in your school? How many computers—one in each classroom, a few in the computer lab, one on each desk? At what grade level will you introduce the computer? What will be your guidelines for choosing the software for your computers? Will you demand empirical evidence of the effectiveness of the programs, or will you be satisfied that you are merely providing computers for your students?

Summary

In this chapter we introduced you to six instructional strategies. Five of these strategies are firmly grounded in principles of behavior analysis and present recurring themes. Frequent active responding, mastery, teacher accountability, student-centered learning, and reinforcement are important themes in Precision Teaching (PT), Personalized System of Instruction (PSI), Direct Instruction (DI), Programmed Instruction (PI), and Peer Tutoring. These themes may or may not be found in Computer Assisted Instruction (CAI) as the computer is simply a medium for delivering instruction. Only if the instruction being delivered is behaviorally based, would you expect to find these themes in a particular CAI program. Therefore, as we review the five recurrent themes, we will review them only for the five instructional strategies that are considered distinctly behavioral–PT, PSI, DI, PI, and Peer Tutoring.

Educators not trained in behavior analysis often suggest that behavioral strategies are simply a matter of trying to pour information into students' heads, that is, trying to fill the empty vessel. This analogy of filling a vessel is a misconception of behavior analysis. Each of the behavioral strategies presented here calls for frequent active responding based on research evidence that there is a high positive correlation between opportunity to respond and academic achievement. Precision Teaching provides for responding during daily timed fluency drills. In PSI, the rates of responding are not nearly as high as in some other strategies presented here, but with quizzes for each of 15 to 18 units each academic term, they are higher than what is typically found in the classroom. Direct Instruction accomplishes frequent active responding with its choral responding throughout the presentation of a lesson. One of the driving principles of PI is the opportunity to respond frequently, which is accomplished when students generate answers to individual frames of instruction. Similarly, Peer Tutoring was designed primarily as a way to increase opportunities to respond and provide immediate feedback (Shapiro, 1988).

This frequent active responding facilitates mastery, the second theme that is evident in each of these strategies. The main purpose of PT is to evaluate the effectiveness of the instruction. If students are not mastering or becoming fluent in the content, the instruction is changed. Personalized System of Instruction requires mastery of each unit before moving on to the next unit. Similarly, mastery tests are built into DI programs so that they are usually administered weekly to be certain the instruction is effective. In PI, students must correctly answer each frame in order to advance to the next frame and in Peer Tutoring students take weekly tests of content to assess mastery.

Requiring mastery is not unique to behavior-analytic strategies. What is unique, however, is to require mastery and if students are not mastering the content to hold the teacher and the instruction accountable rather than to blame the students. In PT, if the charts do not show an acceleration in academic skills, students are not mastering the content and the instruction is changed. Remember, the student is always right. If students in a PSI course do not demonstrate mastery on a unit quiz, they study more, and take another form of the quiz without penalty until they master the content. In DI, if students are not mastering the objectives, it is assumed that the communication is faulty and needs to be changed or the students need to be placed in a different instructional group. If more than 5% of the students miss a frame in PI, the frame is rewritten or broken into smaller steps to ensure mastery with few errors in the process. The weekly tests in Peer Tutoring assess student mastery of the content and if mastery is not occurring, teachers quickly make the necessary changes in instruction.

Students are actively responding, mastering the content, and when they are having difficulty with this mastery, the teachers are taking the responsibility for making the necessary changes so that instructional time is not wasted and students learn as much as they can. This is clearly instruction that places students in the center of the learning. The instruction is geared to students' success and carefully monitored so that all students succeed. Students are met at their entering level of development in each content area and carefully guided to more advanced levels. There is no blame placed on the students or on their circumstances in life. This is enough to make most learning environments very reinforcing.

The five strategies also include a reinforcement component. Each of these strategies suggests that learning is often a great deal of work requiring substantial effort from the students. Initially, the efforts may have to be reinforced extrinsically to help students put forth the effort. However, when students begin to succeed, it is the success that reinforces the efforts. Since mastery is required and changes are made so that all students succeed, all students have the opportunity to experience the powerful reinforcement of success. The evidence tells us that if teachers properly implement the strategies presented here, students will be academically successful— an important reason for all teachers to learn to use the strategies in this chapter.

Another good reason to learn the strategies in this chapter is so they can be used in combination to meet different academic needs. Precision Teaching can be used with all the other strategies introduced in this chapter to chart student progress and guide decisions. However, other strategies in this chapter can also be integrated. For example, DI may be used to teach reading and math while CAI may be used to teach social studies in the same classroom. In addition, PSI may be used to teach science and some of the written material of the PSI course may be presented as PI or CAI.

This same PSI course may include a fluency component. Good PI can often be programmed to be presented on a computer to become CAI. The implementation of any one of these strategies does not eliminate the possibility of implementing others of these strategies. We strongly recommend the combination of these strategies in a behavioral classroom. As long as teachers are using PT to assess and guide instruction, they will know when to implement which strategies.

Annotated Bibliography

Binder, C., & Watkins, C. L. (1990). Precision Teaching and Direct Instruction: Measurably superior instructional technology in schools. *Performance Improvement Quarterly, 3* (4), 74-96.

> Discusses what PT and DI have to offer education, a brief history of the development of each, and how they can be used together to produce measurably superior instruction.

Engelmann, S., Becker, W. C., Carnine, D., & Gersten, R. (1988). The Direct Instruction Follow Through Model: Design and outcomes. *Education and Treatment of Children, 11,* 303-317.

> Presents the assumptions, principles, and components of DI along with a summary of research findings.

Johnson, K. R., & Layng, T. V. (1992). Breaking the structuralist barrier: Literacy and numeracy with fluency. *American Psychologist, 47,* 1475-1490.

> Presents convincing evidence of the importance of fluency in tool skills and effective strategies for achieving this fluency.

Journal of Precision Teaching and Celeration published by the Standard Celeration Society.

> Provides an excellent resource for classroom teachers as well as a vehicle for them to showcase their results. The editor, Dr. Claudia McDade, will be happy to address questions you might have regarding the journal. She can be contacted at the Center for Individualized Instruction, Houston Cole Library, Jacksonville State University, Jacksonville, AL, 36265.

Keller, F. S., & Sherman, J. G. (1974). *PSI: The Keller Plan handbook.* Menlo Park, CA: W. A. Benjamin.

> Presents the development of PSI, how it came to be, by whom, when, and why as well as a clear description of the defining features of PSI.

Miller, L. J., Kohler, F. W., Ezell, H., Hoel, K., & Strain, P. S. (1993). Winning with Peer Tutoring: A teacher's guide. *Preventing School Failure, 37* (3), 14-18.

> Provides very specific guidelines for teachers interested in implementing Peer Tutoring in their classrooms.

Potts, L., Eshleman, J. W., & Cooper, J. O. (1993). Ogden R. Lindsley and the development of Precision Teaching. *The Behavior Analyst, 16,* 177-189.

> Traces the history of the development of PT from Lindsley's work with Skinner to the development of the Standard Celeration Chart, the inclusion of inner behavior, and the adoption of plain English for communication.

Singh, N. N. (Ed.). (1991). *Journal of Behavioral Education, 1* (2).

Offers four excellent articles that examine four of the instructional strategies presented in this chapter. "Direct Instruction: What it is and What it is Becoming" by Diane Kinder and Douglas Carnine, "The Life and Times of PSI" by William Buskist, David Cush, and Richard J. DeGrandpre, "Programmed Instruction: What it is and How to do it" by Ernest A. Vargas and Julie S. Vargas, and "Precision Teaching's Unique Legacy from B. F. Skinner" by Ogden R. Lindsley.

West, R., & Hamerlynck, L. A. (Eds.). (1992). *Designs for excellence in education: The legacy of B.F. Skinner.* Longmont, CO: Sopris West.

Provides three excellent chapters each of which presents a clear description of a different one of three of the instructional strategies examined in this chapter: "Programmed Instruction and Teaching Machines" by Ernest A. Vargas and Julie S. Vargas, "Direct Instruction: A Twenty Year Review" by Wesley C. Becker, and "Precision Teaching" by Richard P. West and K. Richard Young.

Chapter 5

Classroom Management

Classroom management refers to managing the time and behavior of students as well as teachers in the classroom. In this chapter we begin with a description of time in the school day. We discuss the number of hours the student spends in school, the amount of this time that is allocated for instruction, and the amount of allocated time teachers and students are actually engaged in the teaching and learning process. We follow this with suggestions for increasing the time teachers and students are engaged in the teaching and learning process. These suggestions develop along two lines of thought, the first is the use of instructional strategies that in themselves increase the amount of engaged time; the other is the use of classroom procedures that result in more time to engage in academic tasks because less time is spent off-task. In addition to these classroom procedures, we suggest discipline procedures teachers may use to reduce inappropriate behavior that may occur in spite of carefully planned classroom procedures. Finally, we close with a brief look at how teachers can analyze their classrooms to design their own classroom management procedures.

The School Day

The length of the school day ranges from four to seven hours with the typical school day lasting six hours (Karweit, 1988). During this six hours, there are classroom routines such as attendance, lunch counts, and dismissal procedures in elementary schools, and homeroom in middle and high schools. There are academics, and there is lunch. Classroom routines/homeroom typically take about 30 minutes. In elementary schools lunch takes another 30 minutes, while in middle and high schools it is a "period." That leaves approximately five hours for academics in the elementary school where this time is often spent in one classroom with one teacher. In middle and high schools, homeroom is typically followed by seven 45-50 minute periods, one period for lunch and six (approximately five hours) for academics.

The five hours for academics, whether in the elementary, middle, or high school is called **allocated time**. This time is often dictated to some extent by federal, state, and local guidelines. For example, students in elementary school are often required to have 30 minutes of physical education each day; in some parts of the country students in elementary school are also required to have 30 minutes of Spanish instruction every day. A typical elementary school also provides classes in music and art at least once a week, sometimes twice. Many also provide weekly computer classes. The remainder of the time, approximately four hours, is allocated for language arts, math, social studies, and science. For the sake of example, let's say

45 minutes is allocated for math, 30 minutes each for science and social studies, and two hours and 15 minutes for language arts, which includes reading and writing (some schools use separate spelling, handwriting, and English lessons as part of writing, others do not). In the typical middle or high school, each class period is considered allocated time for a particular subject.

One can easily identify allocated time in a teacher's lesson plan book, which typically includes a schedule of what is taught when–this is especially true in elementary school where students do not follow the same schedule each day. "Specials" such as art and music are often taught once or twice a week by the art teacher and the music teacher, leaving classroom teachers to design their schedule for academics around these "specials." While two hours and 15 minutes may be allocated for language arts, it is possible that on Monday and Friday students have language arts for two hours and 15 minutes, on Tuesday they only have it for one hour and 45 minutes because they also have music on Tuesday, and on Wednesday and Thursday they have language arts for two hours and 30 minutes. It is easy to see how the schedule quickly becomes complicated. However, our main concern is not with how the allocated time is scheduled, but with how the allocated time is utilized. In middle and high schools, the schedule of periods may change such that the periods proceed in order from first to seventh on Monday, Wednesday, and Friday and then follow a reverse order on Tuesday and Thursday. Once again, however, the length of each period–the allocated time–usually remains the same and is rarely under the teacher's control.

What teachers control is not *how much* time is allocated, but how they and their students use this allocated time. Some portion of allocated time is **engaged time**, the time students spend actively doing academic tasks such as reading, writing, answering questions, and problem solving. Unfortunately, students do not spend all of their allocated time engaged in academics (Clough, Smasal, & Clough, 1994; Evertson & Harris, 1992; Hollowood, Salisbury, Rainforth, & Palombaro, 1994). For example, Ms. Perry may be presenting a math lesson to the entire class when Shantis says, "I don't have a pencil." Ms. Perry may stop the math lesson, scold Shantis for interrupting, and then ask if anyone has a pencil Shantis can borrow. At this point several students are likely to bury their heads in their desks looking for extra pencils. Before long, students begin calling out, "I have one." Eventually, Shantis gets a pencil and Ms. Perry gets back to the math lesson, but not before several minutes of potential engaged time are lost. Throughout the course of a school day, the teacher may be ready to present a lesson, or give instructions for independent work only to find that one student is not attending to the lesson or instructions. Frequently, the teacher will wait for that one student producing a loss of engaged time for the entire class. Not surprisingly, engaged time is associated with student achievement (Stainback, Stainback, & Froyen, 1987).

Our goal then, is to increase the amount of engaged time, because increased engaged time increases learning opportunities and decreases the inappropriate behaviors commonly found when students are not engaged in academic behavior (Stainback et al., 1987). There are two approaches to achieving this goal–we suggest teachers use both. One approach is to utilize instructional strategies that are designed to provide large amounts of engaged time. The other approach is to design classroom procedures that increase engaged time. As some inappropriate behavior is likely to occur in spite of carefully designed classroom procedures, the teacher must also be prepared to implement carefully conceived discipline procedures and to analyze what is happening in the classroom.

Instructional Strategies to Increase Engaged Time

As you recall, in Chapter 4 we presented six instructional strategies based on behavior analysis—Precision Teaching, Direct Instruction, Personalized System of Instruction (PSI), Programmed Instruction, Peer Tutoring, and Computer Assisted Instruction. We examined common themes across these instructional strategies and we did not include Computer Assisted Instruction as such instruction may or may not be behaviorally based. However, for the remaining five strategies we reviewed five recurrent themes—frequent active responding, mastery, teacher accountability, student-centered instruction, and reinforcement.

When we consider the features that facilitate engaged time, we find these same five themes. Frequent active responding keeps students engaged in the learning. While Precision Teaching is really an assessment procedure to track student progress and make changes as necessary, it requires daily oral or written responses so that rate and accuracy can be charted. This daily responding is an example of engaged time. As suggested earlier, this assessment procedure is often paired with one or more of the other strategies discussed in the Chapter 4. For example, Precision Teaching is commonly paired with Direct Instruction.

With the scripted lessons and fast-paced teacher presentations in Direct Instruction, students remain actively engaged in the lesson. They respond frequently—several times a minute—and they respond in unison (choral responding) so that all students are answering all questions and frequently reading orally in unison. When students respond this way, there is a high level of engaged time, especially compared to instruction in which one child responds while others wait for their turns. Students waiting for their turns are likely to be daydreaming or disrupting others while they are waiting, these students are not "engaged" in academics and cannot be expected to learn much during allocated time.

Allocated time designated for implementing PSI produces a high percentage of engaged time as students are not sitting in the classroom passively waiting for teachers to deliver information. Students using PSI spend their time reading, writing, performing experiments, and discussing with classmates, teacher, and proctor until they believe they are prepared to demonstrate mastery of the content they are studying. At that time, they take a test and if they demonstrate mastery of the content, they move to the next unit. However, if they do not demonstrate mastery, they must actively engage in more academic tasks until they can demonstrate mastery and move on to the next unit.

In Programmed Instruction, students read small amounts of information and write an answer to a question about that information. This is immediately followed by feedback for their answer. If they are correct, they are presented with the next bit of information to read, if they are incorrect, they return to an earlier place in the program for review. This is active responding that requires students to be engaged in the instruction. Peer Tutoring also requires active responding from students throughout the lesson while they are either writing their own responses or checking their partner's responses.

The mastery feature, common to behaviorally-based instructional strategies, also facilitates engaged time. One very good way to keep students engaged is to be sure they are working at the appropriate level (Smith & Misra, 1992; Stainback et al., 1987). That is, they should be working on something they have not yet mastered, but have the prerequisite skills to master. Requiring mastery assures that students do not continue until they are ready and that they are not held back once they demonstrate mastery. Tied to this feature is the student-centered learning feature. When instruction is geared to success and teachers are clearly working to make that happen, it is quite easy to keep students engaged in the learning process. They have good reason to invest their energy because they are likely to be successful, and if they have difficulties, they will not be blamed for them. Teachers are accountable in all behavioral strategies, and work to facilitate learning by requiring frequent active responding and mastery at the appropriate level of instruction and by facilitating this process through reinforcement. Initially, this is extrinsic reinforcement provided by the teacher for demonstrating mastery of predetermined skills. Eventually, having mastered many components of a content area, such as math, doing math becomes intrinsically reinforcing because students are successful.

All instructional strategies based on behavioral principles presented in this book produce high levels of engaged time and are recommended as a good use of allocated time. When resources are not available for teachers to offer these strategies, their recurrent themes can still be implemented to facilitate high levels of engaged time. For example, frequent active responding can be accomplished when students read in unison regardless of what reading program is used. Similarly, all students can increase active responding by answering all questions either with choral responding, by indicating with motions (thumbs up or down), or with response cards.

Response cards provide a way for all students to respond every time and a way for teachers to see quickly who has the correct answer without singling out any one student. Response cards can be used with any text or curriculum teachers are asked to implement An excellent demonstration of the use of response cards to increase active responding, and hence, engaged time, was conducted by Narayan, Heward, Gardner, Courson, and Omness (1990) with fourth grade students during social studies in a regular education class in an urban public elementary school. A comparison was made between students raising their hands to respond with only one student being called on to respond to each question, and all students writing their responses on a response card and holding up their cards at the same time. When using response cards, students had more opportunities to respond, their performance on daily quizzes improved, and they did not "give up" as they often do when raising their hands to respond. When students raise their hands to respond and are not called on (because the teacher can only call on one at a time), students may become discouraged and stop raising their hands.

The response cards were made from laminated particle board and the students wrote on them with dry erase markers. This provides a low cost alternative to choral responding. Three advantages of response cards over choral responding are that response cards reduce the noise level, allow teachers to see individual responses that can be hard to detect in choral responding, and allow students to practice writing answers.

Just as active responding can be implemented without the specific behaviorally based strategies presented in this book, the other recurrent themes of these strategies (mastery, teacher accountability, student-centered learning, reinforcement) can be implemented without the specific instructional strategies offered in this book. Mastery, teacher accountability, and student-centered learning are closely related themes that become apparent when teachers meet students at their current level of development and understanding and then teach in a way that facilitates mastery from that level regardless of the instructional strategies and/or programs provided by the school.

Keeping the instruction student-centered, requiring mastery, and holding the teacher accountable are all ways to increase engaged time. Another way to keep students engaged in the learning is to keep their attention. Three effective ways to keep students' attention are to maintain a quick pace, make sure students are prepared for what you are attempting to teach, and prepare your lessons well. Maintaining a quick pace means not letting students take you off the topic, not letting them ramble when only a short response is needed, and not over-explaining– if it takes too many words or too long to explain, it is best to find a different way to present the information.

To be sure students are prepared for what you are trying to teach, always consider prerequisite skills when designing your lessons. What do students need to already know in order to learn what you are trying to teach next? How will you check to be sure they have these prerequisite skills? Once you have checked and you know students have the prerequisite skills, remind the students of what they already know that will help them learn the new material. For example, students already know that when they are trying to subtract 27 from 52 they cannot subtract 7 ones from 2 ones. They have learned they must get an additional 10 ones from the 5 tens. This gives them 4 tens and 12 ones making it possible to subtract 2 tens and 7 ones. A reminder of how they use an understanding of place value to solve these problems makes it easier to learn how to subtract 386 from 642. The process is the same, earlier they changed 1 ten into 10 ones to subtract the ones. Now they will do that and a similar procedure to change 1 hundred into 10 tens to subtract the tens. Sometimes students find it difficult to make the connections themselves. If they do not readily make the connection between what they already know and what you are teaching now, they may quickly disengage themselves from the lesson either by tuning out quietly or by becoming disruptive.

Finally, regardless of the materials or strategies you have available, prepare your lessons well. Know exactly what you are going to do and what you want your students to do. Have your materials prepared in advance and in easy reach, and arranged in the order in which you will use them. Carefully planned, well organized lessons, delivered in a systematic fashion reduce interruptions, confusion, and backtracking making it easier to keep students' attention (Smith & Misra, 1992).

Will You Reconsider the Instructional Strategies for Your School?

Now that you see how the instructional strategies introduced in Chapter 4 affect classroom management as well as academic achievement, will you reconsider their use in your school? If you do not choose any of the strategies suggested here, will you try to incorporate their themes to facilitate engaged time? Will you try to include all five themes, or begin with just one or two? How will you determine the effect that the incorporation of these themes has on engaged time?

Classroom Procedures to Increase Engaged Time

Keep students focused by maintaining a fast pace, by being sure they are prepared for what you are teaching, by carefully planning your lessons, and by using instructional strategies that require high levels of active responding. This is one very effective direction to take to increase the amount of engaged time in the classroom. In addition, teachers can increase the amount of engaged time by carefully planning their classroom procedures: the complete day-to-day running of the classroom. It is what many call classroom management. We make the distinction only because we believe classroom management includes both classroom procedures and instructional strategies as discussed earlier.

If you will recall from Chapter 2, the big picture of the classroom is the environment within which the behavior analyst works to shape appropriate behavior. Appropriate behavior in the classroom is any behavior that facilitates learning for a student and does not interfere with learning for any other student. The behavior analyst in the classroom is looking to identify the contingencies of reinforcement in effect—what behaviors are occurring, what is prompting those behaviors, and what is maintaining those behaviors? To the extent that the behaviors are appropriate the environment provides an effective classroom. However, sometimes the environment is prompting and maintaining behaviors that are inappropriate and interfere with learning. When that is the case we try to rearrange the environment, which we discuss later in this chapter. The alternative is to try to design, at the start of the school year, a classroom environment that prompts and maintains only appropriate behaviors. We begin with such a design.

Room Arrangement

The physical space is probably the first design teachers complete in their classrooms—sometimes it is the only thing they design, leaving the rest to chance. A design for the physical space in the classroom begins with the arrangement of the desks. It is common to see desks placed in small clusters or neighborhoods to facilitate cooperative learning activities. However, such an arrangement often creates problems. It is probably better to arrange desks in a way that is conducive to learning for the largest part of the school day. Desks can be readily moved to accommodate cooperative activities and then returned to their standard location. We recommend desks face the chalkboard and that when teachers present information they do so from near the chalkboard. If there is an overhead projector that will be used frequently, it should be placed so that the image is also reflected near the chalkboard. This does not mean desks have to be in rows, although rows allow easy access for teachers to walk among the students and provide assistance while students are practicing what they are learning.

The reason for having the desks face the chalkboard, teacher, and overhead is that it is easiest for students to engage in the learning when they are facing the instruction. We can attend better when we can see the speaker and any visual aids being presented. Picture the students sitting in clusters of four desks—two pairs of two desks facing each other. The result is that two students frequently have their backs to the instruction. They can either use this as a signal to disregard the instruction, or they can turn around in their seats to face the instruction. However, turning around often leads to slipping out of chairs, dropping pencils, and poking and/or talking to the person sitting in the adjacent seat. Suppose that there are some very conscientious students who do not engage in slipping, dropping, or poking, but instead carefully turn around and face the instruction. At the very least these students are uncomfortable. When students have to move to face the instruction, we unnecessarily prompt many inappropriate behaviors that interfere with learning. An alternative is for teachers to arrange their students' desks facing instruction, and mark the position of the two front legs of the desks with tape on the floor so that desks can be moved to facilitate other learning activities and then readily placed back for large group instruction and independent work time.

The desk placement above is recommended for elementary, middle, and high schools. In addition, at all levels the teacher's desk should be placed out of the way. Teachers rarely have time to sit at their desks except when students are not in the room. Therefore, the placement of the teacher's desk should be someplace where it does not interrupt the flow of traffic or take up any more room than is absolutely necessary.

Teachers in middle and high school often only need to place student desks and the teacher's desk as that is typically all they have in their classrooms. They rarely have tables for small group instruction or centers for independent and small group activities. In elementary school, however, teachers have to place more than just desks, and the younger the students, the more furniture teachers often need to place. Based on the instructional strategies suggested in this book, we would expect teachers to have a reading table where they meet small groups of students for reading instruction. This table should be placed so that the students sitting at the table have their backs to the other students. The teacher should be sitting across the table from the students in reading group such that the teacher is facing the students in the reading group. Typically, the teacher's back should be near a wall at one end of the room so that the teacher has a clear view of the classroom and of all the students who are not in the reading group at that time. Within easy reach from the reading table should be a small shelf or table to hold the reading materials.

Common to many elementary school classrooms are learning centers. These are areas in the room where students can work independently or in small groups to practice, extend, and/or experience something they are learning. Centers often include areas for reading, writing, math, science, social studies, and art. In each of these areas teachers usually have a small table or desks holding all the necessary materials so that students can gather without direction from the teacher. These centers should be placed as far from the reading table as possible so as not to distract students during reading instruction. Typically they are placed around the perimeter of the room, often with the wall as a display area for suggested activities to be completed at the center.

Finally, teachers need to decide where to place materials that students will need, the pencil sharpener, the basket where students submit their finished work, the trash can, tissues, etc. These should be placed away from the reading table so that they do not prompt distractions during reading instruction, and away from where students form a line to leave the classroom. It is very tempting for students, when standing in line, to play with materials that are in easy reach.

It may begin to sound as if you need a very large room for placing all of this furniture. In fact, you don't. What you need is careful placement of furniture and materials within the space you have. Careful placement of these items does not signal inappropriate behaviors such as playing with classmates during instruction, or distracting students working at their desks, in the centers, or at the reading table. Proper placement does not provide many opportunities for students to engage in inappropriate or off-task behavior. To check for proper placement after you arrange the furniture, position yourself at the various locations in the room and try to picture

What Will the Classrooms in Your School Look Like?

Will you design a school with classrooms that accommodate all the necessary furniture and still allow for easy movement around the room with as little distraction to other students as possible? Will there be some master plan to help teachers design the physical space to create a classroom in which appropriate behaviors rather than inappropriate behaviors are signaled? Will the physical space be readily changed if teachers find that students are easily distracted?

students working where you are and around you. This will help you spot problems and change them before the students arrive.

Scheduling

With the furniture placed, we begin to consider how we will "run" the classroom. From the perspective of the behavior analyst, our goal is to achieve the most engaged time from our allocated time. A good place to start is with the schedule. Your furniture is in place and you are sitting quietly at your desk looking at the parts of the schedule you do not control—lunch, art, music, physical education, etc. Write those in your plan book to see what you have left. Now look for blocks of time around these controlled times to find the best way to schedule the academics you want to teach. Start with the biggest available blocks of time and schedule your language arts followed by math and the other disciplines. Consider activities that may interfere with these academic disciplines if they immediately precede or follow them. It is often difficult to get students' attention after lunch, art, music, and physical education. One strategy is to follow these activities with academic tasks that require high levels of active student responding. That is, this is not a good time to lecture and/or explain. It is a good time for students to be reading, writing, and responding chorally. Once you prepare your schedule, post it in a prominent place so that students know what materials to have ready when and can more efficiently move through the day's activities (Smith & Misra, 1992; Stainback et al., 1987).

How Will Scheduling be Determined in Your School?

Will you design a school in which teachers do all their own scheduling around the "specials" that are scheduled by someone else? Will the principal schedule the "specials" such that there are large blocks of uninterrupted time available for language arts and math? Will you schedule reading for the entire school at the same time with a commitment to no interruptions? Will you do the same for math? Will you schedule assemblies and such during prime instructional time, or will you insist they be scheduled in the afternoon just prior to dismissal?

Transitions

Your room and your schedule are prepared. Your instructional materials were purchased long ago and are waiting for you. You know what instructional strategies you will try to implement, how to implement them, and you have prepared any materials necessary to implement these strategies. What's left are the rules and routines and how you will help students follow them. Perhaps the most important consideration is with **transitions**. Transitions are any changes students make from one activity to another. The change from reading instruction to math instruction is a transition just as a move from the classroom to the lunchroom is a transition. In middle and high school, most of this transition time is accounted for while students change classes between periods. However, transitions also occur between the bell to signal the start of class and the actual beginning of academic activities as well as from the end of academic activities to the bell to end the period (Clough et al., 1994). In addition, there is transitioning between activities within the period—from collecting homework to starting the lesson, and from giving an assignment to the actual start of that assignment by the students.

In the elementary school, no time is scheduled for moving from the classroom to the lunchroom or the gymnasium as in the middle and high school. In addition, no time is scheduled for changing from one subject to another. For example, teachers may schedule 45 minutes for science, but by the time the instruction begins, five to ten minutes may be lost in preparing for the lesson. Similarly, academic activities may stop ten minutes before the end of the allocated science time to allow for clean up before moving to the next subject. Even within one subject, time is lost to transitions. Teachers may schedule three, 30-minute blocks of time to provide reading instruction to small groups of students. However, from the time the teacher calls students to the reading group to the time students begin reading instruction, time is lost to transitioning. Add this across three groups, coming and going as well as starting and stopping and in the hour and a half scheduled for small group reading instruction there may be only an hour of actual instruction, or 20 minutes for each group rather than 30. According to Paine, Radicchi, Rosellini, Deutchman, and Darch (1983), transitions frequently take from five to twenty minutes each to complete. Calculating that students make about ten transitions a day, Becker (1986) points out that about 20% of the school day, or one day out of each week is lost to transitions. Clearly, it is not possible to eliminate transitions. They are necessary; therefore, they must be managed efficiently. As you prepare your classroom, you will want to design routines that reduce the amount of time spent on transitions. Having a routine will help. If there is some standard way you want students to transition, teach them to do it this way, and you will find transitions can be completed more quickly.

While just having a routine will help, some routines are more efficient than others. A good beginning for a transition is to have a signal that lets all students know it is time to stop what they are doing and to listen for a direction to transition. Sometimes, at this point, you may tell them to leave what they are doing and line up to transition out of the room. This is sufficient if their next transition is back to the activity they are leaving now. Other times, you may ask them to put away what they are working on before moving to another activity because they will not be coming back to the first activity until another day. After you tell them this, you will give the signal to actually transition. For example, your first signal may be to turn out the lights. You teach students to stop what they are doing when the lights go out. You follow this signal with "Please put away your work and line up for music." Then you give the second signal, which might be to state "Do it now." If the transition requires leaving the room, you must decide how and where you want your students to form a line. If the transition requires a move to another part of the room, you must decide how they will make that move—all at once, when you call their group, or individually. All at once transitions are usually more efficient and we recommend them.

You also want to decide what you want your students to do at the new location or scheduled activity while they wait for their classmates to join them and for scheduled instruction to begin. For example, if students are transitioning to a math lesson, they may be taught to get out their math books and a pencil as quickly as they can and to practice math flash cards while they wait for everyone to finish the transition. At this point the teacher immediately begins instruction. The teacher does not answer any questions unrelated to math, or deal with issues such as broken pencils, or the need for a tissue. Rather than using allocated time for such concerns, there should be clear rules for what a student should do in these different situations (Stainback et al., 1987). For example, if a pencil breaks—one such rule is to take another pencil from a can of less-than-perfect pencils, another rule is to sharpen the pencil and get back to the group as quickly as possible. The rule for the teacher is not to wait, but to begin the instruction *immediately*. The student will quickly catch up and be prepared next time if the teacher is not going to wait. Teachers waste excessive amounts of time waiting "for the class to be ready." The signal (unintentional, of course) is that "I won't start without you, so take your time."

Having a routine for transitions is only the first of three steps to managing transitions. The next step is to teach the routine to the students. It is one thing for teachers to know how they want students to behave during transitions, it is quite another to relay this routine to the students. Teach the routine and have the students practice the routine (Smith & Misra, 1992). To teach the transition example above, students practice stopping and listening when the lights go out. They also practice waiting for the teacher's signal "Do it now" so they are sure to get all the instructions before they begin the transition. Finally, they actually follow through with the transition as a practice. Time spent doing this is minimal compared to time lost without a routine or with a routine that students do not completely understand. Suppose, however, that you have a routine, and that you have taught the routine to the students—you know they know what you want them to do, but they are not doing it.

This brings us to the third part of preparing for transitions. There need to be consequences for following the transition routine and other consequences for not following it. These consequences will have to be taught along with the transitioning routine. As the transitions are practiced, students should learn the designated consequences for their behavior. If students do not follow the transition procedures during early practice of the routine, follow through with the designated consequence for not following the procedure. This sends a clear message that what you are practicing is important and you, the teacher, are willing to implement the consequences you said would be forthcoming. What these actual consequences should be or could be are discussed below under "Discipline Procedures."

Will You Establish Standard Transitions Procedures in Your School?

Will you call teachers together to discuss the importance of establishing procedures for transitions or will you just expect teachers to establish such procedures? Will you have teachers brainstorm ways to transition efficiently and then test those procedures? Will there be some consistency in the way transitions are accomplished across different teachers and classes so that students know what is expected of them regardless of whose class they are in at the time? Will you encourage the art, music, and physical education teachers to use the same transition procedures that different teachers use with different groups of students?

Routines

While transitions utilize a substantial amount of allocated time, other classroom routines can also interfere with allocated time—these are the morning routines. They frequently extend past the 30 minutes allocated for routines and in fact, could be completed in less than 30 minutes, thus allowing more time for academics. It is rare that students file quietly into the room in the morning all at the same time in neat, orderly lines. Instead, students arrive off the bus, from car pools, on their bicycles, and on foot. Some schools require that students who arrive before a designated time report to a designated place in the school, often the cafeteria, until the time they are allowed to proceed to their classrooms. The children arriving from the cafeteria are all arriving in the classroom at about the same time, but they rarely arrive in an orderly fashion. It is more typical that they are running, talking loudly to each other, or calling to friends they see down the hall.

This loud, less than calm behavior in the hall can signal many inappropriate behaviors that set the tone for more such behaviors in the classroom. To the extent possible, classroom teachers should take control of this situation and arrange an environment that sets the tone for appropriate behaviors in the classroom. We suggest this be accomplished by having at least two places for students to gather in the morning—one place for grades kindergarten through second, and another place for grades for third through fifth in the elementary school. In the middle school all students can gather in the same place. The gathering place should have a planned activity that students can join at any time without distracting students who have already gathered. Reading, writing, and brain teasers are appropriate activities. Students should be met at the door by an adult and required to state the activity they will engage in while they wait for dismissal to their classroom. Picture a large space, such as a cafeteria, with four clearly marked activity areas—one for listening to a story (including novels for the older students), one for reading silently any books students bring with them, another for writing—simply filling a journal with thoughts, feelings, plans, etc, and one for brain teasers where students can work independently or in pairs. The story reading area will require a second adult, and a third adult is probably needed to oversee the other three areas.

Placing three adults in a room where we often only have one adult "on morning duty" may seem excessive because very few teachers like morning duty. However, the reason teachers do not like morning duty is not because they do not want to give up some of their time, but because morning duty is typically stressful. It is likely to set teachers a little off their mark for the remainder of the day. If teachers had morning duty in an environment like the one described above it would not be stressful and would not make their day more difficult. Therefore, they may be quite willing to have morning duty more often.

As the time comes for students to go to their classrooms, transition procedures should be followed. These procedures will have to be planned, taught to the students, and practiced in the gathering area, just as they are practiced in the classroom. With such procedures in place students can quickly and calmly leave for their classrooms. We are not suggesting that students walk silently to their classrooms. For safety reasons, walking should be required, but silence is not necessary. As adults we rarely walk from place to place with another person and not talk to that person—humans are social creatures, talking is normal and expected. Children should be allowed to talk quietly to each other during this time. In fact, if quiet talking is allowed, they are likely to make less noise than if silence is requested. Since this is morning arrival time, quiet talking in the halls will not interfere with lessons occurring in classrooms.

As some students are arriving from the morning gathering area, others are just arriving from home. Typically a ten to fifteen minute time interval is allocated for arriving in the classroom on time. During this time, students hang up their coats, unpack their bookbags, put away their lunches, and generally prepare for the day. Here again, is an opportunity for noisy, high levels of inappropriate behavior that will make it difficult to get students on track for the academics that will soon follow. The best way to utilize this time is to have specific procedures in place for students when they arrive. Yes, you guessed it, you will have to plan these procedures, teach them to the students, and practice them during the first few days of school. It is always a treat to see how readily students will follow procedures when they know what the procedures are and they see that following those procedures is beneficial to them.

Begin with a firm rule for yourself that as soon as the bell rings or it is time to begin, all students who are not yet in the classroom are late. Begin without them. If you wait for late comers your message to the others is that this is not valuable time and they—students present—are not important enough for you to begin. When late comers realize no one is going to wait for them they often begin to make the extra effort to be on time. Most students do not like to miss out on class activities. Even students who arrive in car pools and do not directly determine their arrival time can manage to get the car pool there earlier.

The school day often begins with a moment of silent reflection, the Pledge of Allegiance, and announcements. As the classroom teacher you will not directly control the amount of time spent on morning announcements. However, you can suggest to the administration ways to keep these announcements to a minimum. For example, announcements that are to be made can be posted in the office when teachers arrive in the morning. Then teachers can read these announcements to their individual classes. The students are actually more likely to hear and respond accordingly if the announcements are made in the classroom by the teacher rather than delivered through the speaker system.

The last two morning routines include taking attendance and completing the lunch count. Neither of these need to occur after the announcements. Both can be accomplished very efficiently as students are arriving. Again, there needs to be a procedure and you need to teach this procedure to the students. For example, in some easy to reach area, near where students hang up their coats and put away their lunches and bookbags, provide individual student names on something durable—popsicle sticks and tongue depressors work well. These should be arranged in a manner that makes it easy for students to find their own. Pockets can be attached to a poster board in the same arrangement as the seating arrangement so that each morning students go to the poster board, find their tongue depressor (with their name on it) in a pocket that reflects their seat in the classroom. We do not recommend writing the students' names on the pockets as you are likely to change students' seats periodically and would have to make a new poster board with pockets. When students arrive, after hanging up their coats, putting away their lunches and bookbags, they step up to the poster board, take their tongue depressor and deposit it in one of four small containers, each clearly marked: buying lunch choice A, buying lunch choice B, buying a drink only, have lunch from home. These containers should be labeled to reflect whatever options your students have.

When the announcements are finished, students begin their transition to the first scheduled activity while you go to the poster board and containers and do a quick count. You will easily see who is absent by who still has a stick on the poster (this allows you to complete the attendance form). Then you count the number of sticks in each container to get the lunch count that is usually written on another form. A student who has earned the privilege of delivering these forms, quickly takes them to their designated places. An alternative to offer to the administration is to place a folder outside of each classroom for the attendance form and the lunch count. Sometime after the designated time to have the forms in this folder, clerical staff from the office can walk down the halls and pick up all forms to deliver the lunch counts to the cafeteria and the attendance forms to the office. Following the morning routines as outlined here is likely to reduce the time from about 30 minutes to 10 minutes. In addition, that 10 minutes is likely to be calm and to facilitate the start of a productive academic day.

Just as there are morning routines there are dismissal routines. These routines present a different concern. That is, it is rarely the case that we have spent too much time on dismissal routines resulting in students losing engaged time in what is scheduled to follow. The concern here involves designing a dismissal routine that facilitates students leaving with the necessary materials to complete their homework and the necessary messages to parents from the school. This routine, like all the others, should be planned, taught to the students, and practiced. Here's a possible procedure. Ten minutes before students are to be dismissed have students transition to their desks to prepare for dismissal. Once at their desks, have students take out and open their assignment tablets to that night's assignment—we recommend that all students, starting in second grade, have assignment tablets. With their tablets open, ask students to place on their desks all materials they need to complete these assignments. Once their materials are stacked, pass out any parent communications you have. Only then should students be asked to get their coats, lunch boxes, and bookbags. They pack their bookbags with the books and messages stacked on their desks and they are likely to have everything they need to complete their homework. Two important things are happening here. You are increasing the likelihood that homework will be completed because students have their assignments and the necessary materials, and you are sending the message that homework is important. Assigning time and a procedure for this activity tells students that the activity is important and they, the students, are important because you don't want them to miss this activity.

What Morning and Dismissal Routines Will You Establish?

Will you plan morning activities that set the tone for a productive academic day? Will these activities be determined by the individuals responsible for morning duty from week to week? Will you, instead, plan as a faculty for the types of morning activities that will be avaielable? Will you separate primary grades from intermediate grades? Will they have the same or different activities? What dismissal routine will you establish? Will it be a school-wide routine or will each teacher design an individual routine? How and when will you teach morning and dismissal routines to your students?

Independent Work Time

A very important activity in many classrooms is for students to work independently for portions of the time allocated for instruction. This typically occurs while the teacher provides specific instruction to individuals or small groups of students. Teachers commonly provide small group reading and math instruction geared to the reading and math needs of small groups of students. This is a very efficient and effective way to provide such instruction. While the students are not working in a small group with the teacher, they must be working independently. This independent work time usually begins with **seatwork** or work that students are expected to complete independently while teachers are instructing individuals or small groups of students. In some schools, students have individual folders with their seatwork. However, it is more common to have this work listed on the board and explained at the beginning of the day. Keep in mind that this independent work time is part of the allocated instruction time, and as such, our goal is to arrange an environment in which the engaged time during independent work time will be a high percentage of the allocated time.

When students are not engaged in learning during independent work time they are off- task and likely to be interfering with others who may be trying to work. How then do we keep students actively engaged during independent work time? It should come as no surprise that there need to be procedures in place and these procedures should facilitate the recurrent themes from behaviorally based instructional strategies that increase engaged time during group instruction–frequent active responding, mastery, teacher accountability, student-centered instruction, and reinforcement.

Reinforcement refers to the consequences for remaining engaged in the learning process during independent work time. The other four themes are addressed in the assignments given for students to complete during this time. Assignments that require active responding and a product to be submitted to the teacher help students remained engaged (Evertson & Harris, 1992). Asking students to "study" during this time is not likely to be as effective as asking students to write answers to questions. For what students need to study, provide questions and ask students to write the answers to those questions. After they are finished writing the answers, ask them to find a partner who is finished writing answers, quietly compare their answers, and where there are differences work together to determine which answer is better. These independent activities must be activities that students are capable of completing on their own (Smith & Misra, 1992; Stainback et al., 1987) and that serve some academic need. Independent work activities that serve no academic need are not student-centered and are not likely to be taken seriously by the students. Independent activities that incorporate the themes of frequent active responding, mastery, teacher accountability, and student-centered learning are likely to be activities that students will engage in and complete.

Not all students will complete these activities at the same time. What will students do when they finish their seatwork? Once again, we want them to be academically engaged during this time; therefore, teachers often provide centers where students can independently or in small groups engage in supplementary academic activities. Common centers found in the elementary school include reading, writing, math, social studies, science, and art. Some schools are fortunate enough to also have a technology center in each classroom; these are especially rewarding if they provide access to the Internet. Teachers may change the activities every week or two, they may design long term projects to be completed at a center, or they may just leave materials for free exploration. Art centers typically contain materials to complete a variety of creative projects of the students' own design.

Science centers may provide an opportunity to conduct an experiment. Social studies centers may offer an opportunity to research a culture while the math center may provide practice activities for math concepts being taught. These practice activities may be in the form of games students play in pairs or in small groups, they may be "beat the clock" activities in which students practice math facts and time themselves to see their improvement, or they may be math brain teasers that allow students to practice problem solving. Writing centers often provide a story starter or question to help students focus their writing. Reading centers may take two forms—one a listening center for stories on tape for younger children and books on tape for older children, the other an assortment of reading materials for students to read. The technology center has endless possibilities. For example, with electronic mail students can have pen pals in various countries. Consider the thrill of checking e-mail each day to see if your pen pal has written!

Like everything else in the effective classroom, there are procedures for using the centers. Usually, the number of students in a center at any one time is limited for logistical and safety reasons. This is easily monitored by providing a badge of some kind that students must wear in the center. When a student goes to a center, if there are no more badges available, that student may not join the center until a badge becomes available. Students may not go to any centers until all their seatwork is completed and turned in. Teachers often find this is a problem as students may simply go to centers without finishing their work or they may rush through their work carelessly in order to get to a favorite center quickly.

We suggest two procedures to arrange an environment where this is less likely to happen. One procedure is taught to the students while the other is for the teacher to follow. The student procedure is for students to write on a piece of paper at their desks the seatwork to be completed before going to centers. Teachers usually list all independent work on the board, which is a good idea, but maybe not sufficient to arrange an effective classroom environment. As you explain each independent activity, ask students to write that activity on the paper at their desks. Next to each activity on the board write the names of two children who can answer questions and assist other students who may need help. These should be two students who are not in the same small instructional groups. Students at their desks also write these names on their papers next to the activities.

When students have the activities listed at their desks they are less likely to skip past one the way they might by looking back to the board. In addition, as they finish each activity they can put a check beside it. When all activities are completed, they attach the list of activities to the completed work and deposit it in a designated basket. This basket should be located away from centers and away from where the teacher is working with small groups of students. As you call the next small group for instruction, step over to the basket, and flip through finished papers to check for completeness and neatness. Any papers that are not acceptable should be returned immediately. Students who do not complete their assignments satisfactorily should have to leave the center and not be allowed back in that particular center until the next day. Students typically learn one of two things from their classroom environments. They may learn that if they finish their work quickly and in any manner, they can have additional time in the centers, or they may learn that the only way to access the centers is to carefully complete their assigned work. What do you want the students in your class to learn?

An additional concern teachers typically have is that students will go to centers without turning in *any* work. Here's a procedure you might try. Place the basket for independent work near the poster that holds the tongue depressors with the students' names. When you flip through the papers in the basket, place the tongue depressors back in the pockets on the poster for those students who have turned in acceptable work. Then with a quick glance, you can look up from the small group instruction and see that the only students in centers are the ones who have their tongue depressors back on the poster. These activities may sound time consuming but they are really accomplished very quickly. All the materials you will need to teach all your small groups are gathered and ready near the small group area before the students arrive in the morning. Regardless of how quickly students learn to transition to the small group area when called, time elapses and you can use the minute to do this check.

One final concern of teachers using small group instruction is that of interruptions. Sometimes it does not matter how clear the directions are to you, there are still students who have legitimate questions that they do not realize they have until they begin the activity. That is why you might want to list the names of two students next to each activity. These are students who can answer questions about the activity. These names on the board are a signal that if students need help they should get it from the students listed.

The preceding are suggestions for arranging a classroom in which students receive signals for appropriate behavior and when they behave accordingly, that behavior is reinforced. The suggestions are primarily procedures and routines to be taught to and practiced by the students at the beginning of the school year. Students' behavior that is consistent with the established procedures and routines should be reinforced. Much of this reinforcement comes from the teacher smiling frequently, and the classroom providing a calm, enjoyable atmosphere of mutual respect. This

---

How Will You Handle Independent Work Time in Your School?

Will you expect your teachers to conduct small group instruction? If not, independent work time will not be a problem as teachers will be available to monitor this time. If, however, you are going to have small groups, what plans do you have for the students who will be working independently while you are teaching the small groups? Will you have teachers get together by grade level to plan centers so that it is a reasonable amount of work for each and not an overwhelming task for one or two? What materials will your school supply to support these centers?

is natural reinforcement of appropriate student behavior. Before students realize and appreciate this type of reinforcement, however, it may be necessary to provide more obvious reinforcement, such as access to preferred activities, recognition, and points to be exchanged for other reinforcers. This point procedure will be discussed under token economy.

Rules

While arranging a classroom as described above is likely to result in an efficient, effective classroom where engaged time is maximized, it will not provide a classroom in which students always behave appropriately. Some students will behave inappropriately early in the school year just to test the limits. You will need to be prepared to quickly and consistently demonstrate what those limits are. Therefore, just as there is reinforcement for following procedures and routines, there must be consequences for not following the procedures and routines or for breaking classroom rules. It is recommended that you provide as few classroom rules as possible and that they cover a broad range of possible inappropriate behaviors. For example, a rule that calls for treating classmates and teachers with respect does not allow pushing, shoving, hitting, tripping, talking to a student who is trying to work, talking while another person is talking, talking with anyone if it distracts another from work, running through the classroom distracting others, or doing anything that interferes with anyone actively engaging in academics during the allocated time. A second rule could call for respect of other people's property. This does not allow tearing or marking other people's work, writing on the desks or walls, leaving a mess in the restroom, overturning desks, throwing or kicking books, etc. Those two rules may be sufficient in any classroom at any level provided students fully understand them—you will have to teach what the rules mean at the beginning of the school year. In addition, having these rules posted will serve as a reminder of appropriate behavior and of your expectations for students' behavior (Smith & Misra, 1992).

A problem teachers often face in the classroom is that they *expect* students to respect others' and their property. This may not be a realistic expectation depending on the students' past experiences. Students may come from an environment in which they were not treated with respect nor taught how to treat others with respect. You will have to teach students what you mean by treating others and property with respect and provide consequences (reinforcement) for doing so with different consequences (punishment) for not doing so. Without such initial teaching, it will do little good to try to punish students' disrespectful behavior. If students do not know which behaviors are respectful and which are not, you may have to punish many different inappropriate behaviors all year. As you punish one effectively, it may be suppressed for a while only to reappear again later. In addition, while that particular one is suppressed, it will probably be replaced by another inappropriate behavior if you do not teach the alternative appropriate behaviors.

> ## Will You Have School-Wide Class Rules?
>
> Will teachers write individual rules for their individual classrooms or will there be school-wide class rules that apply in all classrooms and in the hall? Will there be some requirement for teachers to post their rules in the classroom regardless of whether there are school-wide or individual rules? Do you see any advantages to having school-wide rules? If you have school-wide rules, will you have school-wide consequences for following and for breaking those rules?

Discipline Procedures

Implementing the suggestions above will do much to reduce the need for punishment procedures in your classroom and that should be our goal. However, students may still behave inappropriately at times and it will be necessary to decrease that behavior immediately. Therefore, you will want to have procedures in place at the start of the school year. Many different effective punishment procedures are available, we present seven here: reprimands, time out, extinction, response cost, satiation, overcorrection, and positive practice. The procedures you choose should be only the ones you feel most comfortable implementing correctly and consistently. In addition they should be only the ones that are approved by your administration.

Reprimands are strong negative verbal responses. This is when teachers usually raise their voices or get very close to students and scold them. Reprimands should be specific to the student and to the inappropriate behavior. In addition, they should provide clear direction as to what the student should do now. For example, if Jamie is talking to a student who is trying to work you may say "Jamie, stop talking to Art and return to your work." Be aware, however, that the effectiveness of reprimands varies greatly with students. Some students come to you from an environment in which most of what is spoken to them is in the form of reprimands—yours are not likely to have an impact on the behavior of these students. Other students come to you from an environment in which no one ever raises their voices or reprimands them. These students are likely to become emotionally upset by your reprimand. They may not engage in the inappropriate behavior again. However, they may not trust you or feel comfortable in your classroom for a long time afterwards. In addition, for students who do not receive reprimands at home, just hearing reprimands delivered to another child is often enough to make them feel very uncomfortable in your classroom. Reprimands seem to do more for the person delivering them than for the recipient of them. If you have an effective discipline procedure in place, one with clear rules and appropriate consequences, reprimands may not be necessary. When there is an infraction of the rules, simply follow through calmly with the predetermined consequences. Strong negative verbal responses are not needed. If you choose to use a reprimand, you may have to deliver it in combination with other punishment procedures.

While reprimands are not derived from the behavioral literature, the remaining six procedures are. They are based on principles of behavior analysis and have been carefully researched by behavior analysts at all levels of instruction. Possibly the one you are already familiar with is **time out**. Time out is the removal of the opportunity for reinforcement. This is a very specific definition that is often ignored when teachers say they are using time out. As presented and researched in the behavioral literature, time out requires that students do not receive any reinforcement for a period of time—usually a very short period of time such as three to five minutes. Time out may take one of two forms, it may be **exclusionary** or **non-exclusionary**. Exclusionary time out means the student is removed from the learning environment—possibly to another part of the room or to another room. While away from the learning environment in time out, students are not allowed to earn any reinforcement.

This notion of not earning any reinforcement is critical for the correct implementation of time out. That is, teachers often have a time out space in their classrooms. Students who behave inappropriately are sent to time out where they read books that may be near by, and/or chat with classmates who walk by. These books and classmates often provide reinforcement. Therefore, students sent to time out in such a situation are not being removed from the opportunity for reinforcement—they are receiving plenty of reinforcement. Similarly, when teachers send students to the hall or the office for time out, students have significant amounts of reinforcement available, possibly more than what is available in the classroom.

Non-exclusionary time out eliminates the opportunity for reinforcement, but the student remains in the learning environment, usually in the same seat, and is expected to continue with the academic activity in progress—whether it is a teacher-directed activity or a student-directed activity. In order to accomplish this, there needs to be a signal to let others know that this student is temporarily not eligible to earn reinforcement. Students can all wear a bandana or a pin of some sort that they put on when they arrive in the morning. When they engage in inappropriate behavior, they must remove the bandana or pin, which signals that they are not to receive any reinforcement until their bandana or pin is returned. This is more cumbersome to implement and since time out is for such a short period of time, we recommend you use a space in your classroom for exclusionary timeout and be sure there are no reinforcing stimuli available in that space.

One of the main problems of time out is that in many classrooms, being in time out is not much different from not being in time out. That is, if there is not much reinforcement available in your classroom on a regular basis, to remove the opportunity to earn reinforcement for a few minutes is not likely to have much impact on the student's behavior. If you are going to try to implement time out, we suggest you first consider how different being in time out is from not being in time out. If you cannot establish a clear and important difference between the two, time out is probably not a good procedure to implement to reduce inappropriate behavior.

Another common disciplinary procedure used by teachers is **extinction**. Extinction is the withholding of the reinforcer that maintains the behavior. Behavior is maintained because it is reinforced. Therefore, if a behavior is occurring in your classroom something must be reinforcing it. One strategy to eliminate the undesirable behavior is to withhold the reinforcer that is maintaining it. However, such a procedure poses two challenges to the teacher. In order to withhold the reinforcer maintaining a behavior, you must be able to *identify* the reinforcer. If you do not know what it is, you cannot withhold it. If you can identify the reinforcer, your next challenge is whether you can *control* the reinforcer. If you cannot control whether the reinforcer is delivered (e.g., in the case of student attention), you cannot withhold it. If you cannot withhold the reinforcer, you cannot use extinction as the definition of extinction is to withhold the reinforcer maintaining the behavior.

Teachers frequently confuse extinction with ignoring a problem behavior. That is, they work from the premise that if you want a behavior to go away, simply ignore it. Sometimes that works and sometimes it doesn't. When analyzed from a behavioral perspective, it is easy to know when ignoring will function as extinction and when it will not. If your attention is the reinforcer maintaining the behavior, then when you ignore you are withholding the reinforcer–you are actually using extinction. If your attention is not the reinforcer maintaining the behavior, ignoring is not extinction and will not eliminate the behavior. We will talk more about extinction when we examine functional analysis later in the chapter.

Response cost occurs when students, because of inappropriate behavior, must forfeit something they have already earned. Besides social reinforcers that cannot be removed, students often earn privileges, prizes, and points. Any of these can be removed if students engage in inappropriate behavior. At the same time, however, you will want to be sure students have the opportunity to earn additional reinforcement. If your classroom is one in which there are not many opportunities to earn reinforcement for appropriate behavior, you may find that when students engage in inappropriate behavior they have no reinforcers to forfeit. If this is the case, response cost will probably not be an alternative for you. We will briefly return to response cost when we discuss the token economy.

It is quite likely that you were already familiar with reprimands, time out, extinction, and response cost, even if you were not clear on their specific definitions and requirements of effective implementation. The three remaining procedures, however, are not likely to be familiar. The first of these, **overcorrection,** is a procedure in which the student is required to produce positive changes in the environment beyond those required because of the inappropriate behavior. This procedure, like the two that follow, is tied very closely to the inappropriate behavior. For example, if the student's inappropriate behavior is writing on the desk, which defies the respect for property rule, the student may be required to clean not only the desk the student wrote on, but all the desks. Clearly a limitation to overcorrection is that it is probably impossible to *make* a student do this if the student refuses. In addition, some inappropriate behaviors do not produce an environmental change to be corrected. For example, if a student calls out in a way that interferes with other students, thus defying the respect of others rule, there is no physical change in the environment that the student can correct. Finally, you may not be permitted to ask students to do cleaning chores. Be sure to check this with your administration before considering overcorrection as one of your procedures.

Another disciplinary procedure tied closely to inappropriate behavior is **satiation**, a procedure in which teachers can require students to continually engage in the behavior until the reinforcer that is maintaining the behavior loses its reinforcing effectiveness. A reinforcer is more effective if the person who is to receive it has been without it for a long period of time–the person is in a deprived state. If the person has recently received large amounts of the reinforcer, the reinforcer is likely to temporarily lose its effectiveness as a reinforcer. If you have students engage in the inappropriate behavior continually until they satiate on the reinforcer that was maintaining that behavior, the behavior will eventually decrease in frequency. For example, some students take pleasure in burping. To use satiation, require the student to continue burping until you give permission to stop. You will have to have this continue well past the point at which the student finds it reinforcing to burp. Once again, there is the limitation that you cannot force a student to continue engaging in a behavior. That is, you will need a compliant student to use this procedure.

Our final procedure, **positive practice**, also requires a compliant student; however, it provides an advantage not found in any of the other procedures. It teaches the student an appropriate behavior to replace the inappropriate behavior. Consider for a moment that sometimes students emit inappropriate behaviors in a particular situation because they do not know what the appropriate behaviors are for that situation. In positive practice they may learn such behaviors. To implement positive practice, have the student practice an alternative appropriate behavior that you would like to replace the inappropriate behavior. For example, if a student throws her jacket on the closet floor rather than hanging up the jacket, have her put her jacket back on, go out of the classroom and come in again to practice arriving in the room with her jacket on, taking off her jacket, and hanging up her jacket in the closet. What we frequently do is notice the jacket on the floor in the closet and call the student back to hang it up. This does not change the sequence of responses the student makes the next time she comes in the classroom.

We briefly presented seven discipline procedures that may be used to reduce inappropriate behavior–any behavior that breaks the rules or does not follow the routines and procedures. You will have to decide which of these to try to implement for different behaviors. There are several guidelines to help you make your decision. The first must be what your administration will allow. Next, you should be guided by what you feel comfortable and confident in implementing. One of the keys to successful discipline procedures is consistency. If you are not comfortable or do not feel confident in a particular procedure, you are not likely to be consistent in its implementation. To use timeout and response cost effectively you will need to have many opportunities for reinforcement in your classroom; if that is not the case, timeout and response cost are not alternatives. Extinction can only be used if you can identify and control the reinforcer maintaining the behavior. Overcorrection, satiation, and positive practice all require that you have compliant students who will do what you ask them to do. Whatever you decide about disciplinary procedures you need to decide before you actually implement such procedures. You need to know before the students arrive on the first day which discipline procedures you will use so that you are prepared when the first inappropriate behavior occurs. It is likely that if you are that prepared and you remain consistent, you will not have to implement discipline procedures very often.

In an effort to be prepared and consistent, many teachers design and implement a **token economy**, a system for earning tokens that can be exchanged for privileges and activities. When using a token economy teachers can provide reinforcement for appropriate behavior—following the rules, routines, and procedures, and punishment for inappropriate behavior within a single system. In a token economy students earn tokens for appropriate behavior and return tokens for inappropriate behavior (this paying back of tokens is a response cost procedure within a token economy). To implement a token economy, teachers need to decide what behaviors will facilitate learning in their classroom (e.g., completing homework, completing seatwork in a timely fashion without interfering with others, and staying on task and academically engaged during small and large group instruction). Based on the amount of time and effort involved in these behaviors, teachers assign a number of tokens to be earned for each behavior. It is recommended that the tokens be tangible and difficult for students to counterfeit or give to each other in exchange for favors. In reality, such tokens are difficult to provide; therefore, teachers often use points. These are not tangible, but they meet the other recommendations. One way to assign points is to ask local banks to donate check registers. Students use their registers to keep a record of points they have earned for appropriate behaviors.

Just as there are behaviors that earn points, teachers need to identify the behaviors that interfere with instruction (e.g., interrupting a student who is working, running in the hall, arriving late during a transition, and doing anything other than engaging in the academic activity during instruction). For each of these behaviors, teachers must decide how many points to deduct based on the severity of the behavior. These points are subtracted from the check register. Periodically, perhaps once a week, students are allowed to exchange their points for **backup reinforcers**, those things for which students exchange their tokens or points in a token economy such as the opportunity to be class messenger for the week. The points have no value in and of themselves, just as money has no value in and of itself. However, if students can exchange their points for things they want or need, the points are valuable to them.

Therefore, teachers have another important decision to make about the token economy. What backup reinforcers will be available? These reinforcers need not be items that teachers have to purchase. Sometimes parents and local businesses will donate items to be used as backup reinforcers. However, privileges are often equally or more powerfully reinforcing than possessions. The privileges teachers choose will depend on the age level of the students and the particular likes and dislikes of the students. In the earlier grades privileges such as becoming a line leader, can be earned by the students with their tokens. In addition, many students may find it reinforcing to have lunch with the teacher or the principal. The possibilities for backup reinforcers are probably endless at this level. By middle and high school it becomes a little more difficult to identify the backup reinforcers. Some possibilities are homework passes, extra time in the library to work on a project, extra time to experiment with the computer technology in the classroom, and listening to music during independent work time.

In addition to identifying these backup reinforcers, teachers need to decide how much each will cost. The cost of each reinforcer should be determined by its value, which is driven by supply and demand, just as it is in our national economy. As with the rules, routines, and procedures discussed earlier in this chapter, you will have to teach the token economy to your students at the start of the school year.

Which Discipline Procedures Will You Use in Your School?

Will you choose from among the seven procedures presented here, or will you choose other procedures? What will be your guidelines for choosing? Will you collect data as to how often inappropriate behaviors occur to know if the procedures you chose are effective? Will teachers individually choose discipline procedures, or will a set of procedures be chosen for all teachers to use? Will teachers be expected to report their plans for discipline to the administration at the start of the school year? Does the idea of a school-wide token economy intrigue you? How would you design and implement such a system for the school? What might some of the advantages of such a school-wide system be?

Functional Analysis

All of the discipline procedures presented here, including the token economy, are fairly specific procedures, and if that is all you take into the classroom from behavior analysis you will not be adequately prepared to manage your classroom from a behavioral perspective. The procedures provided here are effective if implemented correctly, but they are just a list of procedures that could become nothing more than a bag of tricks. Unless you understand what is happening in the classroom from a behavioral perspective, the first time you try one of these procedures and you do not get the results for which you are hoping, you will not be prepared to make the kinds of decisions you need to make to affect the management of your classroom.

Therefore, let's look at the big picture of behavior analysis in classroom management. In Chapter 2, we introduced you to the signal, response, and consequence involved in any reinforcement contingency. We discussed the importance of providing signals for the responses you desire from students and for reinforcing those responses. We also considered those signals that tell the student *better not do that now*. When the behavior occurs in the presence of those signals, it is punished because we wish to decrease those behaviors. Throughout this chapter we have offered suggestions for sending signals for the behaviors you want, teaching those signals and behaviors, and then reinforcing those behaviors when they occur. Similarly, we have presented suggestions for decreasing behaviors you do not want. However, if you understand the principles of behavior analysis, you can conduct a **functional analysis** in your classroom and generate your own suggestions and procedures to maximize engaged time.

A functional analysis is a means of gathering information that can be used to design strategies to change behaviors (O'Neill, Horner, Albin, Storey, & Sprague, 1990). It is conducted to determine how behavior functions. When a person behaves in a particular way, what happens—what does the person gain? Doing a functional analysis in the classroom provides three pieces of important information: a clear picture of what the behavior looks like, a good idea of when the behavior will and will not occur, and what the behavior produces for the person (O'Neill et al., 1990). Three ways can be used to gather this information. You can interview the student, directly observe the behavior for an extended period of time, and/or systematically manipulate conditions and observe subsequent changes in the behavior (O'Neill et al., 1990).

When we do a functional analysis under the controlled conditions of the laboratory, we typically gather information in all three ways beginning with the interview, which tells us what to look for during direct observation. When we have some ideas about the function of the behavior from the direct observation, we systematically manipulate the conditions identified from observation and see what happens to the behavior under the different conditions. For example, we may find that a person often engages in inappropriate behavior when provided a difficult task. When this inappropriate behavior occurs several possibilities may follow. To determine the reinforcer that is maintaining the behavior, we design a situation in which we present the student with a difficult task. When the student engages in the inappropriate behavior we systematically provide one of several different consequences to see what happens to the behavior. We may provide attention to the student in the way of encouragement or additional help, we may remove the activity (allowing the student to escape the difficult task), or we may ignore the behavior. During each of these situations we observe and record how many times the inappropriate behavior occurs. If during any one of these situations the behavior occurs more often than it does during the other situations, we have identified the function of the behavior. The function may be to provide reinforcement in the way of attention from the teacher, escape from the task, or stimulation from something intrinsic to the behavior itself. Once we learn what the reinforcer is, we can use extinction thereby reducing the behavior.

If you experimentally manipulate the consequences after the behavior occurs—that is, predetermine which consequences you will apply in what order for the benefit of identifying the functional relationship you will be conducting a functional analysis. Unfortunately, this is not practical, especially in a general education classroom with 25 to 30 students and one teacher.

However, a similar procedure that serves the same purpose can be conducted in the classroom. Rather than systematically manipulating the different consequences in some predetermined order, you can take careful notes of when the behavior occurs, what immediately precedes it (to determine the signal for this person to behave this way) and what immediately follows it (to determine the reinforcer). This gives you a systematic means of analyzing why students do the things they do. If you can identify the signal and the reinforcer for the inappropriate behavior, you can begin to design your own strategies for eliminating the inappropriate behavior.

You may decide to eliminate the signal and the reinforcer for the inappropriate behavior. The simplest example of this occurs when students talk to or play with the student sitting nearest them. For example, Samantha frequently talks to and plays with Damion, who is sitting next to her. Damion may be the signal for Samantha to talk and play because he joins in, reinforcing her inappropriate behavior. If you move Damion's seat, you are removing the signal for Samantha's inappropriate behavior. It is possible, however, that Samantha talks to the person sitting nearest her, no matter who that person is. In this case, it is not possible to remove the signal for talking and playing unless Samantha is asked to sit away from the other students. However, Samantha probably only talks to and plays with students who reinforce this behavior by joining in the behavior. If so, your job is to find students who will not acknowledge Samantha when she talks to them and have these students sit near Samantha. While Samantha may initially talk because the signals are there (the other students), her talking will not be reinforced by their joining in, and it will cease. In addition, these other students will no longer be a signal for Samantha to talk.

A much more subtle signal for off-task behavior is sent when the task is too difficult for the student. You may find that students are not actively engaged in the task because they are not prepared to accomplish the task. Rather than be continually frustrated by a task they are not capable of completing, students frequently engage in behaviors that are disruptive to others. If so, your job is to remove the signal for disruptive behavior by providing only independent activities that students are capable of completing on their own.

If you find yourself correcting the same students over and over, consider that your correcting may be functioning as a reinforcer for the behavior you are trying to eliminate. If students are to be working in centers independently and there are frequent problems, watch to see what is happening. Maybe there are not sufficient materials—an easy problem for you to eliminate. Sometimes the mix of students in a center is a problem, again you can take some control. When you are conducting small groups and students who are assigned to seatwork come and interrupt you, what do you do? Do you answer their questions—if you do, you are probably reinforcing the behavior you want to eliminate. This is true, even if you answer in an "annoyed" tone. If you continue with your small group instruction and refuse to be interrupted, the interruptions eventually will stop. Students may have legitimate questions during seatwork—that is why you have names next to each activity so that students can get assistance from their classmates.

Let's also consider the older students, such as high school students, who may frequently come to class unprepared. What are the consequences for being unprepared? They may vary depending on the way in which the students are unprepared—they come without pencils or pens, they come without their homework, they come sleepy from lunch period, or they come excited and anxious for the end of the school day. First, consider what you typically do and how that affects their behavior. If what you typically do maintains their behavior, you may wish to change what you do, which in turn will change what they do. Middle and high school students are notorious for setting up situations in which they take the teacher off task so that they do not have to work. Consider too, students who come without something to write with—the standard procedure for handling this situation should be established at the start of the year. It is their job to find a pen or pencil, you will not deal with it—which means you do not take the time to scold them for it either. You simply continue. High school teachers have been known to deal with students not being prepared for class by telling the students that it was then not possible to teach them today. For many students this is a very powerful reinforcer for not being prepared.

In general, if what you are doing is not having the desired effect on the students, you need to change what you are doing. The guide for making that change is to keep careful records of when the behavior occurs, what precedes it, and what consequences follow it. With an emphasis on functional analysis and arranging an environment that prompts and reinforces appropriate academic and social behavior, you will have less need to use the discipline procedures presented earlier.

Will You do Functional Analyses in Your School?

Will you encourage teachers to conduct functional analyses for problem behaviors they encounter in their classes? Will you provide training in conducting functional analyses so that teachers are prepared to do them? Will you provide assistance in conducting functional analyses—will teachers have someone who can come to their classrooms to collect the data while they are teaching? Will teachers be allowed and encouraged to conduct functional analyses for each other?

Summary

In this chapter we examined ways to manage time and behavior in the classroom by first defining allocated time and engaged time. In considering the positive academic effect of high levels of engaged time, we examined two broad, complimentary approaches to increasing such time. One approach is to utilize instructional strategies designed to produce large amounts of engaged time through frequent active responding, mastery, teacher accountability, student-centered instruction, and reinforcement. While strategies such as Precision Teaching, Direct Instruction, PSI, Programmed Instruction, and Peer Tutoring have these features built in, it is also possible to offer such features without these particular strategies.

A second approach teachers can take involves designing their classrooms for maximum utilization of allocated time, including the physical space and procedures and rules for dealing with transitions and routines in the classroom. With such procedures and rules carefully designed, taught to students, and practiced, it is still likely that some inappropriate behaviors will remain. We described several discipline procedures and how they might be implemented to eliminate behaviors that interfere with instruction. Finally, we suggested ways in which you may analyze the environment of your classroom and design your own efficient, effective procedures to increase engaged student time.

Annotated Bibliography

Becker, W. C. (1986). *Applied psychology for teachers: A behavioral cognitive approach.* Chicago, SRA.

    Presents an excellent, easy to understand introduction to the principles of behavior analysis and how they may be applied to classroom management.

Clough, M. P., Smasal, R. J., & Clough, D. R. (1994). Managing each minute. *The Science Teacher, 61* (6), 30-34.

    Offers many excellent strategies teachers can use to make the most of allocated instructional time.

O'Neill, R. E., Horner, R. H., Albin, R. W., Storey, K., & Sprague, J. R. (1990). *Functional analysis of problem behavior: A practical assessment guide.* Pacific Grove, CA: Brooks/Cole.

    Presents clear guidelines for conducting a functional analysis along with many blank forms students may use in conducting their own functional analyses.

Smith, M. A., & Misra, A. (1992). A comprehensive management system for students in regular classrooms. *The Elementary School Journal, 92*, 354-371.

    Provides a comprehensive classroom management system by clearly addressing antecedents, reinforcement, and punishment, and how teachers can take control of each to develop a system that supports appropriate academic and social behaviors.

Stainback, W., Stainback, S., & Froyen, L. (1987). Structuring the classroom to prevent disruptive behaviors. *Teaching Exceptional Children, 19* (4), 12-16.

    Suggests practical considerations in designing the classroom to prevent or minimize inappropriate behaviors.

Chapter 6

Assessing Academic Performance

Public school systems vary significantly from each other in terms of the number of schools, students, teachers, class size, fiscal budget, and demographics. Yet, the primary mission of all school systems is the education of their children. Although many parents and politicians seem interested in the outcome of the educational process, the attainment of this goal is, for the most part, left in the hands of classroom teachers. In order to determine if children are learning and the mission is being met, at least at the classroom level, teachers must engage in the periodic **assessment** of their students' academic performance. Assessment has many definitions but is generally agreed to entail the processes involved in obtaining information in order to make informed educational decisions. Some of these processes consist of paper-and-pencil tests, oral questioning of students, evaluation of individual student records, and formal or informal observations of student performance.

According to the *Standards for Teacher Competence in Educational Assessment of Students,* which was jointly developed by the American Federation of Teachers, National Council on Measurement in Education, and the National Education Association (1990), "student assessment is an essential part of teaching and good teaching cannot exist without good student assessment" (p. 1). We wholeheartedly concur with this statement. Assessment techniques provide information to make informed, data-based decisions regarding the learning process. Recall from Chapter 1 that we hold teachers accountable for the academic failure and success of their students. Unless students are learning, teaching is not occurring. The only way to determine if teaching is occurring is through the assessment of student performance.

The traditional assessment instrument most commonly used by teachers is the paper-and-pencil test. Well constructed tests are designed to sample only a small part of a student's skill in a particular area. The skill area being assessed is usually referred to as a learning or content domain while the questions that make up the test are referred to as items. Based upon the student's answers to the test items, data-based decisions are made that infer some level of competence in the sampled learning or content domain. For instance, if Mary correctly answered all items on a test designed to assess her skill in adding fractions, you would likely infer that she has mastered this learning domain.

The type of paper-and-pencil tests we are referring to in this context are usually created by individual teachers for use in their own classrooms and typically consist of fill-in-the-blank, multiple choice, matching, or short essay items. It is common to find two or more teachers presenting the same instructional material to similar classes but employing quite different tests to assess their students' performance. Hopefully, these differences are due to the purpose of the test. For example, tests may be employed to find out if individual students are making progress toward instructional goals, to determine if instruction needs to be modified, to motivate students, or to provide feedback to students. Typically, the kinds of data-based decisions made from the outcome of tests are grade assignments, curriculum modifications, or student placement into or out of special programs.

When constructed properly, the information gleaned from paper-and-pencil tests can provide a teacher with a general idea of a student's skill level in the learning domain. Unfortunately, few teachers ever receive formal training in test construction and much has been written about the drawbacks of teacher-made tests. Perhaps the biggest drawback, however, is not in how they are constructed but in the frequency with which they are employed. Test results are like snapshots. They reflect the performance of a student at a single moment in time. If a student does poorly on a test, perhaps that student didn't really have a firm grasp of the material. On the other hand, perhaps that student really did have a grasp of the material but some other factor was responsible for the observed poor performance. A major problem inherent in single assessments of student performance is that unknown influences might effect the outcome and lead to decisions that do not accurately reflect the student's true level of skill in the learning domain.

Occasionally, teachers might administer a test at the beginning of some instructional lesson to determine the entry level skills of students, but in general they usually give tests only after the lesson has been completed. Often, the time lag between beginning the lesson and assessing student performance may be days or even weeks. Typically, the student and the teacher have no idea "how they are doing" until the test results are analyzed. Unfortunately, even though teachers may have an opinion about their individual students, the assessment process does not begin until the data are collected. If the data consist solely of performance on a single test given many days or weeks after the instructional process has begun, changes in the instructional plan are usually too late since the class has moved on to other topics or the time left in the school year is too limited to "back up." The end result, which is an atrocity to behavior analysts, is that some students learn while others do not. The following vignette, taken from Alberto and Troutman (1995) may help to illustrate this point.

Ms. Waller Goes Electronic

Ms. Waller was ecstatic. After months of complaining that she had no materials to use to teach reading to her most challenging reading group, she had received a computerized teaching machine. The salesman proudly demonstrated the machine and pointed out the features that justified the hundreds of dollars invested.

"All you have to do," he assured her, "is hook the little, er, students up to these here headphones, drop in a cassette, and turn this baby on. Everything else is taken care of . . . you don't do a thing."

Ms. Waller briskly administered the pretest included in the materials, scheduled each student for 15 minutes a day on the machine, and assumed that her worries were over.

At the end of the school year, Ms. Waller administered the posttest. Imagine her distress when, although several members of the group had made remarkable progress, some students had made none at all.

"I don't understand," she wailed. "The machine was supposed to do everything. How was I supposed to know it wasn't working?"

"Perhaps," suggested her principal kindly, as he wished her success in her career as an encyclopedia salesperson, "you should have checked before now." (p. 103)

How Behavior Analysis Can Help

Behavior analysis can provide assistance in the assessment process by suggesting to teachers various methods that will result in more frequent collection of information so that scenarios like the one just described can be prevented. As already mentioned, observations of a single instance of student performance at some particular moment in time can sometimes lead to decisions that do not accurately reflect the student's grasp of the material. A more accurate method of assessment involves repeatedly observing and recording student performance over time. This process is at the heart of behavior analysis and allows data-based decisions to be made that are more realistic than those made based upon a single measure.

For example, on a test to assess multiplication skills involving single digit numbers, Johnny may not answer many of the problems correctly for many reasons besides his lack of skill in this area. Perhaps he was ill on the day the test was administered, in a bad mood, skipped breakfast, or had a fight with a classmate. By attempting to assess Johnny's skill level at a single moment in time, the effects of these potential and extraneous conditions cannot be known. Yet, by repeatedly measuring Johnny's ability to multiply single digit numbers over some course of time, a more accurate picture of his skill in this area can be detected since the effect of extraneous variables, such as those just described, tends to be transitory. Figure 6.1 provides a graphic example of this point.

Suppose that a test was administered on Thursday. Notice that Johnny's percentage of correct multiplication problems was at its lowest point of the week (10%). Yet, during the other week days his performance was relatively consistent; it appears that he can correctly multiply from 50 to 60 percent of the problems. If you made a decision about Johnny's performance based on only Thursday's information, your conclusions would be substantially different from a decision made by incorporating all of the information collected during the week. By inspecting Figure 6.1, you might draw the conclusion that something other than Johnny's lack of skill in this area was affecting his performance on Thursday.

Behavior analysts frequently employ graphical representations of student performance or behavior. Graphs tend to be much easier to inspect than tables of numbers. Additionally, once the graph has been constructed it is very easy to add new information on student performance in order to keep abreast of trends or changes in performance. The remainder of this chapter will focus on some of the issues and techniques behavior analysts have developed for conducting educational

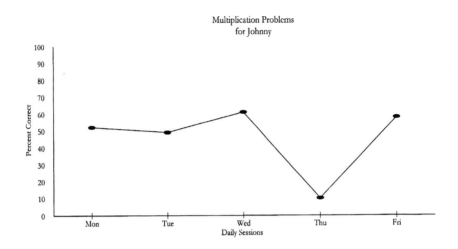

Figure 6.1. Example of repeated mesurements of behavior

assessments. They all meet the three driving forces suggested in the first chapter of this book–they are data-based, individualized, and practical.

Collect Information That is Valid, Reliable, and Practical

Before engaging in observations of student performance and before you begin to collect your first piece of information, you need to be aware of the concepts of validity, reliability, and utility as used by behavior analysts. **Validity** is simply the degree to which what you are measuring reflects what you want to measure. This may seem like common sense but you would be surprised how many educational decisions are made with information that is invalid or only tangentially relevant to the topic under scrutiny. If you are trying to gather information on Tony's reading comprehension skills, observing him walking around with books under his arm is not a valid index of this skill. You need to consider the specific behavior you want to measure. If you are interested in reading comprehension, give Tony something to read that matches your curriculum's current reading level. He could read a passage for some specific period of time and you could measure the number of questions he can correctly answer about that passage. If you are interested in his ability to decode words, you could have him read aloud and you could then count the number of words he misprounounces as a ratio of total words. If you need to obtain information about the number of sit-ups one of your students can perform, counting the actual number of sit-ups over some number of days is probably a valid measure. Always measure the behavior that relates to the purpose of your assessment. For example, measuring some other physical education activity, such as pull-ups or push-ups when your interest is in sit-ups, will not provide you with the type of information you require. Even though there may seem to be some relationship between sit-ups, pull-ups, and push-ups, measuring one is not necessarily a valid measure of the others.

Once you have decided on a behavior to measure that is valid with respect to the type of question you are attempting to answer, your next step is to insure that the manner in which the information is collected produces reliable results. Behavior analysts do not use the term reliability in exactly the same way as those involved in traditional approaches to measurement. For behavior analysts, **reliability** refers to the consistency of your measurements over time regardless of *how* or *who* collects the information. One way behavior analysts attempt to insure reliability is by avoiding terms or categories that are vague or ambiguous. By critically reviewing the aspects of both the classroom and the behavior that is to be measured and stating these aspects in unambiguous terms, behavior analysts strive to clarify the behavior such that two or more individuals will agree that the behavior in question did or did not occur. Behavior analysts refer to this process as operationally defining behavior. **Operational definitions** help to pinpoint the specific behavior and the conditions in which an instance will be considered to have occurred.

In order to obtain reliable measurements, two or more observers who have mastered the content of the operational definition are required. One observer, referred to as the primary observer, records the behavior of interest during all observation periods. The remaining observers are typically employed during a certain percentage of observation periods. The data collected by the observers are then compared and a reliability index is calculated. This index, often referred to as **interrater reliability**, can be calculated in many ways and is typically a reflection of the number of agreements and disagreements between both observers regarding the occurrence of the target behavior. In behavior analysis when two or more observers agree on at least 80% of the recorded information, the data are considered acceptable for decision making purposes. Values less than 80% are indicative of low reliability in the way your observations yield data and render the issue of validity moot.

Once you are assured that your measurements will yield valid and reliable results, you must gauge the practicality or **utility** of the process in terms of your own classroom. The most reliable and valid procedures for gathering needed information will be useless to you if they are too expensive or cumbersome to implement. As the classroom teacher, you are the sole judge regarding the utility of the process. If it is easy to implement and produces the information you need to make informed decisions about your students' progress or a program's effectiveness, you may feel that implementing the data collection process is well worth the time and effort. On the other hand, if you are not convinced that the needed information can be readily and easily obtained you might reject the process for lack of utility and seek some other process that meets these three points.

Dimensions of Behavior

Before we present the various methods for observing student behavior, we must first discuss the issue of behavioral dimensions. If Roderick's parents told you he had "severe tantrums" when he didn't get his way, you might ask questions about these tantrums. If his parents then told you that he had one per day, you might not consider this type of behavior as problematic as his parents. If, on the other hand, they told you he had one tantrum per day that lasted six hours, your perspective on this problem would certainly be different. In the first instance, the dimension of behavior discussed is **frequency**. In the second instance, the dimension is **duration**. Depending upon the particular dimension of behavior that is measured, different types of information emerge and different decisions are made. Before you begin the data collection process, you must select an appropriate behavioral dimension. What follows is a brief description of five behavioral dimensions that can easily be assessed in classroom settings.

Force

If you are interested in measuring and changing the strength of some behavior, *force* is usually the dimension of choice. As an example, suppose you have a student in your classroom who talks so softly that she is barely audible. If one of your goals is to have her speak louder, measuring the loudness of her vocalizations would be appropriate.

Duration

If your interest lies in determining how long some behavior occurs, *duration* is the appropriate measure. Suppose Angela completes very little of her independent work and you suspect it is because she is frequently off-task. You may be interested in determining how many minutes she spends working on assignments during independent work time.

Topography

Interest in the form or shape of some behavior might best be quenched by measuring *topography*. Topography is the term behavior analysts use to talk about the overt pattern of behavior. Suppose you are teaching American Sign Language (ASL) to hearing impaired children. The various hand postures, movements, and locations are critical for effective ASL communication. For example, the ASL signs for coffee and clown share certain finger, hand, and movement characteristics. They differ significantly, however, in terms of where, in relation to the torso and head, they are emitted.

Rate

If you need to evaluate a student's proficiency in some area, *rate* of reponse is often the appropriate dimension to evaluate. In fact, rate measures are at the heart of Precision Teaching, which was discussed in Chapter 4. It is calculated by simply dividing the frequency with which a behavior occurs by the allocated time period. Knowing that Kevin answered all 10 math problems correctly might lead you to conclude that he has learned to solve problems of this kind. However, if it took him two hours, his rate would be one problem every 12 minutes. If you allocated 30 minutes for a 10 question math test, Kevin would only answer two questions. In this light, you may not consider mastery of the math topic to be met.

Locus

A final, and often overlooked, dimension of behavior is location or *locus*. This involves a contextual evaluation. Yelling "fire" in a crowded movie theater, when there is no fire, is an inappropriate and illegal behavior. On the other hand, yelling "fire" when the house is burning down is absolutely appropriate. If another teacher tells you that Kathy is a whirling dervish who constantly runs around, your initial reaction may be disdain. However, if you later find that this behavior only occurs on the playground during recess, your opinion may be significantly different.

Behavior analysts often consider locus of control to be a subset of **stimulus control.** When a particular behavior occurs only in the presence of a certain stimulus but never in the presence of other stimuli, the behavior is said to be *prompted* by or under the control of the antecedent stimulus. This type of behavior is usually the outcome of discrimination training in which a response is reinforced in the presence of one stimulus but never reinforced in the presence of other stimuli. Innumerable instances of stimulus control occur in your daily life. For example, when driving, why do you stop at red lights but not at green lights? When you see a police car on the highway, why do you immediately depress the brake pedal even if you are not exceeding the speed limit? Why do very young children call any female "mommy" while older children reserve this term only for mom? These are all instances of stimulus control which is an area of behavior analysis that has received considerable attention over the years.

Before you begin the task of observing behavior and recording data, you need to identify the particular dimension of interest. The previous examples should indicate to you that the type of question you are asking may only be answered by measuring an appropriate behavioral dimension. Depending on the dimension of behavior you need to quantify and the logistics involved in gathering needed information, one dimension may be more appropriate than another. However, there is no implicit order or ranking associated with these categories; they are simply different aspects of student performance.

Define Behavior To Avoid Ambiguity

If the behavior you are attempting to record or the conditions in which it occurs are vaguely or ambiguously stated, the reliability and validity of your measurements will be low. Imagine what would happen if you asked two different people to count the number of times during each class period that Loretta appeared "frustrated." If you provided no further specification of "frustration," what characteristic behavior on Loretta's part would indicate to these individuals that Loretta is frustrated? Everyone has his or her own personal definition of the various emotional states but not all of these personal definitions are congruent with each other. Unless the observers have some *a priori* agreed upon observable behavior to record, the reliability between the observers is likely to be very low. If you don't know what you're looking for, how will you know it when you see it?

Earlier we suggested that one way to overcome this potential problem, before time and effort are expended in recording information, is to operationally define behavior. Behavior analysts develop operational definitions that objectively state the behavior and the conditions in which an instance will be considered to have occurred. Over the years, many different suggestions have been put forth regarding the development of operational definitions (Gelfand & Hartmann, 1984; Jenson, Sloane, & Young, 1988). However, there is no general consensus or behavioral taxonomy that is employed. Rather, definitions are created by referring to the student's current behavior, expected behavior, and classroom setting (Alberto & Troutman, 1995). If one of your students is chronically running around and not working on assigned tasks very often, you might wish to gather information on his "on-task" performance. How would you define this behavior so that each occurrence could be recorded? You would most likely define "on-task" by referring to some objective criterion that you as the teacher believe represents this pattern of behavior. The point to keep in mind is that however you operationally define "on-task" behavior, it should be specific enough to insure that two or more observers will agree on its occurrence or lack of occurrence.

Establish Assessment Routines for Your School

Will you establish assessment routines that all teachers in your school are expected to follow? How often will teachers be expected to assess student performance? What types of behaviors will be assessed regularly? Will you assess both academic and social behavior? How will these behaviors be defined? For which behaviors will you be primarily concerned with force, with duration, with topography, with rate, and with locus? Will teachers be encouraged to serve as second observers for each other? How will you schedule this? Will teachers be expected to meet regularly to help each other make informed, data-based decisions for their students? How will parents be kept informed of these assessments?

Behavioral Observation and Recording Techniques

Behavior analysts have developed and employed numerous methods for collecting information about behavior, such as real-time observations, behavioral interviews, behavioral checklists, anecdotal reports, permanent products, self-reports, and direct observation techniques. Along with each type of recording technique various coded systems have been developed in order to expedite the data collection process. While there are many techniques for observing and recording student behavior, we will concentrate only on those that are most useful to teachers in the classroom. However, excellent descriptions and examples of all the techniques developed by behavior analysts can be found in other sources (Barlow & Hersen, 1984; Jenson et al., 1988; Johnston & Pennypacker, 1993).

The four observation and recording techniques we will present in this section are relatively easy for the individual classroom teacher or aide to implement. The first three techniques are usually employed when the behavioral dimension of interest can be expressed numerically. The final technique is employed when temporal dimensions of behavior are of interest. Deciding which technique to employ is usually based on whether the behavior of interest is discrete or continuous and whether it occurs at a high or a low rate.

Event Recording

At various times this technique has been called event recording, frequency recording, the tally method, or the trial method (Barlow & Hersen, 1984). Regardless of its name, event recording simply involves counting the number of occurrences of a target behavior during some specified period of time. This method is probably the easiest method that can be employed in the classroom. It can be used to record behavior as it occurs or the outcome of behavior that has already occurred. Discrete behaviors such as spelling words, math problems, letter recognition, completed assignments, trips to the bathroom, and so on can easily be measured with this method. Even the individual items that make up paper-and-pencil tests can be viewed as a form of event recording.

Since a count of the behavior in question is all that is recorded, this method is often practical and easy to implement in the classroom. If the duration of the observation session is also recorded, a rate of behavior can be easily obtained by dividing the frequency of occurrence by the length of the observation session. Rate measures are often used to infer the "fluency" a student has in performing some behavior, such as math problems, and is at the heart of Precision Teaching.

Event recording may not be practical for the classroom teacher if the behavior being observed and recorded tends to occur quite frequently. If so, actual occurrences of the target behavior may not be accurately recorded and result in an underestimate of the true frequency. Additionally, the more frequently the behavior occurs, the more time the classroom teacher must spend observing and recording the behavior, which takes time away from the teaching process. One way to free up the teacher's time is to employ another individual, such as a teacher's aide or another student, to observe and record the behavior. However, the problem of accurately recording high frequency behaviors is not eliminated by employing a second party observer. Instead, other recording methods might need to be considered. Two other observation and recording techniques that evolved from event recording may help overcome this potential problem. They typically require at least one additional person besides the classroom teacher to conduct the observations. The first technique is referred to as interval recording. The second technique is called time-sampling.

Interval Recording

In order to employ interval observation and recording, the time period in which the student is to be observed is typically broken up into discrete intervals of equal duration. These intervals usually range from a few seconds to a minute or more.

During each interval only one of two outcomes is recorded–the behavior of interest either occurred or did not occur. Regardless of how many times the behavior is observed to occur during each interval, it is only recorded once. If the student is observed to emit the behavior in question at the beginning of the interval, no further observations during the remainder of the interval are necessary. At the end of the observation period, the number of intervals in which the behavior was observed can be divided by the total number of observation intervals in order to calculate a percent or proportion of occurrence of the target behavior. Figure 6.2 provides an example of a hypothetical recording sheet which covers a five minute observation period broken up into 10-second intervals. If the target behavior was detected during this brief observation, a plus (+) sign was placed in the appropriate cell otherwise a slash (/) was placed to indicate the absence of the behavior. Notice that these data suggest the behavior being assessed occurred over 67% of the total observation period.

Although interval observation and recording techniques are frequently em-ployed, they do not provide information that is as accurate as the information gleaned from event recording techniques. For example, notice that the first interval of the first minute in Figure 6.2 is marked as indicating that the target behavior occurred. Since only a single instance of behavior need be observed to score the interval, you have no way of knowing if the target behavior occurred only once, more than once, or began in that interval and continued into the next interval. However, if your goal, as a classroom teacher, is to obtain a general overview of your students' performance in order to make data-based decisions about their progress, the advantages of interval observation and recording techniques often outweigh this minor disadvantage.

Time-Sampling

The observation and recording technique known as time-sampling is very similar to interval recording. Once again, the observation period is divided into equal intervals and the target behavior is scored as having occurred or not occurred. However, with time-sampling methods, observation and recording is made only at the *end* of each interval. Figure 6.3, which is similar to Figure 6.2, provides an

10" Intervals

	1	2	3	4	5	6
Minute 1	+	+	/	/	+	/
Minute 2	/	+	+	+	+	/
Minute 3	+	+	+	+	/	+
Minute 4	+	+	+	/	/	/
Minute 5	/	+	+	+	+	+

+ = occurrence of target behavior   / = nonocccurrence of target behavior
% occurrence of target behavior = 20/30=67%

Figure 6.2. Example of a 10-sec. interval recording data sheet

example of a recording sheet for use with time-sampling methods. The dark areas indicate that the student *was not* observed while the white areas indicate that a momentary observation of the student was made.

Since a student only has to be observed briefly at the end of each interval, time-sampling methods make it easy to observe and record several students during the same time period. However, time-sampling observation and recording methods have the same drawbacks as interval observation and recording in that they may underestimate the occurrence of the target behavior (Repp, Roberts, Slack, Repp, & Berkler, 1976). Yet, if the behavior of interest tends to occur continuously or with a very high frequency, time-sampling may be a more practical method compared to interval recording.

Duration Recording

Classroom teachers are often interested in finding out how long students engage in various activities rather than how often. When this is the case, duration observation and recording techniques are usually appropriate. For example, a teacher may be interested in determining how long students work on math problems, reading assignments, computer activities, or social interactions. Duration observation and recording techniques can often provide a fairly accurate measure of these activities. With this method, the elapsed time between the beginning and end of the behavior of interest is simply measured.

15" Intervals

	1		2		3		4
Minute 1	+		+		+		+
Minute 2	+		/		+		/
Minute 3	/		+		+		+
Minute 4	+		/		/		+
Minute 5	+		+		+		+

+= occurrence of target behavior /= nonoccurrence of target behavior
% occurrence of target behavior = 15/20=75%

Figure 6.3. Example of a 15 sec. time-sampling data sheet. If the target behavior was detected during this brief observation, a plus (+) sign was placed in the appropriate cell otherwise a slash (/) was placed to indicate the absence of the behavior.

Duration recording always provides you with both a frequency count and a temporal measure of behavior. However, the frequency of the behavior is not usually relevant since the individual emissions of the observed behavior can vary tremendously across occurrences and make day-to-day comparisons difficult or meaningless to compare. For example, assume that during the course of a 30-minute recess period on Monday, Wednesday, and Friday, you observed Alan engaging in "appropriate play." Suppose his behavior conformed to your operational definition during the following time periods: 11:15-11:18, 11:20-11:22, 11:24-11:26, 11:28-11:31, 11:33-11:36, 11:39-11:43 on Monday (17 minutes - 6 occurrences), from 11:15-11:17, 11:20-11:30, and 11:40-11:45 on Wednesday (17 minutes - 3 occurrences) and from 11:20-11:37 on Friday (17 minutes - 1 occurrence). Although the total duration of appropriate play was identical across each day, if the information was reported as the outcome of event recording, it would suggest that Alan's appropriate play during recess was steadily declining. Data-based decisions regarding Alan's appropriate play during recess would be quite different if made based on event recording as opposed to duration recording. Remember, an ongoing record of behavior is important *but* if the behavioral dimension chosen for the behavior is not appropriate, you might end up with data that are meaningless or misleading.

Figure 6.4 graphically displays this point. The height of each grey bar represents the total duration of appropriate play on each day while the black circles represent the outcome of measuring the same behavior using event recording. Although it has been reported that duration recording is not employed as often as other recording procedures (Kelly, 1977), it is probably the most useful observation and recording procedure for gathering information when the temporal nature of behavior is important.

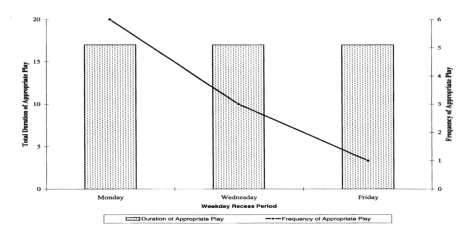

Figure 6.4. Example plot of measures of two different dimensions of the same behavior

Choosing and Using Observation and Recording Techniques

Of the types of behaviors you decided to assess regularly, decide for which of these behaviors you will probably use event recording, interval recording, time-sampling, and duration. How will you train your teachers to use these techniques? Will you video tape some classroom interactions and then practice each observation and recording technique? Will you try to hire teachers who are already skilled in the use of these techniques?

Graphically Portraying Collected Information

Regardless of the method employed for recording information, graphical representations often make data easier to interpret and understand. Although tables and raw data sheets can contain the same information portrayed by graphs, they are usually much more difficult to read and interpret than graphic "pictures" of information. Furthermore, unless you have extensive experience using tables, it is very difficult to spot trends or changes in behavior that might indicate the need to make changes in the instructional process.

In this section we provide some very rudimentary conventions for creating graphs in order to develop a "picture" of the target behavior. All graphs have two basic components: a vertical axis and a horizontal axis. The vertical axis is scaled in units that reflect the way in which the target behavior will be portrayed. For instance, if your data will be converted to percentages, the vertical axis might be scaled from 0% to 100%. The horizontal axis is scaled in units that reflect the time periods during which behavior was recorded. For example, if you recorded data daily for 10 consecutive class periods, the horizontal axis might be scaled from 1 to 10. It is customary to indicate exactly what is being portrayed along both axes. Figure 6.5 provides an example of the information just discussed.

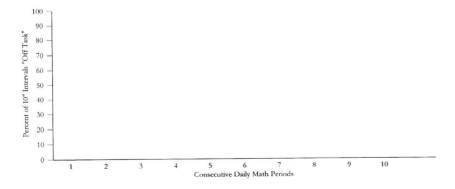

Figure 6.5. The components of a simple graph

When you construct a graph, you should employ labels for both the horizontal and vertical axes that are as descriptive as possible. Additionally, the scales you employ for the vertical axis should cover the range of expected results. To plot the collected data, a mark (circle, triangle, square) is placed at the point at which behavior and time intersect. As subsequent marks are placed on the graph, they are connected by a line to indicate the continuity of the measure. Following these recommendations makes it much easier for others to understand the information that is portrayed and also makes it easier for you to see what is happening to the behavior. For example, suppose you gave Jamie 10 problems on Monday, Tuesday, and Wednesday that involved adding two fractions and employed event recording to measure the number of correct problems she completed. Further suppose that you recorded the following number of correct math problems on each of those days: three, four, and two. Figure 6.6 provides one possible way to portray this information.

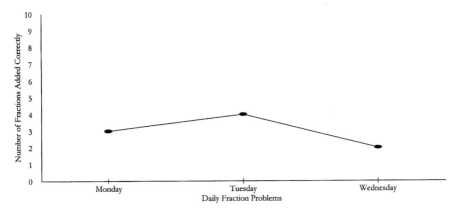

Figure 6.6. Example of a correctly labeled line graph

Although other types of graphs such as bar, histogram, cumulative record, and logarithmic plots are employed by behavior analysts, the most frequently used graph is the simple line graph. For example, line graphs can be used to display the behavior of more than one student at a time or multiple behaviors of the same student. Figure 6.7 provides an example of each of these uses. Once you have practiced making and using this type of graph a few times, you will probably wonder how you did without them for so long.

Making Data-Based Decisions

Recall from Chapter 4 that various strategies for teaching were discussed that are either rooted in behavior analysis or share characteristics with behavior analysis. Four of the strategies presented were the Personalized System of Instruction (PSI), Direct Instruction (DI), Peer Tutoring (PT), and Programmed Instruction (PI). Each of these methods, although different from each other in terms of instructional presentation, share the common premise that students can learn if instructional

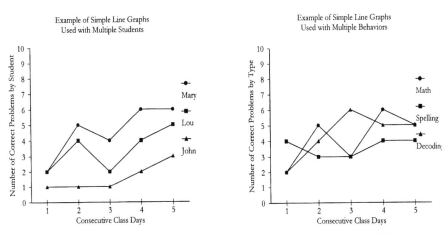

Figure 6.7. Examples of simple line graphs used with multiple students or behaviors

material is properly sequenced, participation is active, feedback is frequent, and modifications to the instruction are made based upon assessment of each student's performance. Not all instructional strategies share these characteristics, but the good ones do. This section will concentrate on the last characteristic that these methods share—when to make modifications in the instructional strategy based upon student performance.

Remember the dilemma Ms. Waller encountered when she waited until late in the year to assess her students' reading progress? Had she collected information on her students' reading performance sooner and more frequently, she would have been in a better position to make an accurate assessment of her students' reading progress. This is an area in which behavior analysis can provide help. Over the years, behavior analysts have developed various techniques that are useful in making decisions regarding the effects of instructional strategies on individual student behavior. Understand, however, that these techniques *do not* insure that your particular decision is the best decision. They do, however, insure that whatever decision you make is grounded in valid and reliable data.

With the exception of Precision Teaching, the techniques we discuss are subsumed under the heading of *single-subject research designs* to distinguish them from the more traditional *quasi-experimental designs* that are also employed in education and the social sciences. The differences between these categories are too numerous to discuss in this chapter and their underlying philosophical positions are beyond the scope of this book. However, suffice it to say that if you are interested in gathering information in order to make informed, data-based decisions about individual students based upon their own behavior and not the average behavior of some aggregate, single-subject designs can provide you with insights not available in quasi-experimental designs. Several outstanding sources are available that detail the unique aspects of each of the various single-subject (Barlow & Hersen, 1984; Johnston & Pennypacker, 1993) and quasi-experimental designs (Cook & Campbell, 1979).

Although single-subject designs *do not* require that only a single student be evaluated, their strength lies in the conclusions that can be drawn about a single student's behavior. With the more traditional quasi-experimental designs, no statements can be made about the behavior of any single student. The analysis of information gathered from employing quasi-experimental designs is subjected to statistical manipulations so that all conclusions are couched in language based on such statistical quantities as means, standard deviations, confidence intervals, and levels of significance. Knowing that Jesse was a member of the class whose average reading ability was significantly higher than any other class in the entire school system gives you no idea whatsoever about *his* level of reading. He could be the best or the worst reader in the group.

The purpose of this section is to provide some of the data-based decision tools used by behavior analysts. As with the various methods of recording data addressed earlier, we will not present all of the single-subject designs that have been developed since some are not well suited for classroom environments. We will, however, present two specific decision making strategies referred to as A-B and Multiple Baseline designs. For each we provide an example and discuss the strengths and weakness. As you read through the following material, try to think of examples from your own experiences in which these methods of analysis might have been helpful. However, before we present the two designs just mentioned, we return to a short discussion of Precision Teaching and touch upon some of the advantages of employing this method for making data-based decisions.

Precision Teaching

Precision Teaching was earlier grouped with the various teaching strategies that are rooted in behavior analysis or closely linked to behavior analysis (see Chapter 4). Recall, however, that we stated Precision Teaching is *not* a true teaching strategy. Rather, it is a method of analyzing student performance and making data-based decisions. If you employ Precision Teaching, whatever behavior is of interest is recorded and the outcome is converted to a rate measurement. For example, if John correctly completed 5 math problems in 5 minutes, his rate of correctly solving math problems would be expressed as 1 problem per minute. This rate would then be plotted on a semi-logarithmic chart, which reflects a more accurate representation of behavior when compared to such other measures as percent correct or number correct. Figure 6.8 provides an example.

With traditional graphical representations, the y-axis is usually scaled according to some interval scale. For example, if the y-axis is scaled from 0% to 100%, the distance from 10% to 20% is the same as the distance from 70% to 80%. On a semi-logarithmic chart the distances between values on the y-axis represent ratios, which result in a smoother plot of behavior and a more accurate representation of behavior over other types of scales. Figure 6.9 portrays the rate of solving math problems for two students, John and Mary, across five days of instruction. The filled circles depict John's rate per minute while the triangles represent Mary's rate per minute. Notice that John consistently had higher rates than Mary but *both* students showed increases

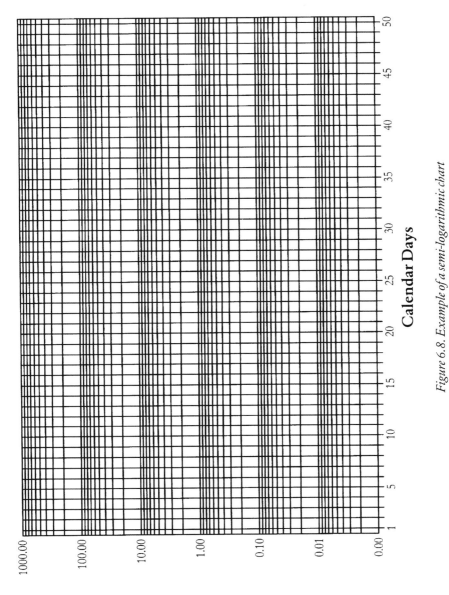

Figure 6.8. Example of a semi-logarithmic chart

in their respective rates over the course of the week's instruction. These data represent both students' fluency with math problems. In John's case, he could solve approximately 0.17 math problems per minute on the first day but increased this rate to 1.0 math problem per minute by the fifth day. Similarly, Mary's rates changed from approximately 0.03 to 0.17 over this same time period. If you were these students' teacher, would you continue your instructional strategy in this area? The data suggest that each student is rapidly becoming more fluent in this area so you probably want to keep your strategy intact—it's working. Recall from the earlier

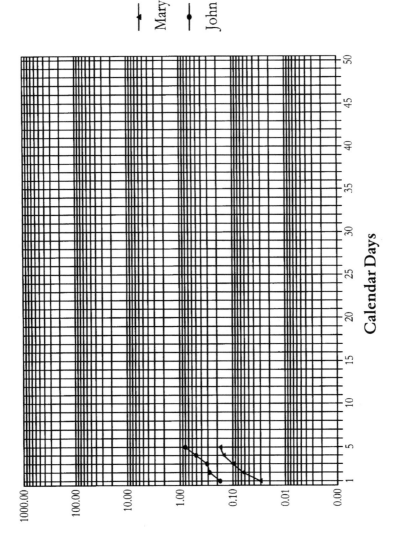

Figure 6.9. Rate of solving math problems for John (closed circle) and Mary (closed triangle)

discussion that PT mandates a change in instruction if three consecutive data points show no change. That is to say, if fluency does not improve across three consecutive days, change your approach since it's not working.

We mentioned that plotting on a semi-logarithmic chart makes comparisons between students much more realistic when compared to other types of graphic representations. Figure 6.10 provides a graphical description of this statement. The plot in the upper left of Figure 6.10 represents John's performance in math expressed as a percentage of math problems correctly solved; the information in the upper right of this figure represents the same information for Mary. On each of the five days, both students were given 30 minutes to work on math problems.

A cursory glance would seem to suggest that Mary was doing much better than John over the course of five consecutive days of instruction. Mary's graph shows a clear linear increase in her percent of problems solved correctly; each day she has improved by twenty percent. On the other hand, John did not seem to make as much improvement during the first three days. He started out solving 10% of the math problems and reached 20% on the third day. By the fifth day of instruction, John could only solve 50% of his math problems. However, the graph at the bottom of Figure 6.10 depicts each student's behavior with respect to math problems completed correctly, plotted on a semi-logarithmic chart and depicted as a rate measure. Notice that John's rate of solving math problems exceeded Mary's on each day by a factor of ten. This apparent discrepancy is explained by advocates of Precision Teaching as the "gee whiz" effect and is an inherent limitation of graphical representations that scale the y-axis in units that reflect percentages or proportions. Notice under the titles of both John's and Mary's individual graphs that the maximum number of problems each student was working on during each day is listed. John was working on 50 problems each day while Mary was working on only five. This additional information is required if you are trying to make comparisons

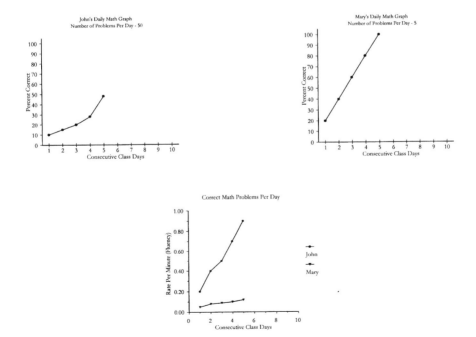

Figure 6.10. Comparison of percentage plots with plots on a semi-logarithmic chart.

between John and Mary, since without it your conclusions regarding whose performance is better or worse are clouded by a lack of critical information.

This method of analysis has many advantages and some disadvantages over more traditional methods of portraying collected information in order to make decisions. We will not reiterate those points since they were presented in Chapter 4. However, we will state that rate of performance is not the *only* method of portraying data in order to make decisions. We now turn to two of the more traditional strategies for making decisions that have been developed by behavior analysts.

A-B Designs

A-B designs, often called case studies, are the weakest of the single-subject designs for making statements about cause and effect relationships but are probably the most frequently employed and easiest to use by classroom teachers. These designs consist of two conditions that are generally referred to as *baseline* (A) and *treatment* (B). All designs, whether single-subject or quasi-experimental, seek to hold constant as many factors as possible that might effect the behavior you are interested in evaluating. The degree to which alternative explanations of observed changes in behavior can be ruled out is a measure of the internal validity of a particular strategy. If you can't assert *and* support your instruction as the reason student behavior changed, you cannot discount any, no matter how seemingly absurd, alternative explanation.

For example, suppose you are an algebra teacher and decide to administer an algebra test to each of your students prior to beginning instruction on this topic in order to determine their entry level skills. After a few weeks of instruction, you decide to give them the same test again to see if they are learning the material. Your decision as to whether they are learning will be based on the differences between each student's score on the pretest and posttest. This type of arrangement is really a quasi-experimental design referred to as a one-group pretest posttest strategy. To your satisfaction, everyone has made progress (how much progress is not critical in this example), as measured by the differences between these test scores, and you conclude that your instruction is effective.

However, you are unaware of the fact that some people actually learn from the pretest and, thus, will score higher on the second administration of the test *even in the absence of instruction*. In a situation such as this, you really do not know if a student's observed improvement is due to your instruction, the pretest phenomenon, or some combination of both. This is an example of a threat to internal validity. (There are other possible threats to internal validity but we will not address them in this book.) The point to consider now is simply that you may observe changes in student performance or behavior that you hope are due to your teaching strategy. However, the A-B design does not allow you *categorically* to dismiss other potential explanations for the observed differences in behavior. Nevertheless, classroom teachers are usually not terribly concerned with internal validity threats and we will pursue this issue no further.

In order to make a decision about the effectiveness of your instructional strategy, you need a comparative index. **Baselines** provide this index. Typically, baselines refer to a period of time during which multiple observations are made and information is collected *but* treatment or instruction has not yet been implemented. For example, suppose you are a math teacher and are going to institute a new strategy for teaching linear algebra next week. During baseline, you have no idea of the skills your students have with respect to linear algebra. So, you decide to administer a short quiz on the Monday, Wednesday, and Friday immediately before you introduce this topic so that you can sample the various skills required to complete linear algebra problems. The scores, recorded as percent correct, that each of your students receive on these quizzes represent their baseline level of performance of linear algebra calculations. Once you implement the teaching strategy (treatment), you continue to assess each student's performance by administering similar quizzes on Monday, Wednesday, and Friday. Again these scores are recorded as the percent correct of linear algebra problems. By plotting these recorded values on a graph, you can immediately ascertain if student progress is being made with respect to baseline skill levels. Figure 6.11 provides an example.

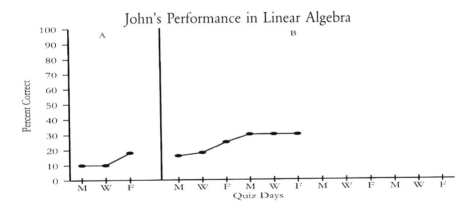

Figure 6.11. Example of an A-B design with three days of baseline and six days of treatment

Let's closely examine the "picture" represented by this graph. Notice during the baseline phase (A), John's percent correct ranged from 10 to 20 percent and averaged around 16 percent. (The thick vertical line is placed on the graph to easily discriminate baseline from treatment phases.) On the first Monday on which the linear algebra teaching strategy was implemented (B), his percentage did not change appreciably from baseline. This was to be expected since he had only been exposed to a single day's instruction. Over the course of the first two weeks of instruction in linear algebra, two things are immediately noticeable from the graph. First, the data collected over the first four tests indicate a clear linear trend and corresponding increase in the percent of problems correctly completed. Second, the data for the second week suggest that John has made no progress in linear algebra, as measured by quiz scores, since his percent correct has remained unchanged over the three successive observations made during this week. What should you do since it appears that he is not progressing? Should you immediately change your instructional strategy for John? Should you try to obtain some further information about "other factors" that may be effecting John's performance?

Recall from Chapter 4 that the rule used in Precision Teaching states that three consecutive measurements with no improvement mandate change in instruction. However, you may not be evaluating student performance according to the mandates of PT and are not obligated to follow their rule. Still, what would you do? If you make no changes, continue to measure his performance and obtain similar results, you will waste valuable instruction time during which John is not learning the material. Figure 6.12 depicts continuing the instruction for two more weeks with no modifications. Notice that in this case your decision to continue the instructional strategy was not beneficial to John's learning. After four weeks of instruction, you

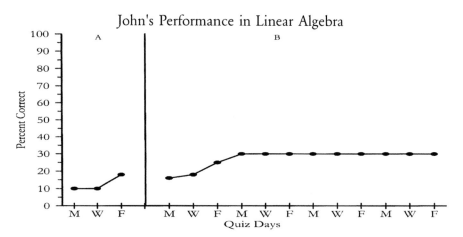

Figure 6.12. Example of an A-B design with three days of baseline and twelve days of treatment

conclude that the instruction was not effective and decide to make changes. If you had simply waited until the fourth Friday of instruction and administered a test, you would have been presented with the same dilemma: John did not learn.

Alternatively, suppose that you decided to make modifications in your instructional strategy based upon the information from Figure 6.11. By continuing to collect and graphically portray John's performance, you might find the following scenario depicted in Figure 6.13. Behavior analysts would refer to the conditions represented by this graph as A-B-C, where C represents the point in time that you made a change in your instructional strategy. Notice that whatever changes you made in your strategies were apparently successful: John appears to have learned the material.

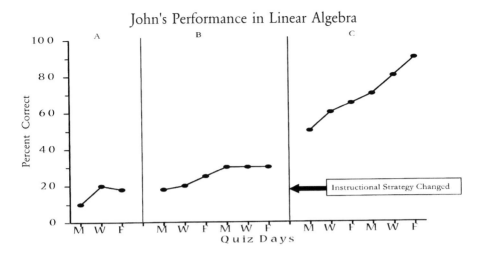

Figure 6.13. Example of an A-B-C design

Although the A-B design has some inherent weaknesses, it is a very easy design to implement and allows for evaluations based upon actual student performance, that is to say, data-based decisions. Its advantages over traditional tests given at the end of some course of instruction should be obvious. The frequent observation and measurement of student performance places you in a position to make "immediate" decisions regarding both the student's performance and the effectiveness of your instructional strategy. If your analysis of the student's performance indicates a need to change your method of instruction, you can do so immediately and not lose valuable time from the school calendar. By changing instructional strategies at the point in time in which students cease to make progress, you accomplish two interrelated goals. In the first, students can return to being active participants in the instructional process. Being more active increases the likelihood that more reinforcement will be forthcoming, which tends to support and sustain further active participation. This is one of the major goals espoused by behavior analysts. Regarding the second goal, active participation tends to minimize the need to implement strategies to deal with inappropriate classroom behaviors. If students are not actively engaged in the instructional process, they are usually actively engaged in some other, often misguided or unacceptable, process. The advantages of being able to make immediate decisions, grounded in the data that reflect *actual student behavior or performance* are inherent in all good assessment techniques that are concerned with the behavior of an individual as opposed to merely the behavior of a group.

Multiple Baseline

Like the A-B design just discussed, multiple baseline designs share similar characteristics in that they usually consist of a baseline and treatment condition. They differ from the A-B design in that multiple behaviors, students, or settings can be evaluated simultaneously. By employing the multiple baseline design, you can assess the effectiveness of changes you make in your teaching strategies and make conclusions about these changes with a greater degree of confidence than you can with the A-B design.

For example, suppose you are a classroom teacher taking a course in behavior analysis at the local university and have just learned about the principle of reinforcement. You are anxious to see if you can apply this information to your own classroom. You decide to begin reinforcing your students' attempts at completing the problems you assign in the hope that the number of completed problems will increase. Before you begin, you realize that the individual attention you will have to provide to each student may limit the time you have to engage in other classroom activities so you decide to evaluate this idea before you implement it for all students.

To see if reinforcement works, you select three students: John, Mary, and Ted. Each time they complete the assignment you provided, you reinforce their individual efforts with praise and special recognition. You are aware that you need to collect information on the number of problems they currently complete (baseline) so that you will have a comparative index to evaluate your reinforcement strategy.

When you discuss your idea with your instructor at the university, she suggests that you stagger the introduction of praise across each student rather than introduce praise at the same time for each. Your instructor points out that if you implement this idea at the same time for each student, even if the number of problems they complete increases over the number they completed before praise, you really will not be able to determine if your procedure was responsible or some other unknown factor was the cause. However, if the number of problems solved correctly only increases after the reinforcement strategy is introduced to each student, then you may safely conclude that it was the reinforcement strategy and not some other variable that produced the change. Figure 6.14 graphically portrays this point. The line that divides each individual graph and continues through all graphs designates the change from baseline to the introduction of your reinforcement strategy.

Notice that each student increased the number of problems completed only after your reinforcement strategy was implemented. During the baseline conditions, each had a relatively low frequency of completed problems but all had higher frequencies once your strategy was employed. Of particular note is the fact that no student increased the frequency of problems completed *until* your strategy was put in place for each student. This is one of the strengths of the multiple baseline design. If behavior or performance changes only after you implement your strategy, the confidence you have with regard to your strategy is eminently strengthened as compared to the A-B design. Based on the collected data and analyses conducted with the multiple baseline design, you now have evidence to suggest that praising students for completing problems appears to result in an increase in the number of problems completed. If you decide to implement this procedure for all students in your second period class, you have empirical evidence to suggest that the procedure will work and you will not be wasting valuable time and effort that could be applied elsewhere.

Will You Look for Evidence of Regular Assessment?

How will you know that teachers are conducting regular assessments of students' academic progress? Will you provide blank graphs or computer graphing programs for teachers to use? Will you expect teachers to bring graphs to meetings to share their teaching strategies and successes? When a teacher asks for assistance with a student, will you expect to see a graph of current behavior and the teacher's attempts to improve it? Will teachers be expected to provide graphs of student behavior at parent/teacher conferences? Will you expect to see graphs posted in the classrooms?

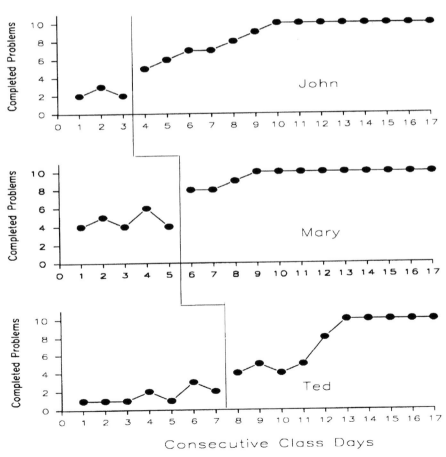

Figure 6.14. Example of a multiple baeline design

Summary

Throughout this chapter we have supported a data-based decision making process for assessing student performance. We have stressed the need to perform frequent observations of student performance in order to have sufficient and relevant data on which to make informed decisions. Unfortunately, words like "sufficient" and "relevant" are subjective. Your unique circumstances may not lend themselves to use "the best" assessment technique for a given situation. Do not despair!

The methods and techniques discussed in this chapter are simply tools that allow you to better assess your teaching techniques. Behavior analysts offer these tools freely and encourage their use. The more you use these techniques, the more light you will shine on the effectiveness of your instruction.

Always keep in mind that the data you collect speak for themselves. By constantly trying to understand your data, you will evolve into a data-based decision maker. At times you may not like the story your data tell, but you must accept the fact that they are honest.

Annotated Bibliography

Alberto, P. A., & Troutman, A. C. (1995). *Applied behavior analysis for teachers* (4th ed.). New York: MacMillan.

    Provides an excellent introduction to the science of behavior analysis for teachers by presenting the major topics of behavior analysis in a clearly written, easy to follow style.

Barlow, D. B., & Hersen, M. (1984). *Single case experimental designs: Strategies for studying behavior change* (2nd ed.). Elmsford, NY: Pergamon Press.

    Examines various single case experimental designs with many excellent examples of each, providing an excellent resource for anyone interested in behavior analysis. Included is an excellent chapter on statistical analysis written by Alan Kazdin.

Johnston, J. M., & Pennypacker, H. S. (1993). *Strategies and tactics of human behavioral research* (2nd ed.). Hillsdale, NJ: Lawrence Erlbaum.

    Is an intermediate text on behavior analysis for students who have a relatively strong background in behavior analysis.

Chapter 7

Training Teachers

In this chapter we begin with a brief history of teacher education to understand changes in the focus of teacher education over time and how these changes led us to the teacher education programs we have today. We then examine typical teacher education degree programs for the elementary, middle, and secondary grades to identify the current thinking in teacher education and how that might be changed with an emphasis on behavior analysis in teacher training programs. We conclude with a comprehensive model of teacher training whose primary purpose is to prepare teachers to be more successful in tomorrow's classrooms.

History of Teacher Education

Free public education available to all was started during the early nineteenth century in the common schools in New England, which created a need to prepare teachers. This need was met with the public normal schools, the first formal teacher preparation schools (Urban, 1990). While the normal school was intended to be a single purpose institution, in reality students could continue their studies without necessarily preparing to teach; however, our focus on the normal school will be on its preparation of teachers. The official curriculum was primarily geared to teacher education with an attempt to make school and instruction systematic.

Most of the normal school students were women who came to these schools after completing various levels of education. Some only attended elementary school while others had some high school education before attending the normal school. Therefore, the normal school had to provide instruction at the students' individual levels of academic training and require students to demonstrate mastery of content areas such as "reading, writing, spelling, geography, grammar, and arithmetic" (Urban, 1990, p. 62) before beginning any professional teaching courses. The professional sequence that followed these academic courses included history of education, science of education, methods in elementary branches, and mental science (Pangburn cited in Urban, 1990). This basically provided a technical approach to teacher education.

While the normal schools were available and busy educating teachers, most elementary teachers at that time received no special training for their positions. Many continued to teach or began teaching without attending the normal school. Even with normal schools available, "the major qualification for getting a teaching job was being approved of by the local authority" (Urban, 1990, p. 63). This is not surprising given that the normal schools were not very effective in improving the teaching in common schools.

The admission of too many immature and unqualified students had forced the normal schools to make up for the deficient common-school education of their pupils. It had prevented them from carrying out their real business, instruction in the art of teaching. (Herbst, 1989, p. 220)

A gradual shift in emphasis from the practical aspects of teaching toward an academic training took place in the normal school from the middle to the end of the nineteenth century. Several reasons for this shift have been suggested. It is possible the normal school began to emphasize academic training because there was no "core of theoretical knowledge which could guide professional practice" (Johnson, 1989, p. 248). In addition, the normal school was already concentrating on academics with the students who arrived underprepared. Finally, while normal schools were originally established to prepare teachers for common schools, many students took advantage of the opportunity to continue their studies in the normal schools but then taught for only brief periods before moving on to other careers. The normal schools actually provided educational opportunities that ultimately led to many different careers. With this shift in emphasis came changes in identity as normal schools became teachers colleges, and finally colleges offering liberal arts programs.

The changes in the normal school also may have been an attempt to keep pace with the departments of education that arose with the establishment of universities during the post-Civil War period. These departments of education increased enrollments, demonstrated to the taxpayer the support of public education, allowed women to enter the universities while keeping them contained in education departments, and prepared high school teachers, which the normal school did not do (Urban, 1990). Teacher preparation in the university represented a shift in focus away from practical, nontheoretical kinds of training to a scientific study of teaching. On the surface, this appeared to be an improvement in the training of teachers. However, departments of education and colleges of education were not readily welcomed within colleges and universities where many were convinced there was not much to teach about teaching (Clifford & Guthrie, 1988). In addition, professors in education departments were frequently more concerned about research for its own sake than in offering any practical information for teachers. Ultimately, the push for professionalism in the education departments of universities brought a focus on school administrators, psychologists, and researchers. The classroom teachers, mostly women, were left behind (Herbst, 1989). Even with the first Master of Arts in Teaching (MAT) offered in 1936 as a fifth year of education "the academic courses offered during the fifth year were rarely tailored or even adjusted with prospective teachers in mind; they remained designed for potential scholars and researchers" (Clifford & Guthrie, 1988, p. 179).

Laboratory schools, based on the medical model of the teaching hospital, were in existence at many universities, but did not function for teachers in training the way teaching hospitals functioned for doctors and nurses in training (Clifford & Guthrie, 1988). Where laboratory schools were available, teachers in training were typically required to observe teachers and their students, but only for short periods, often not more than a week. These experiences appear to have been unpleasant based on what has been reported about them. It is not clear why they were unpleasant, but it is speculated that possibly it was because of a mismatch between what students were learning in their university classes and what they observed to be the realities of teaching in laboratory schools.

Some might argue that the problem with teacher preparation programs is that the university has not yet found the best approach or even an adequate approach to teacher training. However, it has not been for lack of trying. The 1950s called for more stringent academic training to improve teacher education, but provided no model for accomplishing it. Since it appeared that teachers could not be adequately prepared, teacher-proof programs were designed to improve instruction. During the early 1960s, the public agreed that teachers needed more intensive academic training, but could not agree on *how* teachers should be trained or what should be included in more intensive academic training. In the mid-1970s, performance-based teacher education and competency-based education were introduced suggesting teachers could be taught a set of skills thought to be necessary and sufficient for effective teaching. In the 1980s it became popular to test children by providing criterion-referenced tests at different grade levels that required students to demonstrate mastery of content before allowing them to move from one grade level to the next or to graduate from high school. At the same time teachers began taking certification tests (Clifford & Guthrie, 1988). Now five-year teacher preparation programs are available which allow teachers to earn both initial certification and a masters degree; however, there is no empirical evidence that five-year programs prepare teachers any better than four year programs (Nicklin, 1994). At the close of the twentieth century, after having had teacher preparation available since the early nineteenth century, there is still no clear direction for professional training, leaving it open to prevailing fads and theories.

Interestingly, however, there are aspects of teacher training that have remained constant over time, including admission to teacher education programs, teachers leaving the profession, and professors' research practices. The first represented a concern in normal schools; that is, students attending the normal school often arrived ill prepared from their common school education. As a result, there was too much time spent teaching academics in the normal school, making it difficult to get to the purpose of the institution, "instruction in the art of teaching" (Herbst, 1989, p. 220).

To what extent today are we still accepting students into teacher preparation programs who do not have a solid academic background from high school and the first two years of college? Entrance into teacher education programs may require an undergraduate grade point average of as low as 2.0. These are "C" students. Possibly, students choose to become teachers because their weak academic record leaves them few other options. How committed are these students? Possibly some students are very committed to teaching, but academically are not capable of more than "C" work. How well will these students perform in a teacher education program? Will the requirements of the teacher education program be lowered to accommodate these students? How well do these students read and how well-read are they? How well can they write? If we find that the students in our teacher education classes do not write well, do we reduce the number of writing assignments because reading and providing corrective feedback on poorly written papers is very time consuming? When we consider the importance of reading and writing in every subject, how well prepared will these students be to teach others? The problem of admitting "too many immature and unqualified students" in the normal schools has changed very little. "From the very beginning of pedagogical education the policy of colleges and universities has been to produce teachers to fill jobs, rather than to produce quality personnel" (Smith, 1980, p. 39). Teacher education programs are still providing the many teachers needed to fill classrooms, often turning out large numbers of teachers who are not very well prepared (Kramer, 1991; Labaree, 1996; Smith, 1980). One encouraging change from the days of the normal school, however, is that now students must eventually complete the teacher preparation requirements to earn a teaching certificate.

Unfortunately, many students who complete teacher preparation requirements and earn teacher certification do not stay in the teaching profession. This is similar to teachers, who, after studying at the normal school, taught for a few years, and then left teaching. Easy access to teacher preparation programs allows many students the opportunity for a college education that they frequently do not use for teaching. Teachers may leave the profession because they are not well prepared. The normal schools did not do a very good job of preparing teachers for the common school making it difficult for them to teach. Similarly, we often send teachers into the classroom ill prepared for teaching and then find that these teachers quickly quit teaching and move on to other careers.

Perhaps the reason some teachers are not well prepared for teaching is because of the mismatch between professors' research practices and teachers' needs. Professors then, as now, are frequently more concerned about their research for its own sake than for the practical information it can provide teachers. Professors at major universities are required to publish research if they expect to keep their jobs and what really counts in publications is not demonstration research in the classroom, but research that advances theory. As professors strive to conduct and publish such research, it is often with little thought as to how it might inform the classroom teacher. When professors teach their classes they are often more interested in discussing theory and how the research is conducted to advance that theory than in how the theory may be applied in the classroom. Further, many have not been in an elementary or high school classroom since their own or their children's days as a student. If they want to spend time in the classroom to guide what and how they teach students who are preparing to teach, they must use time that could be spent doing research to be published. According to Johnson (1989) schools of education in universities are not very interested in the "training and concerns of classroom teachers." Their "research agenda has not often produced knowledge useful to the practitioner." They "have produced no permanent, durable models of teacher training" (p. 243).

This brief summary of aspects of teacher training that have remained constant throughout the history of teacher education is not meant to be a criticism of teacher preparation programs. They receive more than their fair share of criticism from the public as well as from their own administrators without much guidance in how to improve. Some of this criticism came from the approximately 100 deans from research-oriented colleges of education in major universities who started the Holmes Group in 1985 for the purpose of promoting educational reform. But educational reform, as we know from Chapter 1, is difficult to accomplish. The first Holmes report in 1986 encouraged professors in schools of education to focus their energies on advancing scientific knowledge in the university and then sending that knowledge into the schools (Labaree, 1996). Nine years later, however, in their 1995 report, they argued "that the ed school should turn its back on the academic life of the university and bury itself in the world of daily practice within the public school classroom" (Labaree, 1996, p. 42).

Schools of education are in a difficult position, walking the fine line between theory and practice. By profession they are concerned with the development of theory, yet they are preparing teachers to go out in the schools where practice is more important. Working on the border brings criticism from both sides. "Professors dismiss them as unscholarly and untheoretical while school people dismiss them as impractical and irrelevant" (Labaree, 1996, p. 43).

How Does History Affect Your Program?

What is the history of teacher preparation at your college or university? Do you recognize any aspects of the early teacher preparation programs in your program? Consider the aspects of teacher training that we suggested have remained constant throughout history: accepting ill prepared students into the program, teachers leaving the profession, and professors' research practices. To what extent are these present in your teacher preparation program?

Teacher Education Programs

In this section, we will examine typical teacher education degree programs at the early, middle, and secondary grade levels to identify common features across these programs as well as any features that have been in place throughout the history of teacher education. As is the case with most undergraduate degree programs, students begin their studies with courses in mathematics, English, history, science, and possibly a foreign language before moving into their major area of study, typically in the beginning of their junior year in college. In order to be accepted into teacher education programs students usually must have a cumulative grade point average of 2.0 or better at the end of first two years of study, although this requirement may be as high as a 3.0 depending on the college or university. Once accepted into a teacher education program, students have moderately different requirements depending on whether they are preparing to teach in the early, middle, or secondary grades, or to teach art, foreign language, or music in grades K-12. In universities, this preparation often comes through the college of education for early and middle grades and through the college of arts and science for the secondary grades. Regardless of the grade level students are preparing to teach, they frequently take a core set of courses required for all prospective teachers.

A teacher education core may consist of at least one course in educational media and microcomputer applications in education as well as a foundations in education course, a human growth and development course, a course in exceptional children, and a course in issues related to school health. In addition to these courses, students preparing for certification in early childhood education or middle childhood education take pedagogical courses appropriate for the particular grade levels they will be teaching. These courses are typically driven by the requirements for certification in the state in which the student is attending college. The requirements necessary to meet certification in one state are often the same or similar in other states. Over 30 states are party to the Interstate Certification Compact, which qualifies students certified in any one of those states to be certified in all of the states in the Compact.

Some states offer certification in elementary education and middle grades education while others offer certification in early childhood education and middle childhood education; however, they are very similar. The first level of teacher preparation programs is preparation for elementary education or early childhood education which share several requirements—a foundations of education course that focuses on the history and philosophy of education along with policy issues in education; courses in the teaching of mathematics, science, social studies, and reading; and a course in human growth and development. In addition, students preparing to teach at this level are usually required to take courses in music, art, and physical education for the elementary school and a course in school related health issues. Students also are typically required to take a course in computers and their use in facilitating teaching and learning in the elementary school. Finally, students are required to have many field-based experiences along with their course work. These field-based experiences often begin with simple observations in the schools, and gradually become more involved until students do their student teaching during their senior year. Student teaching usually begins with observations for a week or two followed by teaching one lesson a day and gradually adding more lessons until the student teacher takes total responsibility for the teaching in that classroom (see Table 7.1).

While there is much in common in teacher preparation programs in the early grades, two noticeable differences stand out between programs in different states. Some states require a course in exceptional children and youth and a course in cultural diversity while other states do not make these requirements. Typically, states that do not require specific courses in exceptional children or in cultural diversity infuse this content throughout all their courses.

Many similarities can be seen between teacher certification programs in middle grades education and in middle childhood education, the second level of teacher preparation programs. Once again, a computer/technology course is required along with a foundations in education course, a course in human growth and development, a course in instructional issues in the middle grades, and a course in contemporary health problems and issues in schools, as well as a fine arts course. In addition, all programs require one or more student teaching experiences. It is interesting to note that some programs require a course in classroom management for students preparing to teach in the middle grades, while others do not. Once again, some programs include discussions of exceptional children throughout their courses while others require a specific course in exceptional children, just as some programs infuse cultural diversity throughout their program while others teach this topic in an independent course.

A similarity across programs preparing teachers for the middle grades is the completion of two subject area concentrations that are usually offered in social studies, mathematics, science, and language arts. Some programs require students to complete methods courses only within the student's areas of concentration. For example, if social studies is chosen as an area of concentration, along with the required social studies courses students are required to take a course in social studies methods and materials for middle grades. Other programs, regardless of the student's choice of subject area concentration, require students to take courses in the methods of teaching language arts, mathematics, science, and social studies (see Table 7.1).

The third level of teacher preparation program is preparation for secondary teaching. Here too, we find similarities across programs leading to certification. Most secondary teacher education programs require students to complete a major in a discipline such as biology, chemistry, English, history, mathematics, or social studies. In addition, students are required to complete a core of education courses that usually include foundations of education, a curriculum planning course or strategies course for teaching high school, a computer course for teachers and an educational media course. As with teacher preparation for early childhood and middle childhood, students are typically required to complete a course in human growth and development and may also be required to complete a course each in educational psychology and exceptional children. Finally, depending on the discipline of the student's major, students are required to take a methods and materials course for the particular content area they are planning to teach and they must complete a student teaching experience (see Table 7.1).

As we presented typical programs at each level of teaching we pointed out similarities and differences in programs for a particular level. We will now compare and contrast preparation requirements across the three levels. We will then look at similarities and differences in teacher preparation requirements throughout history. As noted earlier, almost without exception, teacher preparation programs require courses in the foundations of education, human growth and development, and computers and their use in the classroom. Exposure to exceptionalities in children and youth and to cultural diversity are provided in all teacher preparation programs

Table 7.1. Courses Typically Required in Teacher Preparation Programs By Grade Levels

EARLY CHILDHOOD	MIDDLE GRADES	SECONDARY GRADES
foundations of education	**foundations of education**	**foundations of education**
human growth & development	**human growth & development**	**human growth & development**
school health	school health	curriculum planning
computer use in education	**computer use in education**	**computer use in education**
teaching of mathematics	instruction in middle grades	educational media
teaching of science	fine arts	educational psychology
teaching of social studies	classroom management	**exceptional children**
teaching of reading	**exceptional children**	methods course (1)
music in the elementary school	cultural diversity	**student teaching**
art in the elementary school	methods course (1)	
physical education in the elementary school	methods course (2)	
exceptional children	**student teaching**	
cultural diversity		
student teaching		

Note. Courses in bold are those courses usually required across all teacher preparation programs.

either as stand alone courses or infused within all courses. Also, some noticeable differences are found among course requirements for early grades, middle grades, and high school. For example, most teacher preparation programs for the early grades require courses in the methods and materials of teaching in all content areas (e.g., mathematics, science, social studies, and reading). However, at the middle grades level some programs require methods of teaching all of these content areas while other programs only require the methods of teaching for the content areas in the student's areas of concentration. Yet, in all secondary teacher education programs students are only required to complete a methods course for their discipline area. Finally, when a course in classroom management is required, it is usually only required for students preparing to teach in the middle grades (see Table 7.1).

Other differences in teacher education programs are found at different institutions—typically in different states. Some institutions require a course in educational psychology in all their teacher preparation programs. Other institutions do not require it for all teacher preparation programs but may require it for some of their programs, while still others do not require educational psychology for any of their teacher preparation programs. Without exception, though, teacher preparation programs require a student teaching experience. This experience may be one or two terms; it may or may not include an "opening school experience."

How are today's teacher education programs different from early teacher preparation programs? One difference is that teacher preparation programs are now available as separate and different programs for students preparing to teach in the early grades, middle grades, and secondary grades. These options evolved from the early normal schools that only prepared teachers for the common schools (which were elementary schools). Preparation for teaching in high school did not become available until normal schools became teachers colleges. From then until about 25 years ago, teachers could prepare for elementary school teaching or high school teaching. In the past 25 years, however, a third option has been available, preparation for teaching the middle grades. This option emerged as educators began to realize that students' needs and abilities change as they enter adolescence. The methods and materials used to teach students in the middle grades are thus different to some extent from the methods and materials used to teach students in the early grades or in high school. In addition, formal education is beginning at an earlier age than it did in the common school. Kindergartens for children age 5 and pre-kindergartens for children age 4 are common throughout the United States. These developments brought with them the need for specialized teaching methods and materials. As a result, many states no longer offer certification in elementary school (K-8); instead they may offer certification in pre-kindergarten to grade three or four with a different certification for grades five through eight or nine, and a secondary certification for high school teaching.

Another change in teacher preparation is seen in required field experiences. In the early years of teacher education there was no required field experience or student teaching. Eventually some universities had laboratory schools available, but students only observed in them for short periods of time. Gradually a student teaching requirement of one term during the student's senior year was added to teacher preparation programs. However, it became clear that this was probably too little field experience too late in the student's program. Students who waited until their senior year for a field experience frequently learned at the end of their studies that they were not well suited for teaching. Even many of the fortunate ones who found they were well suited for teaching felt their student teaching experience was too short to effectively prepare them for assuming the full responsibility of a classroom. Today most students preparing to teach are placed in schools during their junior year. Many teacher preparation courses are now taught with a field experience component so that, for example, students who are studying the methods and materials of teaching language arts in the college classroom are also observing such methods in the school and possibly teaching lessons. Human growth and development courses may require a field experience in which students observe child or adolescent behavior in the classroom as examples of what they are learning in their corresponding college course. Similarly, foundations of education courses typically include a field experience that allows students to experience first-hand how policy and philosophy drive what happens in schools.

Many teacher preparation programs also require an opening school experience during which students are in the schools with the cooperating teacher for a week of preplanning to learn how to prepare for the first day of school. In addition, they remain for the first week or two of school to gain practical experience with many of the potential problems of meeting new students and establishing the initial climate for an effective classroom. Recall the suggestions made in Chapter 5, Classroom Management, and the importance of a first-hand exposure to the start of the school year to learn how to implement those strategies.

We do not know much about the specifics of what was offered in the early teacher preparation programs, but there are two types of courses that seem to have been offered since the normal schools and are still offered today. One of these is the foundations of education course, which usually includes the history and philosophy of education as well as policy issues in education. The other course is the methods course. A course in educational psychology has sometimes been included in teacher education preparation programs over the years driven primarily by certification requirements in different states. The common course requirements regarding technology, cultural diversity, and exceptional children and youth are all fairly new to prospective teachers' coursework.

Teacher Preparation Based on a Behavior Analysis Model

In this section, we propose a behavior-analytic model of teacher preparation. This model begins after students have successfully completed the sophomore year in college. To be eligible for this teacher preparation program students must have a 2.8 grade point average or higher. Teachers are a constant role model for students, therefore, it is important that teachers be academically competent. As we have seen, teacher preparation programs vary based on the grade level students are preparing to teach. Therefore, our proposal will begin with the early grades, make some changes for middle grades, and even more changes for secondary grades. In some cases, we suggest keeping a course but changing the focus or content of the course. In other cases, we suggest consolidating two or more courses into one course or taking some independent courses and incorporating aspects of them into all courses. Finally, we add some new courses. The intent is to keep the number of courses about the same as what is currently required, knowing that the actual number may vary from one institution to another.

Examine Your Teacher Preparation Program

What courses have you taken that you feel will be particularly helpful to you when you begin teaching? What was missing from those courses that you think might better prepare you for teaching? What courses have you taken that don't seem to have much practical application for when you begin teaching? Could these courses have been revised to make them more valuable? How much field experience will you receive in your teacher preparation? Do you think it will be adequate?

Teacher Preparation for the Early Grades

As noted earlier, a typical preparation program for the early grades includes a foundations of education course, courses in the teaching of mathematics, science, social studies, and reading, a course in human growth and development, courses in music, art, and physical education for the elementary school, and courses in computers, exceptional children, school-related health issues, and cultural diversity. Typically there are about 13 courses plus a student teaching experience required in teacher preparation programs for the early grades (see Table 7.2).

A behavior-analytic model of teacher preparation for the early years would keep a course in the foundations of education and in that course would require that students examine the history of education, how that history is a reflection of the philosophy of education at that time, what the public had identified as weaknesses in education at that time, how these weaknesses were a reflection of the policy issues in place at that time, and the likelihood of avoiding similar problems in the present.

This course would be followed with a course in human growth and development. However, rather than requiring a life-span development course, which usually begins with biological foundations and birth and continues through old age and dying, our course would consider development from birth through pre-adolescence and address the topics in more depth than is possible when teaching a life-span course.

Early in their program students would be required to take a course in applied behavior analysis in which they would learn about the three-term contingency and functional analysis. They would learn how to analyze a learning environment and to create effective learning environments. They would also learn how to collect data. As part of this course, students would be required to complete a field experience in which they conduct a functional analysis of the classroom in which they are completing their field experience. This course would be followed by a course in instructional strategies. According to Binder (1990) "there is a general lack of awareness of the existence of measurably superior instructional methods" (p. 34), or those strategies that produce rates of academic achievement far greater than what is typically achieved in most schools. This course would be an introduction to Precision Teaching, Direct Instruction, Personalized System of Instruction, Peer Tutoring, Programmed Instruction, and Computer Assisted Instruction. Students would read the empirical evidence of the effectiveness of these strategies with different student populations to determine when it would be appropriate to use which strategies. Students would learn how to implement these strategies, how to evaluate the effectiveness of these strategies, and how to integrate several different strategies. This course would include a field experience during which students observe master teachers implementing the strategies being taught in the college course.

Students would still take courses in the teaching of mathematics, science, social studies, and reading. However, these courses would be reconfigured such that students had one course in methods and materials of teaching mathematics, one course that combined methods and materials of teaching science and social studies, and two courses in the methods of teaching reading. In her 1996 Benjamin E. Mays Memorial Lecture at Georgia State University, Barbara Sizemore suggested that colleges of education are not preparing teachers to teach reading. Without reading children cannot succeed or even compete academically with their peers. Without reading many will not graduate from high school. Those who do graduate from high school will find it difficult to be admitted to colleges or to have many career options open to them. Children need to be able to crack the code to be able to read. They need to know what sounds to put with which symbols, to know what the words are on the page. This is especially true if their language or dialect is different from the printed text they are expected to read. Therefore, we would put an additional emphasis on reading such that one course would be devoted strictly to the process of reading, cracking the code and understanding the message, and the other course would address aspects of reading in conjunction with all of the language arts (writing, grammar, literature, etc.).

In each of the proposed methods courses students would learn several strategies for teaching particular content. Students would learn the strategies, practice implementing the strategies, and research the empirical evidence of their effectiveness. Each of these courses would include a component on the use of computers in the classroom for the particular content area rather than requiring only a general course on the use of computers. These methods courses would also include a field experience in which students observe instructional strategies in the classroom, implement different strategies in the classroom with children, and then report on their effectiveness.

Table 7.2. Teacher Preparation For The Early Grades Based on Behavior Analysis

Current Programs	Proposed Program
foundations of education	foundations of education
human growth & development	*human growth & development*
school health	**applied behavior analysis**
computer use in education	**instructional strategies**
teaching of mathematics	teaching of mathematics
teaching of science	*teaching of science and social studies*
teaching of social studies	*teaching of reading (1)*
teaching of reading	*teaching of reading (2)*
music in the elementary school	*music and art in the elementary school*
art in the elementary school	*physical education & health in the elementary school*
physical education in the elementary school	**educational psychology**
exceptional children	**classroom management**
cultural diversity	**assessment**
student teaching	student teaching

Note. Courses in bold are courses not typically required in current programs. Courses in italics are modifications of courses currently required.

Rather than requiring courses in music, art, physical education and school-related health issues, we recommend two courses, one for music and art in the elementary school and one for physical education and school-related health issues in the elementary school. Given that most schools employ a music teacher, an art teacher, and a physical education/health teacher, all of whom are well-versed in their respective disciplines, it seems redundant to require teachers to take four such courses. Music and art in the elementary school should be taught after the methods courses so that students can learn ways of incorporating music and art in their instruction in these content areas.

Students also would be required to take an educational psychology course in which they are introduced to the many theories of learning, how these theories may be applied in the classroom, and the scientific bases for these theories. As noted by Tashman (1996), "scientific research and the classroom are still strangers to one another. Until they join forces, American school-children will continue to receive a second-class education" (p. 67). Our goal would be to make scientific research accessible to the prospective teachers. Rather than keeping the courses in exceptional children and in cultural diversity, we would infuse these topics into all teacher preparation courses, as they are issues that should underlie all of our classroom decisions.

Two final required courses would be classroom management and assessment. A classroom management course would be designed around the issues described in the classroom management chapter in this book (see Chapter 5) and would be taught in conjunction with an opening school experience. This would give students both academic knowledge of classroom management and first-hand experience setting up an effective classroom. Because we believe students are entitled to assessments that allow teachers to make appropriate decisions about instruction and discipline (Barrett et al., 1991), our assessment course would focus on the assessment of both academic and social behaviors and on tracking changes in those behaviors to guide teacher decision making. This would include learning to write good test items, to chart progress, to design assessment instruments that are not paper and pencil tests, to interpret standardized tests, and to use what is learned from assessment to improve learning rather than simply to assign a grade (see Table 7.2).

Finally, teacher preparation would include a term of student teaching with particular requirements during this experience. Students would be required to keep daily data on student achievement and classroom behaviors and to use instructional strategies for which there is empirical evidence of effectiveness. When questioned about their teaching practices, they should be able to explain what they are doing, why they are doing it, and what their data show about their effectiveness with these strategies. They would be assessed on the correct implementation of the strategies and on their ability to facilitate as much engaged time as possible during instructional time. During each observation visit (at least once a week) the supervising professor would randomly choose one student, and with a stop watch track the percentage of the instructional time during which the student teacher academically engages that student. The goal would be at least 80% engaged time. Student teachers also would be required to track and assess their own teaching progress based on their students' progress.

Teacher Preparation for the Middle Grades

As we move to a teacher preparation program at the middle grades level, much will remain the same. We know that in addition to choosing two areas of academic concentration, students preparing to teach in the middle grades typically only take approximately eleven education courses as more course time is allocated for the area of concentration (see Table 7.3). We would require the same foundations of education course for these students as for the students preparing to teach in the early grades. We would require a course in human growth and development, albeit with a different emphasis. This course would only briefly examine development from birth to pre-adolescence; it would concentrate more on preadolescence and adolescence. Once again, we would require the courses in applied behavior analysis and instructional strategies. The applied behavior analysis course would be the same course required of students preparing to teach in the early grades. However, the instructional strategies course may be slightly varied to address particular instructional strategies appropriate for the middle grades while still focusing on measurably superior methods.

Table 7.3. Teacher Preparation For The Middle Grades Based on Behavior Analysis

Current Programs	Proposed Program
foundations of education	foundations of education
human growth & development	*human growth & development*
school health	school health
computer use in education	*computer use in education*
instruction in middle grades	**applied behavior analysis**
fine arts	*instructional strategies*
classroom management	**assessment**
exceptional children	*classroom management*
cultural diversity	**educational psychology**
methods course (1)	methods course (1)
methods course (2)	methods course (2)
student teaching	student teaching

Note. Courses in bold are courses not typically required in current programs. Courses in italics are modifications of courses currently required.

Rather than requiring courses in the methods of teaching all content areas, we would require only the two methods courses that matched the student's two areas of concentration. These would be designed much like the methods courses for early grades preparation in terms of topical issues and field experiences. While the use of computers in instruction would be included in these methods courses, there would also be an entire course devoted to computers in education. A substantial part of this course would focus on accessing and disseminating information via the computer. Classroom management, which is already required in some institutions, would be required in our program, and like the course for the early grades, would follow the topics of the chapter in this book and require a simultaneous opening school experience. Similarly, students would be required to take the same educational psychology and assessment courses that are offered for the early grades, while issues of exceptional children and cultural diversity would be infused throughout all teacher preparation courses. Students would be required to take a course in health issues of particular concern for the preadolescent and adolescent student (i.e., teenage suicide, alcohol and drug use, and sexually transmitted diseases). The focus in this course would be on preparing teachers to help students arrange their environments such that the probability of teenage suicides, alcohol and drug abuse, and sexually transmitted diseases would be reduced among students. As with the teacher preparation program for the early grades, students would be required to complete a term-long student teaching experience during which the concerns would be the same as they are in the early grades.

Teacher Preparation for Secondary School

Our last proposed teacher preparation program is for students preparing to teach in the secondary grades. The typical programs presented earlier required students to complete a major in the discipline they are preparing to teach; we too, would have this requirement in this program. In addition, students usually complete about eight education courses (see Table 7.4). As with the other programs we would keep the foundations of education course with the focus presented earlier. In addition, we would keep the human growth and development course, but would put very little emphasis on birth and early years with a major emphasis on adolescence and early adulthood instead. We would require the educational psychology course, the course in applied behavior analysis, the course in assessment, and the course in instructional strategies that would be required in early and middle grades.

In addition to the instructional strategies course, students would be required to take a methods course for the discipline they are planning to teach. Requirements in this course would be similar to the requirements for the methods courses designed for teachers in the early and middle grades; however, some of the content would be different. Rather than offer a course in exceptional children, exceptionalities would be incorporated throughout their course work as it is in the other programs proposed here. Finally, rather than requiring courses in computers and in educational media, these would be combined into one course. As with the other teacher preparation programs based on a behavior-analytic model, students would be required to

Table 7.4. Teacher Preparation For The Secondary Grades Based on Behavior Analysis

Current Programs	Proposed Program
foundations of education	foundations of education
human growth & development	*human growth & development*
curriculum planning	educational psychology
computer use in education	**applied behavior analysis**
educational media	**assessment**
educational psychology	**instructional strategies**
exceptional children	methods course (1)
methods course (1)	*computers and educational media*
student teaching	student teaching

Note. Courses in bold are courses not typically required in current programs. Courses in italics are modifications of courses currently required.

complete one term of student teaching during which the supervising professor would address the same issues addressed for teachers in other grade levels.

As may be evident to you by now there are several courses we believe are essential for an effective teacher preparation model based on behavior analysis (see Table 7.5). These courses include a course in applied behavior analysis, which would be an expansion on the behavior analysis section of the theory chapter in this book; a course in educational psychology, which is currently required in some programs and states and not in others; a course in instructional strategies, which would focus on measurably superior methods including the instructional strategies found in this book and any additional strategies for which there is empirical evidence of effectiveness; and a course in assessment which teaches students to track their progress on a regular basis so that the approximate 150 instructional decisions they need to make every day can be informed decisions made in a timely manner. In addition, students would continue to take courses in foundations of education and in human growth and development, and to complete a student teaching experience.

Table 7.5. Summary of Proposed Teacher Preparation Programs Based on Behavior Analysis

EARLY CHILDHOOD	MIDDLE GRADES	SECONDARY GRADES
foundations of education	**foundations of education**	**foundations of education**
human growth & development	**human growth & development**	**human growth & development**
applied behavior analysis	school health	**applied behavior analysis**
instructional strategies	**applied behavior analysis**	**instructional strategies**
teaching of mathematics	**instructional strategies**	**educational psychology**
teaching of science and social studies	**assessment**	**assessment**
teaching of reading (1)	classroom management	computers and educational media
teaching of reading (2)	**educational psychology**	methods course (1)
music and art in the elementary school	computer use in education	**student teaching**
physical education and health in the elementary school	methods course (1)	
educational psychology	methods course (2)	
classroom management	**student teaching**	
assessment		
student teaching		

Note. Courses in bold are required across all levels.

Who Will You Hire to Teach in Your School?

Will you consider all candidates with teacher certification for your state and similar grade point averages from their colleges to be equally prepared to teach in your school? Will you examine individual transcripts in search of particular courses that you consider important for teachers, such as classroom management or educational psychology, even if they are not required for state certification? What specific skills or knowledge will you look for when you interview prospective teachers for your school? When teachers have difficulty in their classrooms either with discipline or with mastery of academics, what advice will you have for them?

Who Will Teach These Courses?

A final consideration in proposing teacher preparation programs is the issue of who will teach the proposed courses. To understand the importance of this issue, the politics of the institution need to be considered. In a small college where there is typically only one department of education within the college, faculty tend to specialize in a content area and other courses such as foundations of education, educational psychology, and classroom management may be shared while a course in human growth and development might be offered by the psychology department. In large universities, however, where there is often a college of education and several departments within the college of education, there is likely to be some issue of which department teaches which courses. A second, more important, issue is what expertise will the faculty who teach these courses bring to the program?

As there are not many options in a small department of education within a college, let us instead examine this issue in the universities that have a college of education. A college of education within a university typically has several departments such as early childhood, middle and secondary, educational psychology, physical education and health, foundations of education, and special education. We would recommend that the methods courses be taught within the departments that offer the degree, for example, students preparing to teach in the early grades should complete their methods courses in the early childhood department while those preparing to teach in middle or secondary grades should complete their methods courses in the middle and secondary department. However, courses that are recommended across all preparation programs should be taught outside the department offering the degree. These are considered "umbrella courses" that will prepare students for the particular methods courses taught in their appropriate departments. For example, the courses in applied behavior analysis, educational psychology, instructional strategies, classroom management, assessment, and human growth and development might be taught within a department of educational psychology where one is likely to find broad expertise in the psychology of teaching and learning as well as expertise in development. Computers and educational media might be taught in the department that houses instructional technology. Depending on the university and the configuration of departments within their college of education, different programs of education are housed together. It does not matter in which department the program is housed, what matters is that the professors teaching the courses have the particular expertise needed to teach them well.

Because our programs focus on a behavioral approach to teacher training, several of the faculty would have to be well-grounded in behavior analysis to teach the courses in applied behavior analysis, assessment, instructional strategies, and classroom management. In addition, these faculty should have recent classroom teaching experience. This may be difficult to find at first because most faculty who are well-grounded in behavior analysis were trained in psychology and are not likely to have experience as classroom teachers. However, that could be compensated for if faculty are doing research in the classroom. What is important is that faculty have knowledge of what is happening in today's classrooms and can make their instruction applicable and practical.

The faculty best prepared to prepare teachers in the programs proposed here should be conducting research in the schools on a regular basis. This research should advance practical aspects of teaching, for example, finding ways to increase engaged academic time, identifying effective instructional strategies, examining ways to facilitate classroom management, and investigating ways to meet individual student needs. In addition, their research should take them into schools in different socio-economic areas and into both public and private schools.

This entire chapter is based on the premise that students can be taught to teach, which forces us to consider if teaching is an art or a science. If it is an art, teachers are primarily born and not made. That is, they have a natural talent for helping people learn. If teaching is a science, there are identifiable strategies, skills, and knowledge that facilitate learning and can be taught in teacher preparation programs. We suggest that by temperament and personality some people may be better suited to teaching than others. These are the teacher education students we would most like to see in our teacher preparation programs. However, we do not believe a particular temperament or personality is sufficient. There are skills that any teacher needs to be effective in the classroom. "Students' right to learn is directly tied to their teachers' opportunities to learn what they need to teach well" (Darling-Hammond, 1996, p. 6). What teachers need to know is how to analyze what is happening in the classroom academically and socially and then arrange a classroom environment in which appropriate academic and social behaviors will occur more often. In addition, to be effective, teachers need to know how to present content and skills in a way that will facilitate students' learning. To do this, teachers need to know how to assess learning on a regular basis and to implement effective strategies for change.

It is not enough to care about students and to want them to succeed. Although they are excellent starting points, we would like to add to these, the skills and knowledge outlined above. Students will still not be prepared to be excellent teachers, however, unless they are committed to education. We do not know how to teach commitment, but it is usually easy to spot when it is present. We suspect it must begin with college and university faculty who are committed to education and who can model that commitment for the students who desire to become teachers.

Annotated Bibliography

Barrett, B. H., Beck, R., Binder, C., Cook, D. A., Engelmann, S., Greer, R. D., Kyrklund, S. J., Johnson, K. R., Maloney, M., McCorkle, N., Vargas, J. S., & Watkins, C. L. (1991). The right to effective education. *The Behavior Analyst, 14*, 79-82.

> Outlines students' rights to an effective education as well as teachers' rights in providing this education. A teacher preparation program based on providing these rights would do much to further education.

Kramer, R. (1991). *Ed school follies: The miseducation of America's teachers*. New York: The Free Press.

> Kramer visits teacher education programs around the country interviewing administration, faculty, and students, and sitting in on classes to present to the reader a picture of the philosophy and the approach taken in each of these programs presented in her book. She concludes her book with strong recommendations for what we need to do to achieve educational reform in our teacher education programs.

Labaree, D. F. (1996). The trouble with ed schools. *Educational Foundations, 10* (3), 27-45.

> Provides a refreshing look at the struggles of schools of education. It is true, he tells us, that they are often criticized for doing a poor job of preparing teachers and for not curing the ills of American education, but few have looked at the underlying reasons for this the way Labaree does in this article.

Urban, W. J. (1990). Historical studies of teacher education. In W. R. Houston (Ed.), *Handbook of research on teacher education* (pp. 59-71). New York: Macmillian.

> Traces formal teacher education from the normal schools of the nineteenth century to the rise of the departments, schools, and colleges of education in the university along with the changes that occurred in the normal school as it became the teachers college and later college.

Chapter 8

Excellent Education, Myths, and Behavior Analysis

Schools can work. Schools can be effective. Schools can be places where students and teachers are successful, productive, and happy. Throughout this book we introduced you to many ideas, practices, and methods that are successful for children and schooling. We introduced you to the complex issues of educational theory and showed how behavior analysis presents a coherent, effective, data-based approach to education. We showed how Direct Instruction, Personalized System of Instruction, Precision Teaching, Peer Tutoring, and Programmed Instruction give teachers the necessary tools to help all children become successful learners. In addition, we offered an approach to classroom management that goes beyond the control or correction of misbehavior and considers a design that includes effective instructional strategies, time management, and functional analysis. We also showed you practical ways to assess performance with individual children so that you can be sure students are learning—or make changes if they are not. You have constructed a complete plan for your own school and it could be one of the best schools in the country. And, if you can do it, why aren't all schools improving and becoming excellent?

Americans are well aware that schools need to improve, that more children need to reach higher levels of preparation than ever before—and that, overall, great success is not uniformly available to America's 51 million school-aged children.

Two challenges face American education today: 1) raising overall achievement levels and 2) making opportunities for achievement more equitable. The importance of both derives from the same basic condition— our changing economy. Never before has the pool of developed skill and capability mattered more in our prospects for general economic health. And never before have skill and knowledge mattered as much in the economic prospects for individuals. (Resnick, 1995, p. 55)

If the United States is to be competitive in the 21st Century, our schools must provide effective education for all children.

Effective teaching is the essential ingredient of effective schools. Recently, the National Commission on Teaching and America's Future (1996) released a report entitled *What Matters Most: Teaching for America's Future.* Believing that "what teachers know and can do makes the crucial difference in what children learn" (p. 5), the Commission emphasized the importance of improving teaching as a means of improving learning. In their report are five major recommendations for improving teaching and learning.

I.   Get serious about standards, for both students and teachers.
II. Reinvent teacher preparation and professional development.
III. Overhaul teacher recruitment, and put qualified teachers in every classroom.
IV. Encourage and reward knowledge and skills.
V.   Create schools that are organized for student and teacher success.
(National Commission on Teaching and America's Future, 1996, p. vii)

Each of these recommendations is important, should be a goal of educational reform, and can be facilitated by behavior analysis. High standards for teacher and student performance will help clarify the goals of education. Specific strategies will have to be designed to achieve these goals. We believe behavior analysis can offer guidance in designing these strategies. In Chapter 7 we offered suggestions for redesigning teacher preparation. Implementation of these suggestions must be coupled with data collection so that further revisions are based on data. Teacher preparation based on behavior analysis will help put only qualified teachers in our classrooms.

Throughout this book we emphasized the importance of encouraging students to succeed academically by offering them measurably superior instructional strategies in a well managed classroom with ample reinforcement to maintain performance. In addition, we emphasized the importance of designing systems of reinforcement that foster excellence in every school for every teacher and every child. If you reflected on and answered the questions throughout this book you have probably created, on paper at least, schools in which students and teachers could be successful. It is time to begin investing in such a plan. "In contrast with other countries that invest most of their education dollars in well-prepared and well-supported teachers, half of the educational dollars in the United States are spent on staff and activities outside the classroom" (National Commission on Teaching and America's Future, 1996, p. 5). Unfortunately, although the recommendations above are excellent, this report, like so many before it, will probably lead to little significant change in our children's schools and our nation's colleges of education. In the next section we discuss three interrelated and complicated reasons for this.

How Will You Improve Teaching and Learning In Your School?

How will you address each of the five recommendations above? Will you set high standards and not be satisfied until all your students reach those standards? What types of professional development will you plan for your teachers? How will your hiring practices increase the probability that you hire only qualified teachers? What system of reward and encouragement will you establish for your school? How will you know if your school facilitates success for your teachers and their students?

Theory and Practice

The first of three reasons why recommendations from *What Matters Most: Teaching for America's Future* will not have a significant impact in our schools is the persistent preference for theory over data displayed by the mainstream educational establishment. Believing too strongly in one theory can blind educators to effective practices if they believe that those practices cannot be clearly derived from their theory. Many social scientists also have favorite theories derived from a set of beliefs about people or social settings, rather than from data about the effectiveness of certain practices. But no particular theory necessarily leads to any particular set of practices. Murray (1989) suggests that our educational theories are not precise enough to "permit exact deducible formulations for teaching, curriculum design, or educational assessment" (p. 8).

On the whole, few educational theories are sufficiently well-formulated to permit falsification or unambiguous classroom practices to be drawn from them. Thus, the initiation of a classroom innovation on theoretical grounds alone would need to be made with great caution. (Murray, 1989, p. 12)

Still, too many educators use their theories, rather than data, to justify their recommendations. In their attempts to improve education, many traditional educators believe it is more important to support theory, even flawed theory, than to develop and test effective practices. Sadly, this seems to be increasing not decreasing. "Interest in the use of scientific research methods in education is waning, not growing. Instead of investing in large-scale, long-term evaluations of classroom teaching methods, most research today favors impressionistic studies of individual classrooms and teachers" (Marshall, 1993 p. 29). The lack of a research emphasis leads to the adoption of educational programs for the wrong reasons. "Gullible principals, school boards, and even state legislatures too often jump on the latest educational bandwagons, led by charismatic proselytizers who promote their programs with unsupported or anecdotal claims" (Marshall, 1993, p. 28). Educators are often accused of going with the latest "fad," without basing practice on data, and unfortunately this is often (although not always) the case.

Shanker (1995), when wondering why we do not learn from the successes of other countries in educating their children, asked:

. . .why do we not see what these many different education systems have in common? Why do we not try to learn from their successes? Why do we not translate their textbooks, their examinations, and samples of their students' work? Why, instead, do we constantly try "new," "creative," and "promising"–but totally unproven programs? (p. 47)

The first defining feature of behavior analysis presented in Chapter 1 was **data-based effectiveness**. Any educator who strictly adhered to this criterion would avoid fads and learn from the successes of others. Rather than constantly proposing new and better fads, educators would establish schools and classrooms that use effective, proven practices. Without strict adherence to this criterion, education will remain rudderless and subject to the whims of the most popular current theory.

Still, while criticizing the over-emphasis on theory in American education, it is difficult not to present some critical information that shows that the theory of behavior analysis has recently received some strong support. Recent research on the development of the brain has reaffirmed the importance of environmental experiences in the development of the individual. It is not the case that behavior analysts claim an exclusionary influence on environmental variables. Rather, given the "anatomical, physiological, and biochemical states" (Zeiler, 1996, p. 307) of a biological organism, the environmental variables pose "constraints and opportunities" (p. 307) that strongly influence the development and actions of that organism. "The experiences of childhood, pioneering research shows, help form the brain's circuits—for music and math, language and emotion" (Begley, 1996, p. 55). Begley (1996) explained that:

> ... it is the experiences of childhood, determining which neurons are used, that wire the circuits of the brain as surely as a programmer at a keyboard reconfigures the circuits in a computer. Which keys are typed—which experiences a child has—determines whether the child grows up to be intelligent or dull, fearful or self assured, articulate or tongue-tied. The implications of this new understanding are at once promising and disturbing. They suggest that, with the right input at the right time, almost anything is possible. But they imply, too, that if you miss the window you're playing with a handicap. (p. 56)

Current research clearly shows that it is a child's interactions with environmental variables which are critical to the development of skills and abilities (Donahoe & Palmer, 1989). These studies show that the interactions with the environment are central to understanding how the brain develops and how gene-environment relations operate in the analysis of the development of human abilities. Behavior analysts investigate the exact details of behavior's interactions with the environment and it is from these investigations that effective practices are developed. Human development is more than just maturation, over which we have very little control. Human development is also determined by the many, detailed interactions every individual has with the world. For children to develop their full potential we must emphasize effective practices developed through studying behavior-environment relations.

An ironic corollary to this problem of theory exists, however. While behavior analysts support data-based effectiveness as the single most important criterion for selecting practices for schools, they, too, are often more interested in theory than practice. Many behavior analysts, much like "constructivists" or "developmentalists" are more concerned that educators claim to "believe" in their theory than adopt their practices. In the practical world of teaching, this is a serious flaw. It does not matter if teachers, principals, or superintendents "believe" that behavior analysis is the most accurate theory. Rather, effective practices need to be a part of every teacher's repertoire; only by practicing data-based effective teaching methods, will schools improve and children benefit.

What Will Guide the Educational Practices in Your School?

Will your school be guided by theory? In Chapter 2 you were asked to consider four different educational theories that you might use as a basis for educational decisions in your school. Did you choose one or possibly a combination of theories for your school? Are you still supporting the theory you chose in Chapter 2, or are you considering a different theory for your school? Will you make decisions based on theory and then collect data to determine the effectiveness of your decisions? Will you abandon theory and make all your decisions on data alone? How might you combine theory and data to guide your educational decisions?

Some Myths Harming American Education

A second reason that the report, *What Matters Most: Teaching for America's Future*, will have little impact on improving America's schools is that there are many powerful myths that dominate discussions analyzing teaching, learning, and teacher preparation. These are myths that persist even in the face of substantial data to refute them. If education is to become uniformly effective, we must overcome these myths. Let us look at some of these myths.

Myth Number 1: Teachers Are Born, Not Made

This is a theoretical mistake that is not a part of the belief system of most teacher educators but is prevalent in the general public. Many lay people and it seems most legislators believe that specific training in teaching is not important—that people who are great teachers are simply born that way. While it may be acknowledged that learning is hard work, rarely do people admit that the skills required of excellent teaching are also the result of hard work. Teaching requires expertise that cannot be derived just from common sense or from love of children.

We recognize that learning is not an issue of aptitude, that as Resnick (1995) stated, "effort can create ability" (p. 56). She went on to tell us:

there are five essential features of an effort-oriented educational system: 1) clear expectations for achievement, well understood by everyone; 2) fair and credible evaluations of achievement; 3) celebration and payoff for success; 4) as much time as is necessary to meet learning expectations; and 5) expert instruction. (pp. 57-58)

Learning to deliver the required "expert instruction" is difficult and time consuming. Effective methods of teacher education can turn a mediocre teacher into a superior one. Teachers are made, not born that way.

Myth Number 2: A Teacher Can't Teach, Only Help Students Learn

Teachers who know how to teach do far more than help students learn. They direct and guide instruction. They know when to be directive and when to allow students to discover. They know how to make children active participants in the learning process without allowing students to flounder without knowledge. While many current educational theories have criticized Direct Instruction, the information we have provided shows that Direct Instruction is an essential part of an effective instructional repertoire. More importantly, even discovery learning requires the direct involvement of the teacher.

> In both a discovery learning exercise or a programmed learning lesson, the teacher must sequence the events so that the pupil begins with some response or skill he or she already has. Typically the child responds either to a deliberate statement or a clear direction, or to an artful manipulation of the materials. (Murray, 1989, p. 9)

Sipe and Curlette (1996) completed an informative meta-synthesis of educational productivity. A meta-synthesis examines analyses of groups of similar studies and synthesizes overall effects so that broad, general conclusions can be reached. Sipe and Curlette examined educational productivity across 103 studies in the attempt to identify those sets of teaching procedures that produce the strongest achievement with children.

The findings of Sipe and Curlette (1996) strongly support Direct Instruction on the part of the teacher. They document that the most effective procedures were direct, individual, and data-based. Curriculum interventions with the most impact included vocabulary instruction, accelerative instruction, mastery learning, Direct Instruction, and note taking. These are important sets of skills that teachers need to learn in order to establish and guide effective learning.

In Chapter 1, we discussed how schools often preach the gospel that *all children can learn* but rarely practice what they preach to insure that all students *will* learn. Without reviewing the whole argument, that important distinction can be ignored by mainstream educators if one believes that all teachers can do is help children learn. Until those in charge of schools and school systems take responsibility for the education of all our children and require only the inclusion of data-based, effective practices in our nation's classrooms, much education will remain minimally effective with many of our children.

Myth Number 3: Subject Matter Expertise Makes an Excellent Teacher

Many educational critics believe that anyone with a high level of skill in a subject matter area can be an excellent teacher in that area. For example, if you are a biologist or a mathematician, you could teach biology or mathematics well. One immediate issue questioning that assumption is the quality of teaching in college. College professors must have expertise in their subject matter at the highest levels. Anyone who has been to college can tell you that many of those faculty members are not very good teachers (although many are very good teachers). But if all it took to be an excellent teacher was the subject matter expertise, all college professors would be good teachers. As this is not so, there must be more to teaching than knowing your subject matter. Subject matter experts often lecture on their subject matter, paying little or no attention to effective practice or to the results with students. In fact, it is common in college to "blame the victim"; if students fail, it is their fault (they did not work hard enough or pay attention, or whatever). To their credit, many college professors realize their shortcomings in teaching and are seeking to learn more about effective teaching skills.

These first three myths are concerned with what it takes to be an effective teacher. Excellent teaching is not a part of an individual's birthright and it is not enough simply to oversee a child's ability to learn. Many effective practices discussed in this book are not "natural"—nor are they easy to learn and master. They require hard work and practice to use correctly. The best teachers are always learning how to improve their teaching. Although thorough knowledge of subject matter is important, excellent teaching requires much more. It requires knowing how to structure that knowledge, present it, construct examples and nonexamples to clarify concepts, and assessment procedures to track the progress of individual children. Debunking these three myths from the public's perception of education will advance us toward implementing effective practices in all our nation's schools.

Myth Number 4: Setting High Standards Will Improve Our Schools

The issue of setting high academic standards currently dominates discussions of education. In the last half of this decade, there is no more widely discussed issue than setting higher standards for students and their teachers. It is important to know that setting high academic standards is an excellent and much needed practice, not a myth nor a problem for education. The myth is that by setting those standards, schools will necessarily improve. There are two problems with this myth. First, setting standards alone cannot lead directly to improved teaching and learning. It seems that some educators and many politicians believe that we only need to set high standards and schools will improve. But without much more, they will not. Standards are only a useful and preliminary step. Of course, we should want everyone to perform at high levels. However, unless we give students and teachers the tools to accomplish those expectations, we are guaranteed to fail once again. Teachers cannot teach well if they have not been taught to teach well. Students cannot learn to perform at high levels if excellent teaching is not available.

Second, in the rest of the world where standards are common, there are not single sets of standards like those being discussed for the United States.

The reference to "world-class" is ironic because none of the nations with more successful school systems have a single set of performance standards. They have a common curriculum throughout most or all the elementary grades and a relatively high floor of achievement, but that is not the same as having a single set of performance standards. Moreover, all of those countries put students into different tracks, beginning in the fourth or seventh grade, on the basis of their having met different performance standards. (Shanker, 1995 p. 51)

In other words, other countries rely on multiple standards and meeting any of those standards requires some form of comparable curriculum (how can every student meet a single standard for performance in a subject matter if students study different aspects of that subject matter?). In the United States, we do not uniformly support national standards much less the concept of a national curriculum. Many politicians do not even support the goals of *America 2000* (1991) that require such vague generalities as "all children will start school ready to learn" and "U.S. students will be first in the world in math and science" (p. 19). Those goals are seen by some conservative politicians as damaging to local control of schools and promoting "a federal takeover of education" and a "national school board" (Editorial Board, 1996, p. C6).

Myth Number 5: Tracking Hinders the Education of Children

A corollary idea to setting high standards in Shanker's (1995) statement is that most European countries put students into different tracks depending on how well or poorly they meet those standards. That presents another interesting problem. While many politicians may not agree on setting standards, many educators strongly believe that tracking causes more problems than it solves, which leads us to the next dominant myth in American education—tracking always hinders the education of children. Tracking, as it is currently practiced in the United States, usually assigns students in early elementary school to either a slow, average, or accelerated academic track. When these students enter middle school, they have few educational options available to them. Tracking is ability grouping between classes which differs from ability grouping within classes. Ability grouping within classes allows students at the same level of skill in a particular subject area (e.g., reading or math) to receive instruction for the next skill to be mastered. Students can be in different groups for reading and for math, in addition, they can be moved quickly from one group to another as their skills advance. Students who are in tracks, however, receive slow, average, or accelerated academics for all their courses regardless of the students' particular needs in individual content areas. In addition, once students are placed in a track in elementary school, it is very difficult to move the student to another track.

While parents with children in advanced tracks are supportive of tracking, most educators are not. Educators argue that when students are in separate tracks, the students in the slower tracks have lower standards set for them, and miss important opportunities to learn with and from students with more advanced skills. The parents' argument is that students with more advanced skills can progress more quickly when they are in tracks with students who have similar skills. "Official United States educational ideology is against tracking," however "it is not tracking that causes the problem; it is what is on the track when the student gets there" (Shanker, 1995, p. 50). In other words, there needs to be excellent curriculum and effective instruction for all students no matter what track they are on.

Tracking that is not done well can damage students with lower levels of skill (Slavin, 1994). That need not be the case. Provided all tracks lead to the same standards of excellence and prepare all students for many educational options, they can be very beneficial. Tracks can allow more time for students who need more time.

They can provide different instructional strategies to reach the same goals allowing all students the opportunity to access the most effective strategies. Students who come to school without the necessary skills could receive the needed special attention to gain those skills—attention that may not be available in a mixed class. On the other hand, students who come to school with high skill levels should be constantly challenged to avoid boredom and to achieve to their highest potential. Tracking used cautiously and with constant attention to data, can assist all students in reaching their highest ability.

Myth Number 6: Teachers Should Teach Thinking Skills Rather Than Information

This one is fun. Of course students should learn thinking skills. But what does that mean in practice; how is it accomplished? Many traditional educators today talk about teaching thinking skills as a primary goal of education. Their discussion emphasizes thinking, often with little or no regard to information, and without a careful analysis of what it means to "think." Imagine a classroom where students are going to be taught how to think as a skill separate from other skills. The teacher starts the lesson, "OK, children, today we are going to work on our thinking. I want everyone to close their eyes, concentrate, and think. Then we will talk about it. Now remember children, don't think about anything in particular, just think." What do the children do? How can they just sit there and think without thinking about anything? If you are not sure, try it. Stop reading and think, but not about anything, just practice your thinking skills.

As this exercise shows, "thinking" without "thinking about" is not really possible and that is the flaw in the arguments of the traditional educator. In order to teach children (or adults) to think, educators must start with the mastery of content. In other words, to teach thinking, one must first teach knowledge or information. Johnson and Layng (1992) clarified this issue; they showed that to develop "thinking skills," it is essential to teach facts and to teach them well—until they are automatic. Once children are fluent in these basic skills, thinking skills actually begin to evolve without additional specific instruction. In other words, automatic, fluent performance (practice makes perfect) can lead to thinking. "When presented with new environmental requirements, these behaviors can recombine in new ways that correspond to the higher level complex skills shown by experts" (Johnson & Layng, 1992, p. 1476).

If Johnson and Layng (1992) are correct, thinking skills can be an important goal for teaching but only when they are combined with teaching information to think about. Educators would teach facts and information to very high levels of mastery—to fluency—and this is something most teachers can already do fairly well. Supplemental teaching in *just* thinking may not be very useful or even necessary. This approach can go far in guiding educational accomplishment in schools. By teaching facts, relations among facts, information, and solutions, thinking skills in many different areas will develop. It is an interesting twist that teachers who teach information to high levels of mastery could develop more thinking skills indirectly than teachers who try to teach thinking directly.

Myth Number 7: Extrinsic Motivation Damages Learning

For the past twenty years, some educators have claimed that extrinsic motivation is one of the main problems with our schools. It is said by some that to reward excellence is to inhibit the intrinsic motivation of students (e.g., Balsam & Bondy, 1983; Levine & Fasnacht, 1974). In other words, if you reward someone for doing something, they will do it less. Given what fifty years of research on reinforcement has shown, this position is difficult to accept.

Fortunately, two trends counter the position that reinforcement is detrimental in schooling. First, the data that support these conclusions have been reanalyzed to show that the conclusions are unreliable. Eisenberger and Cameron (1996) stated, "our analysis of a quarter of a century of accumulated research provides little evidence that reward reduces intrinsic task interest" (p. 1162). They also documented that reward can actually increase generalized creativity and that any negative effects of reward that might occur are very specialized and easily avoided.

A second important trend is a growing realization among mainstream educators that reinforcement is an important element in learning. When Shanker (1995) examined the more effective educational practices of other countries, he found

a major difference between our school system and those of other industrialized countries is that they use extrinsic motivation and high stakes for students. This runs counter to much of American educational theory, which holds that *only* intrinsic motivation works. (p. 49)

Resnick (1995) also acknowledged that reward and reinforcement are important to effective education. She supports celebrating hard work and achievement. "Celebration coupled with payoff will keep the effort flowing; achievement will rise accordingly" (Resnick, 1995, p. 60).

Toch (1996) discussed the need for reward for teachers if teachers are to improve the ways they teach. He recommended that incentives be established for effective teaching—unfortunately, such "pay for performance" systems are not well appreciated by many leaders of teacher groups. While it may be a more perfect world if everyone did what needed to be done for the good of others, that is not the way human behavior has evolved. Extrinsic motivation is essential to effective schools and it is time for all educators to acknowledge that fact and begin to change practice.

While the first three myths were concerned with what it takes to be a teacher, these last four myths are more concerned with policies that guide decisions in school systems. We encourage the setting of high standards as long as teachers have the skills and materials necessary to help *all* students achieve those standards. In addition, tracking that leads *all* students to these high standards will not hinder learning. In all tracks, students must begin with basic facts and information to ultimately develop thinking skills for the content area. To help students reach the level of mastery necessary, extrinsic reinforcement should be carefully designed and implemented.

Are Your Ready to Relinquish the Myths?

What are some of your "beliefs" about education? Which of those do you think might be myths? How will you determine if your beliefs are myths or if they are realities? Did you previously believe any of the seven myths presented above? Have some of these myths guided the design you created for your school? What changes will you make now?

Extending Behavior Analysis

The third major reason that *What Matters Most: Teaching for America's Future* will not result in significant changes in schools rests with those who already present the most effective educational practices for schools today–behavior analysts. Behavior analysts have worked hard developing effective teaching practices, but they have not fully addressed other important issues such as curriculum and social dimensions of education. Until effective, data-based educators turn their attention to improvement in these areas, there will remain barriers to improving the education of our children (Deitz, 1994).

The Total School Curriculum

A complete approach to schools and schooling requires a thorough approach to curriculum. Behavior analysts have concentrated primarily on the basic areas of reading and mathematics in the elementary school. They have shown excellent procedures for teaching reading and mathematics but with the exception of those in Direct Instruction, little else is available to guide teachers or administrators. Boyer (1995) showed how schools need a complete curriculum covering, "the life cycle, the use of symbols, membership in groups, a sense of time and space, response to the aesthetic, connections to nature, producing and consuming, living with purpose" (p. 85).

Behavior analysts need to become involved in determining what ought to be taught in schools and should become supporters of common elements in our nation's curriculum, if not a national curriculum. Currently, in the United States there is no common curriculum. It is determined by "teachers, principals, advocates or legislators. The results: discontinuity, confusion, an absence of building blocks of knowledge, and a constant need for teachers to determine if students have the necessary background to proceed with the current work" (Shanker, 1995, p. 52). If those advocating Precision Teaching are correct that higher levels of thinking skills evolve from complete mastery of basic skills (Johnson & Layng, 1992), their knowledge can inform those involved in making decisions about the curriculum of a school.

There is a second important reason for behavior analysts to become involved in a standardized curriculum. If the curriculum is standard, teaching methods have a greater chance of becoming standard. Schools are not now organized so that teachers work with each other to develop effective practices. The calls for standardization in method used to be only from those in Direct Instruction who advocated that teachers follow scripted lessons and develop scripts for lessons as they found them to be effective.

> Equally important, when all teachers ... are teaching a common curriculum, there is a basis for professional discussion and collegiality, which we now lack. ...teachers can be trained to teach a particular subject, texts can be targeted, and many lessons can be standardized and techniques routinized. (Shanker, 1995, p. 52)

There was a time when many teachers found scripted lessons to be insulting. It was said that standardized lessons questioned their creativity and their ability to teach to the unique needs of every child. That idea is changing today.

> Is this "unprofessional"? Quite the contrary. Every profession relies on proven, standard operating procedures. Imagine a doctor, a pharmacist, or an architect—or even a barber—constantly having to be imaginative. Creativity comes into play in difficult, non-routine situations and in developing a better set of routines. The notion that standardization and routinization are evils and that teachers should be creative and innovative every minute of the day is disastrous. It is also a major barrier to transforming teaching into a genuine profession. (Shanker, 1995, pp. 52-53)

There is no better time than now for the ideas of behavior analysts to have an impact on schools. However, to make that contribution, behavior analysts need to become involved in national, state, and local discussions about the total curriculum in our schools.

The Social Dimension of Education

Boyer (1995) clarified that schools are more than places where children learn academic skills. Schools are communities of children, teachers, administrators, parents, and community members. Each group brings its own interests, needs, and expertise to the table. Leadership is a shared enterprise in today's schools. Parents and teachers work with principals in a shared decision-making effort. To understand and be able to affect the total school, behavior analysts need to help create a place that is "purposeful, communicative, just, disciplined, caring, [and] celebrative" (Boyer, 1995, p. 18).

Schools designed and run by behavior analysts meet most of these goals. However, there are often two issues that will require further attention. The first is values. Boyer (1995) discussed values as a commitment to character, to the core virtues of life. Attention to values allows the consideration of "how the school experience shapes the ethical and moral lives of children" (Boyer, 1995, p. 11). According to Boyer, the experiences of schooling need to instill in children the values of honesty, respect, responsibility, compassion, self-discipline, perseverance, and giving. In too many schools, children are unpleasant to each other, disrespectful to adults and other children, and lacking manners. Equally important, these unpleasant and sometimes dangerous actions extend to the playground, social interactions after school, and home. The lack of actions reflective of these values can expand as children become adolescents and adults. Criminal activities of all sorts would be less likely if schools insured that children and teenagers were honest, respectful, responsible, compassionate, self-disciplined, persevering, and giving. Schools have often been hesitant to demand these core values and the political climate in many states makes efforts toward this goal difficult. A further problem that needs to be solved through research is that we are not sure how to teach and maintain these activities. Behavior analysts must research the different ways in which values are an essential part of success for all children and adults.

Discipline is an important part of an effective educational system. Numerous studies have showed how to use positive procedures to eliminate the inappropriate actions of children in schools (Deitz & Hummel, 1978). These studies have been severely criticized for creating children who were still and docile (Winett & Winkler, 1972) and much of the research stopped. In fact, it is now difficult to find studies on discipline in education. But ending such research was not the appropriate solution for the apparent creation of still and docile children. With increases in serious crime in today's schools, it would have been preferable to continue the research on discipline but with a different emphasis. The type of research needed to change; behavior analysts needed to emphasize studies which showed how to strengthen active, involved children who were well behaved.

It is time for behavior analysts to begin that thrust in research on discipline. Specifically, two approaches need to be emphasized. First, behavior analysts should re-establish a strong line of research on the elimination of inappropriate behavior. As the seriousness of those behaviors have increased over the last twenty years, these studies will address those new levels of activity. Teachers need effective skills. Behavior analysts need to move beyond where we are now—where we have very little to offer to teachers when students engage in serious criminal activity beyond hoping that law enforcement officers arrive before it is too late. Second, behavior analysts need to begin to look at ways to teach the behaviors related to the important values listed above. They should develop methods which are effective at teaching children honesty, respect, responsibility, compassion, self-discipline, perseverance, and giving (Boyer, 1995). In everyday language, "self-discipline" is very different from "discipline." Behavior analysts should work to teach children to be disciplined in their own actions, not just subject to discipline. It is not too late to begin.

To impact American education into the 21st Century, there are other issues, as well, that behavior analysts need to address. While these issues go beyond the scope of this book, we thought it important to at least mention them as they are common and constant topics of discussion in education. Behavior analysts must involve the latest, most effective, technology in what they do; the move toward the use of technology in education is rapid and there is a lack of effective, educational software that behavior analysts could supply. They must insure that their methods take into consideration the growing multi-cultural population of our schools. Early in the 21st Century, more than half of the public school children will be members of minority groups. They must acknowledge, study, and document how, when, and under what circumstances cooperative learning is an important dimension. Many behavioral procedures were built only for use with individuals but there is a growing concern that group learning solves problems that individualized instruction does not. They must understand site-based management and school finance and come to grips with issues related to vouchers for both public and private schools and the promise and problems of privatization of schooling in America. They must know, in their own state, how to help schools become charter schools to free them from the bureaucracy of the state and local systems. Many behavior analysts believe that through charter schools, they can have the greatest impact on public education.

> Discipline, high stakes, tracking, common curriculum—these are not feel-good issues. But it is unconscionable that we are willing to run with virtually anything that is novel or "promising" in education while refusing to confront and debate the elements that successful school systems have in common. Romanticism is frequently a characteristic of reformers. Pragmatism would better serve our students and our public schools. (Shanker, 1995, p. 54)

The path is open; mainstream educators and administrators are looking for success; many who once criticized the data-based, individual, and practical approach of behavior analysis are now showing a renewed interest—practices that are effective are necessary when what you are currently doing is not as successful as you would hope. Behavior analysts who expand their scope, get involved in the schools, and document their success can have a great impact on education.

But remember, this book is just the beginning of your study of the effective use of behavior analysis in education. Although you have only just begun, your design of your own school is an excellent beginning. With further fluency in this area, you may become a leader of education in the 21st Century. Our children will reap the benefits and you have no time to lose.

Annotated Bibliography

Deitz, S. M. (1994). The insignificant impact of behavior analysis on education: Notes from a dean of education. In R. Gardner, D. M. Sainato, J. O. Cooper, T. E. Heron, J. W. Eshleman, & T. A. Grossi (Eds.), *Behavior analysis in education* (pp. 33-41). Pacific Grove, CA: Brooks/Cole.

> Explains why behavior analysis is not widely practiced in public schools and identifies what the behavior-analytic community can do to have a greater influence on education practices.

Eisenberger, R., & Cameron, J. (1996). Detrimental effects of reward: Reality or myth? *American Psychologist, 51,* 1153-1166.

> Dispels the myths about the harmful effects of reinforcement by delineating the conditions under which these effects occur and proper procedures for implementing reinforcement to avoid the harmful effects.

Murray, F. (1989). Explanations in education. In M. C. Reynolds (Ed.), *Knowledge base for the beginning teacher* (pp. 1-12). New York: Pergamon Press.

Describes the different types of explanations used in education and points out that vastly different theories frequently have similar practices. He encourages educators to be skeptical of instructional innovations based on theory that has not yet been demonstrated empirically effective.

Resnick, L. B. (1995). From aptitude to effort: A new foundation for our schools. *Daedalus, 124* (4), 55-62.

Describes a five point educational model to produce higher academic achievement: clear, public instructional outcomes; assessments that are tied to these outcomes; a reward structure that reinforces students' achievement; more learning time for students who need it; and empirically based teaching methods instead of constant innovations.

Shanker, A. (1995). Educational reform: What's not being said. *Daedalus, 124* (4), 47-54.

Presents several educational reform issues that have generally been neglected when American schools are compared to those of other industrialized countries and addresses four substantial differences between American schools and its international cohort: better discipline techniques, increased use of extrinsic rewards, improved ability grouping, and higher performance standards.

References

Alam, D. V. (1983). Humanism: A theoretical perspective. *Humanistic Education and Development, 21,* 101-106.

Alberto, P. A., & Troutman, A. C. (1995). *Applied behavior analysis for teachers* (4th ed.). New York: MacMillan.

Alcorn, R. D. (1992). Test scores: Can year-round school raise them? *Thrust for Educational Leadership, 21,* 12-15.

Alexander, K., & Salmon, R. G. (1995). *Public school finance.* Needham Heights: Simon and Schuster.

American 2000: An education strategy. (1991). Washington, DC: U.S. Department of Education.

American Association of University Professors. (1995). Professors explore role as citizens. *Academe, 81* (4), 52-53.

American Federation of Teachers, National Council on Measurement in Education, & National Education Association. (1990). *Standards for teacher competence in educational assessment of students.* Washington, DC: U.S. Department of Education.

Anderson, L. M. (1989). Learners and learning. In M. C. Reynolds (Ed.), *Knowledge base for the beginning teacher* (pp. 85-99). New York: Pergamon Press.

Anderson, L. M., Blumenfeld, P., Pintrich, P. R., Clark, C. M., Marx, R. W., & Peterson, P. (1995). Educational psychology for teachers: Reforming our courses, rethinking our roles. *Educational Psychologist, 30,* 143-157.

Appleman, R. (1995, Spring/Summer). Venturing beyond the default carrot. *Chalkboard, 42* (2), 4-6.

Axelrod, S. (1993). Integrating behavioral technology into public schools. *School Psychology Quarterly, 8,* 1-9.

Bailo, E. R., & Sivin-Kachla, J. (1995). Effectiveness of technology in schools. 1990 - 1994. Washington, DC: Software Publishers Association.

Balsam, P. D., & Bondy, A. S. (1983). The negative side effects of reward. *Journal of Applied Behavior Analysis, 16,* 283-296.

Barker, B. O. (1986). *The advantages of small schools.* Las Cruces: ERIC Clearinghouse on Rural Education and Small Schools. Available URL: http://www.ed.gov/databases/ERIC_ Digests/ed265988.html

Barlow, D. B., & Hersen, M. (1984). *Single case experimental designs: Strategies for studying behavior change* (2nd ed.). Elmsford, NY: Pergamon Press.

Barrett, B. H., Beck, R., Binder, C., Cook, D. A., Engelmann, S., Greer, R. D., Kyrklund, S. J., Johnson, K. R., Maloney, M., McCorkle, N., Vargas, J. S., & Watkins, C. L. (1991). The right to effective education. *The Behavior Analyst, 14,* 79-82.

Bean, E. (1994). The future of education. *Georgia Trend* [Special education edition], 6.

Beck, R., & Clement, R. (1991). The Great Falls Precision Teaching Project: An historical examination. *Journal of Precision Teaching, 8,* 8-12.

Becker, H. J. (1991). How computers are used in United States schools: Basic data from the 1989 I.E.A. computers in education survey. *Journal of Educational Computing Research, 7,* 385-406.

Becker, W. C. (1986). *Applied psychology for teachers: A behavioral cognitive approach.* Chicago: SRA.

Becker, W. C. (1988). A summary of: Becoming a nation of readers: The report of the commission on reading. Prepared by Richard C. Anderson, Elfrieda G. Hiebert, Judith A. Scott, and Ian A. G. Wilkinson. *Education and Treatment of Children, 11,* 389-396.

Becker, W. C. (1992). Direct Instruction: A twenty year review in R. P. West & L. A. Hamerlynck (Eds.), *Designs for excellence in education: The legacy of B. F. Skinner* (pp. 71-112). Longmont, CO: Sopris West.

Begley, S. (1996, February 19). Your child's brain. *Newsweek, 128,* 55-59.

Bell, K. E., Young, K. R., Salzberg, C. L., & West, R. P. (1991). High school driver education using Peer Tutors, Direct Instruction, and Precision Teaching. *Journal of Applied Behavior Analysis, 24,* 45-51.

Bell, K. E., Young, K. R., Salzberg, C. L., & West, R. P. (1991). High school driver education using peer tutors, Direct Instruction, and Precision Teaching. *Journal of Applied Behavior Analysis, 24,* 45-51.

Bijou, S. W. (1970). What psychology has to offer education-now! *Journal of Applied Behavior Analysis, 3,* 65-71.

Binder, C. (1988). Precision Teaching: Measuring and attaining exemplary academic achievement. *Youth Policy, 10,* 12-15.

Binder, C. (1990). Efforts to promote measurably superior instructional methods in schools. *Performance and Instruction, 29* (9), 32-34.

Binder, C., & Watkins, C. L. (1990). Precision Teaching and Direct Instruction: Measurably superior instructional technology in schools. *Performance Improvement Quarterly, 3* (4), 74-96.

Bjork, D. W. (1993). *B. F. Skinner: A life.* New York: Basic Books.

Bostow, D. R. (1995, Winter). Computer-based training. *TBA News, 3,* 2-3.

Boyer, E. L. (1995). *The basic school.* Princeton, NJ: The Carnegie Foundation for the Advancement of Teaching.

Boylan, H. R. (1980). PSI: A survey of users and their implementation practices. *Journal of Personalized Instruction, 4,* 40-43.

Bracey, G. W. (1991). Why can't they be more like us? *Phi Delta Kappan, 73,* 105-117.

Bracey, G. W. (1992). The second Bracey report on the conditions of public education. *Phi Delta Kappan, 74,* 104-117.

Bredekamp, S. (1991). Redeveloping early childhood education: A response to Kessler. *Early Childhood Research Quarterly, 6,* 199-209.

Brown, R. (1993). *Schools of thought: How politics of literacy shape thinking in the classroom.* New York: Basic Books.

Bryceland, J. A. (1995). Rule-governed behavior: Effects of internal versus external instructions on sequential ordering behavior (Doctoral dissertation, Georgia State University, 1995). *Dissertation Abstracts International, 56,* A0865.

Buskist, W., Cush, D., & DeGrandpre, R. J. (1991). The life and times of PSI. *Journal of Behavioral Education, 1,* 215-234.

Canelos, J., & Ozbeki, M. A. (1983). Application of the Keller instructional strategy of personalized instruction for the improvement of problem-solving learning in technical education. *Journal of Instructional Psychology, 10* (2), 61-69.

Carnegie Forum on Education and the Economy. (1986). *A nation prepared: Teachers for the 21st Century.* New York: Carnegie Corporation.

Clendenin, J. L. (1994). Education is business' bottom line. *Georgia Trend* [Special education edition], 14-17.

Clifford, G. J., & Guthrie, J. W. (1988). *Ed school: A brief for professional education.* Chicago: University of Chicago Press.

Clough, M. P., Smasal, R. J., & Clough, D. R. (1994). Managing each minute. *The Science Teacher, 61* (6), 30-34.

Cognition and Technology Group at Vanderbilt (CTGV). (1991). Some thoughts about constructivism and instructional design. *Educational Technology, 31*(9), 16-18.

Cook, T. D., & Campbell, D. T. (1979). *Quasi-experimentation: Design and analysis issues for field settings.* Chicago: Rand McNally College Publishing Company.

Cubberly, E. P. (1920). *The history of education.* Boston: Houghton Mifflin.

Cunningham, D. J. (1991). Assessing constructions and constructing assessments: A dialogue. *Educational Technology, 31* (5), 13-17.

Darling-Hammond, L. (1996). The right to learn and the advancement of teaching: Research, policy, and practice for democratic education. *Educational Researcher, 25* (6), 5-17.

Davies, C. S. (1981). Teaching introductory chemistry: Generality of the PSI approach. *Journal of Chemical Education, 58,* 686-689.

Davis, C. G. (1993). Humanism and anti-humanism: The contest for education. *Improving College and University Teaching, 31,* 155-159.

Deitz, S. M. (1994). The insignificant impact of behavior analysis on education: Notes from a dean of education. In R. Gardner, D. M. Sainato, J. O. Cooper, T. E. Heron, J. W. Eshleman, & T. A. Grossi (Eds.), *Behavior analysis in education* (pp. 33-41). Pacific Grove, CA: Brooks/Cole.

Deitz, S. M., & Hummel, J. H. (1978). *Discipline in the schools.* Englewood Cliffs, NJ: Educational Technology Publications.

Delpit, L. D. (1988/1993). The silenced dialogue: Power and pedagogy in educating other people's children. *Effective School Practices, 12* (2), 42-54. Originally published in *Harvard Educational Review, 58,* 280-298.

Delquadri, J., Greenwood, C. R., Stretton, K., & Hall, R. B. (1983). The Peer Tutoring spelling game: A classroom procedure for increasing opportunity to respond and spelling performance. *Education and Treatment of Children, 6,* 225-239.

Delquadri, J., Greenwood, C. R., Whorton, D., Carta, J., & Hall, R. V. (1986). Classwide Peer Tutoring. *Exceptional Children, 52,* 535-542.

Dickinson, A. M. (1989). The detrimental effects of extrinsic reinforcement on "intrinsic motivation." *The Behavior Analyst, 12,* 1-15.

Dineen, J. P., Clark, H. B., & Risley, T. R. (1977). Peer Tutoring among elementary students: Educational benefits to the tutor. *Journal of Applied Behavior Analysis, 10,* 231-238.

Donahoe, J. W., & Palmer, D. C. (1989). The interpretation of complex human behavior: Some reactions to *Parallel distributed processing,* edited by J. L. McClelland, D. E. Rumelhart, and the PDP Research Group. *Journal of the Experimental Analysis of Behavior, 51,* 399-416.

Duffy, T. M., & Bednar, A. K. (1991). Attempting to come to grips with alternative perspectives. *Educational Technology, 31* (9), 12-15.

Duffy, T. M., & Jonassen, D. H. (1991). Constructivism: New implications for instructional technology? *Educational Technology, 31* (5), 7-12.

Editorial Board. (1996, November 3). No secret agenda to Goals 2000. *The Atlanta Journal/Constitution,* p. C6.

Eisenberger, R., & Cameron, J. (1996). Detrimental effects of reward: Reality or myth? *American Psychologist, 51,* 1153-1166.

Elkind, D. (1989). Developmentally appropriate practice: Philosophical and practical implications. *Phi Delta Kappan, 71,* 113-117.

Engelmann, S. (1991). Change schools through revolution, not evolution. *Journal of Behavioral Education, 1,* 295-304.

Engelmann, S. (1992). *War against the schools' academic child abuse.* Portland, OR: Halcyon House.

Engelmann, S., & Carnine, D. (1982). *Theory of instruction.* New York: Irvington Publishers.

Engelmann, S., Becker, W. C., Carnine, D., & Gersten, R. (1988). The Direct Instruction Follow Through Model: Design and outcomes. *Education and Treatment of Children, 11,* 303-317.

Evertson, C. M., & Harris, A. H. (1992). What we know about managing classrooms. *Educational Leadership, 49* (7), 74-77.

Fantuzzo, J., & Atkins, M. (1992). Applied behavior analysis for educators: Teacher centered and classroom based. *Journal of Applied Behavior Analysis, 25,* 37-42.

Fernald, P. S., & Jordan, E. A. (1991). Programmed Instruction versus standard text in introductory psychology. *Teaching of Psychology, 18,* 205-211.

Fetler, M. (1989). School dropout rates, academic performance, size, and poverty: Correlates of educational reform. *Educational Evaluation and Policy Analysis, 11,* 109-116.

Fredrick, L. D., & Keel, M.C. (1996, May). Making the most of instructional time. In D. E. Bostow (Chair), *Empirically validated education packages.* Symposium conducted at the meeting of the Association for Behavior Analysis, San Francisco, CA.

Friedkin, N., & Necochea, J. (1988). School system size and performance: A contingency perspective. *Educational Evaluation and Policy Analysis, 10,* 237-249.

Gandara, P., & Fish, J. (1994). Year-round schooling as an avenue to major structural reform. *Educational Evaluation and Policy Analysis, 16,* 67-85.

Gelfand, D. M., & Hartmann, D. P. (1984). *Child behavior analysis and therapy.* Elmsford, NY: Pergamon Press.

Gersten, R. (1992). Passion and precision: Response to curriculum-based assessment and Direct Instruction: Critical reflections on fundamental assumptions. *Exceptional Children, 58,* 464-467.

Gersten, R., Carnine, D., Zoref, L., & Cronin, D. (1986). A multifaceted study of change in seven inner-city schools. *Elementary School Journal, 86* (3), 257-276.

Gersten, R., Keating, T., & Becker, W. (1988). The continued impact of the Direct Instruction Model: Longitudinal studies of Follow Through students. *Education and Treatment of Children, 11,* 318-327.

Gersten, R., Woodward, J., & Darch, C. (1986). Direct Instruction: A research-based approach for curriculum design and teaching. *Exceptional Children, 53,* 17-36.

Glickman, C. D. (1993). *Renewing America's schools: A guide for school-based action.* San Francisco: Jossey-Bass.

Goodwin, G. A. (1987). Humanistic sociology and the craft of teaching. *Teaching Sociology, 15,* 15-20.

Graham, P. A. (1992). *S.O.S.: Sustain our schools.* New York: Hill & Wang.

Greenberg, P. (1990). Ideas that work with young children. *Young Children, 45* (2), 70-80.

Greenwood, C. R., & Carta, J. J. (1988). An ecobehavioral interaction analysis of instruction within special education. In E. L. Meyer, G. A. Vergason, & R. J. Wheelan (Eds.), *Effective instructional strategies for exceptional children* (pp. 505-521). Denver, CO: Love.

Greenwood, C. R., Dinwiddie, G., Bailey, V., Carta, J. J., Dorsey, D., Kohler, F.W., Nelson, C., Rotholz, D., & Schulte, D. (1987). Field replication of classwide Peer Tutoring. *Journal of Applied Behavior Analysis, 20,* 151-160.

Greenwood, C. R., Dinwiddie, G., Terry, B., Wade, L., Stanley, S. O., Thibadeau, S., & Delquadri, J. C. (1984). Teacher-versus peer-mediated instruction: An ecobehavioral analysis of achievement outcomes. *Journal of Applied Behavior Analysis, 17,* 521-538.

Greer, R. D. (1992). L'Enfant terrible meets the educational crisis. *Journal of Applied Behavior Analysis, 25,* 65-69.

Gregor, A. (1981). Humanism: A definition of literacy. *The Journal of Educational Thought, 15,* 202-208.

Hardin, J., & Ziebarth, J. (1996). Digital technology and its impact on education. *White paper: The future of networking technologies for learning.* U.S. Department of Education's Office of Educational Technology. Available URL: http://www.ed.gov/Technology/Futures/ hardin.html

Harris, K. R., & Pressley, M. (1991). The nature of cognitive strategy instruction: Interactive strategy construction. *Exceptional Children, 57,* 392-404.

Haughton, E. C. (1980). Practicing practices: Learning by activity. *Journal of Precision Teaching, 1,* 3-20.

Herbst, J. (1989). Teacher preparation in the nineteenth century. In D. Warren (Ed.), *American teachers: Histories of a profession at work* (pp. 213-236). New York: Macmillan.

Heward, W. L. (1994). Three "low-tech" strategies for increasing the frequency of active student response during group instruction. In R. Gardner III, D. M. Sainato, J. O. Cooper, T. E. Heron, W. L. Heward, J. W. Eshleman, & T. A. Grossi (Eds.), *Behavior analysis in education* (pp. 283-320). Pacific Grove, CA: Brooks/ Cole.

Hollowood, T. M., Salisbury, C. L., Rainforth, B., & Palombaro, M. M. (1994). Use of instructional time in classrooms serving students with and without severe disabilities. *Exceptional Children, 61,* 242-253.

Huang, G., & Howley, C. (1993). Mitigating disadvantage: Effects of small-scale schooling on students' achievement in Alaska. *Journal of Research in Rural Education, 9* (3), 137-149.

Huitt, W. G. (1995). *Success in the information age: A paradigm shift.* Valdosta State University. Available URL: http://chiron.valdosta.edu/whuitt/col/context/ infoage.html

Jackard, C. (1983). Humanism: An answer to problems facing education. *The Humanist, 43* (3), 20-23.

Jaeger, R. M. (1992). World-class standards, choice, and privatization: Weak measurement serving presumptive policy. *Phi Delta Kappan, 74,* 118-128.

Jenson, W. R., Sloane, H. N., & Young, K. R. (1988). *Applied behavior analysis in education: A structured teaching approach.* Englewood Cliffs, NJ: Prentice Hall.

Johnson, K. R. (1981). Behavior analysis in instructional design: A functional typology of verbal tasks. *The Behavior Analyst, 4,* 103-121.

Johnson, K. R., & Layng, T. V. (1992). Breaking the structuralist barrier: Literacy and numeracy with fluency. *American Psychologist, 47,* 1475-1490.

Johnson, W. R. (1989). Teachers and teacher training in the twentieth century. In D. Warren (Ed.), *American teachers: Histories of a profession at work* (pp. 237-256). New York: Macmillan.

Johnston, J. M., & Pennypacker, H. S. (1993). *Strategies and tactics of human behavioral research* (2nd ed.). Hillsdale, NJ: Lawrence Erlbaum.

Jonassen, D. H. (1991). Evaluating constructivist learning. *Educational Technology, 31* (9), 28-33.

Kagan, D. M. (1992). Implications of research on teacher belief. *Educational Psychologist, 27,* 65-90.

Kamps, D. M., Barbetta, P. M., Leonard, B. R., & Delquadri, J. (1994). Classwide Peer Tutoring: An integration strategy to improve reading skills and promote peer interactions among students with autism and general education peers. *Journal of Applied Behavior Analysis, 27,* 49-61.

Karweit, N. (1988, February). Time-on-task: The second time around. *NASSP Bulletin, 72,* 31-39.

Katz, L. G. (1988). What should young children be doing? *American Educator, 12* (2), 28-45.

Kazdin, A. E. (1973). The effect of vicarious reinforcement on attentive behavior in the classroom. *Journal of Applied Behavior Analysis, 6,* 71-78.

Keller, F. S., & Sherman, J. G. (1974). *PSI: The Keller Plan handbook.* Menlo Park, CA: W. A. Benjamin.

Kelly, M. B. (1977). A review of observational data-collection and reliability procedures reported in the *Journal of Applied Behavior Analysis. Journal of Applied Behavior Analysis, 10,* 97-101.

Kinder, D., & Carnine, D. (1991). Direct Instruction: What it is and what it is becoming. *Journal of Behavioral Education, 1,* 193-214.

Klonsky, M., & Ford, P. (1994). One urban solution: Small schools. *Educational Leadership, 51* (8), 64-66.

Knox, G. A. (1994). Seven rules to year-round schooling. *School Administrator, 51,* 22-24.

Kondracke, M. (1995, September 4). America's public schools failing. *The Valdosta Daily Times,* p. A4.

Kramer, R. (1991). *Ed school follies: The miseducation of America's teachers.* New York: The Free Press.

Kramlinger, T., & Huberty, T. (1990). Behaviorism versus humanism. *Training and Development Journal, 44* (12), 41-45.

Kulik, C. C., Schwelb, B. J., & Kulik, J. A. (1982). Programmed Instruction in secondary education: A meta-analysis of evaluation findings. *Journal of Educational Research, 75* (3), 133-138.

Kulik, J. A. (1983). How can chemists use educational technology effectively? *Journal of Chemical Education, 60,* 957-959.

Kulik, J. A., Kulik, C. C., & Cohen, P. A. (1979). A meta-analysis of outcome studies of Keller's Personalized System of Instruction. *American Psychologist, 34,* 307-318.

Labaree, D. F. (1996). The trouble with ed schools. *Educational Foundations, 10* (3), 27-45.

Lancioni, G. E. (1982). Normal children as tutors to teach social responses to withdrawn mentally retarded schoolmates: Training, maintenance, and generalization. *Journal of Applied Behavior Analysis, 15,* 17-40.

Levine, F. M., & Fasnacht, G. (1974). Token rewards may lead to token learning. *American Psychologist, 29,* 816-820.

Lindsley, O. R. (1990). Precision Teaching: By teachers for children. *Teaching Exceptional Children, 22* (3), 10-15.

Lindsley, O. R. (1992). Why aren't effective teaching tools widely adopted? *Journal of Applied Behavior Analysis, 25,* 21-26.

Loveless, T. (1996). Searching for legitimacy: Educational reform and education's institutional dilemmas. *Working paper: Taubman Center for State and Local Government, John F. Kennedy School of Government, Harvard University.* Available

URL:http://ksgwww.harvard.edu/taubman/reports/searching_for_
legitimacy.html

Mager, R. F. (1962). *Preparing instructional objectives.* Belmont, CA.: David S. Lake, Publishers.

Marshall, J. (1993, December). Why Johnny can't teach. *Reason,* 27-31.

McDade, C. E., & Goggans, L. A. (1993). Computer-based precision learning: Achieving fluency with college students. *Education and Treatment of Children, 16,* 290-305.

McDowell, C. (1995, August 30). Group trumpets good news about people's attitudes toward schools. *The Valdosta Daily Times,* p. A4.

Meir, D. (1992). Reinventing teaching. *Teachers College Record, 93,* 594-609.

Merrill, M. D. (1991). Constructivism and instructional design. *Educational Technology, 31* (5), 45-53.

Mills, R. K. (1985). Let's keep humanism in the classroom. *The Social Studies, 76,* 108-110.

Molenda, M. (1991). A philosophical critique of the claims of "Constructivism." *Educational Technology, 31* (9), 44-48.

Muirhead, W. M., & McLaughlin, T. F. (1990). The effects of a Peer Tutoring spelling game on academic performance and student attitudes. *Child & Family Behavior Therapy, 12* (4), 1-9.

Murray, F. (1989). Explanations in education. In M. C. Reynolds (Ed.), *Knowledge base for the beginning teacher* (pp. 1-12). New York: Pergamon Press.

NAEYC. (1988). NAEYC position statement on developmentally appropriate practice in the primary grades, serving 5- through 8-year olds. *Young children, 43* (2), 64-84.

Narayan, J. S., Heward, W. H., Gardner, R., Courson, F. H., & Omness, C. K. (1990). Using response cards to increase student participation in an elementary classroom. *Journal of Applied Behavior Analysis, 23,* 483-490.

National Center for Research of Teacher Education. (1991). *Final report of the teacher education and teacher learning study.* East Lansing: Michigan State University.

National Commission on Excellence in Education. (1983). *A nation at risk: The imperative for educational reform.* Washington, DC: U.S. Department of Education.

National Commission on Teaching and America's Future. (1996, September). *What matters most: Teaching for America's future.* New York: National Commission on Teaching and America's Future.

Neuringer, A. (1991). Humble behaviorism. *The Behavior Analyst, 14,* 1-13.

Nickerson, R. S. (1988). Technology in education in 2020: Thinking about the non-distant future. In R. S. Nickerson & P. P. Zodhiates (Eds.), *Technology in education: Looking toward 2020* (pp. 1-9). Hillsdale, NJ: Lawrence Erlbaum.

Nicklin, J. L. (1994, March 9). A plethora of reforms. *The Chronicle of Higher Education,* pp. A16, A18.

O'Loughlin, M. (1992). Rethinking science education: Beyond Piagetian constructivism toward a sociocultural model of teaching and learning. *Journal of Research in Science Teaching, 29,* 791-820.

O'Neil, I. R., & Adamson, D. R. (1993). When less is more. *American School Board Journal, 180,* 39-41.

O'Neill, R. E., Horner, R. H., Albin, R. W., Storey, K., & Sprague, J. R. (1990). *Functional analysis of problem behavior: A practical assessment guide.* Pacific Grove, CA: Brooks/Cole.

Ollendick, T. H., Dailey, D., & Shapiro, E. S. (1983). Vicarious reinforcement: Expected and unexpected effects. *Journal of Applied Behavior Analysis, 16,* 485-491.

Orlansky, J., & String, J. (1979). *Cost-effectiveness of computer based instruction in military training.* Institute of Defense Analysis, Alexandria VA.

Osier, D. R. (1994). Wired for the future. *Georgia Trend* [Special education edition], 38-43.

Paine, S. C., Radicchi, J., Rosellini, L. C., Deutchman, L., & Darch, C. B. (1983). *Structuring your classroom for academic success.* Champaign, IL: Research Press.

Perelman, L. J. (1992). *School's out: Hyperlearning, the new technology, and the end of education.* New York: William Morrow.

Perkins, D. N. (1991). Technology meets constructivism: Do they make a marriage? *Educational Technology, 31* (5), 18-23.

Perkins, V., & Cullinan, D. (1984). Effects of Direct Instruction intervention for fraction skills. *Education and Treatment of Children, 7,* 109-117.

Plecki, M. (1991, April). *The relationship between elementary school size and student achievement.* Paper presented at the annual meeting of the American Educational Research Association, Chicago, IL.

Pogue, J. (1994). Why Georgia can't afford to have poor schools. *Georgia Trend* [Special education edition], 18-23.

Poplin, M. S. (1988). Holistic/constructivist principles of the teaching/learning process: Implications for the field of learning disabilities. *Journal of Learning Disabilities, 21,* 401-416.

Prawat, R. S. (1992). Teachers' beliefs about teaching and learning: A constructivist perspective. *American Journal of Education, 100,* 354-395.

Reboy, L. M., & Semb, G. B. (1991). PSI and critical thinking compatibility or irreconcilable differences. *Teaching of Psychology, 18,* 212-215.

Repp, A. C., Roberts, D. M., Slack, D. J., Repp, C. F., & Berkler, M. S. (1976). A comparison of frequency, interval, and time-sampling methods of data collection. *Journal of Applied Behavior Analysis, 13,* 501-508.

Resnick, L. B. (1995). From aptitude to effort: A new foundation for our schools. *Daedalus, 124* (4), 55-62.

Roberts, S. M., Suderman, L., Suderman, R., & Semb, G. B. (1990). Reading ability as a performance predictor in a behaviorally based psychology course. *Teaching of Psychology, 17,* 173-175.

Sardo-Brown, D., & Rooney, M. (1992). The vote on all-year schools. *American School Board Journal, 178,* 25-27.

Schoen, S. F., & James, D. A. (1991). If at first you don't succeed.... *Journal of Instructional Psychology, 18,* 273-277.

Shanker, A. (1995). Educational reform: What's not being said. *Daedalus, 124* (4), 47-54.

Shapiro, E. S. (1988). Preventing academic failure. *School Psychology Review, 17,* 601-613.

Shaw, R. (1994). State of the art. *Georgia Trend* [Special education edition], 54-60.

Sipe, T. A., & Curlette, W. L. (1996). A meta-synthesis of factors related to educational achievement: A methodological approach to summarization and synthesis of meta-analyses. *International Journal of Educational Research, 25,* 583-698.

Skinner, B. F. (1968). *The technology of teaching.* New York: Appleton-Century-Crofts.

Slavin, R. E. (1994). *Educational psychology: Theory and practice* (4th ed.). Boston: Allyn and Bacon.

Smith, B. O. (1980). *A design for a school of pedagogy.* Washington, D.C.: U.S. Department of Education.

Smith, K. E. (1990). Developmentally appropriate education or the Hunter teacher assessment model: Mutually incompatible alternatives. *Young Children, 45* (2), 12-13.

Smith, M. A., & Misra, A. (1992). A comprehensive management system for students in regular classrooms. *The Elementary School Journal, 92,* 354-371.

Stainback, W., Stainback, S., & Froyen, L. (1987). Structuring the classroom to prevent disruptive behaviors. *Teaching Exceptional Children, 19* (4), 12-16.

Stone, B. L. (1988). Teaching sociology in the humanist tradition. *Teaching Sociology, 16,* 151-159.

Stone, J. E. (1994). Developmentalism's impediments to school reform: Three recommendations for overcoming them. In R. Gardner III, D. M. Sainato, J. O. Cooper, T. E. Heron, W. L. Heward, J. W. Eshleman, & T. A. Grossi (Eds.), *Behavior analysis in education* (pp. 57-72). Pacific Grove, CA: Brooks/Cole.

Stossel, J. (1995, October 13). No frills drills (M. Kenny, Producer). *20/20.* New York: ABC.

Tashman, B. (1996). Our failure to follow through. *Effective School Practices, 15,* 67.

Toch, T. (1996, February 26). Why teachers don't teach. *U.S. News & World Report, 121,* 62-71.

Trends and Ideas. (1994). *Georgia Trend* [Special education edition], 8-13.

Tucci, V., & Hursh, D. E. (1994). Developing competent learners by arranging effective learning environments. In R. Gardner III, D. M. Sainato, J. O. Cooper, T. E. Heron, W. L. Heward, J. W. Eshleman, & T. A. Grossi (Eds.), *Behavior analysis in education* (pp. 257-264). Pacific Grove, CA: Brooks/Cole.

Tucker, K. H. (1994). Education should be everybody's business. *Georgia Trend* [Special education edition], 32-37.

U.S. Department of Commerce, National Telecommunications and Information Administration. (June, 1995). Educational technology improves student performance. Available http://www.aasa.org/TECH4.html

U.S. Department of Education. (January, 1995). *Projections of education statistics to 2005.* (National Center for Education Statistics, NCES 96-169). Washington, DC: U.S. Government Printing Office.

Urban, W. J. (1990). Historical studies of teacher education. In W. R. Houston (Ed.), *Handbook of research on teacher education* (pp. 59-71). New York: Macmillian.

Vargas, E. A., & Vargas, J. S. (1991). Programmed Instruction: What it is and how to do it. *Journal of Behavioral Education, 1,* 235-252.

Vargas, E. A., & Vargas, J. S. (1992). Programmed Instruction and teaching machines. In R. P. West & L. A. Hamerlynck (Eds.), *Designs for excellence in education: The legacy of B. F. Skinner* (pp. 33-69). Longmont, CO: Sopris West.

Walberg, H. (1989). District size and student learning. *Education and Urban Society, 21* (2), 154-163.

Warren, D. (1995). Educational technology and the bottom line. *Chalkboard, 42* (2), 2-3.

Weiner, H. (1969). Controlling human fixed-interval performance. *Journal of the Experimental Analysis of Behavior, 12,* 349-373.

Weiner, H. (1970). Instructional control of human operant responding during extinction following fixed ratio conditioning. *Journal of the Experimental Analysis of Behavior, 13,* 391-394.

Weisberg, P., & Clements, P. (1977). Effects of direct, intermittent, and vicarious reinforcement procedures on the development and maintenance of instruction-following behaviors in a group of young children. *Journal of Applied Behavior Analysis, 10,* 314.

West, R. P., & Young, K. R. (1992). Precision Teaching in R. P. West & L. A. Hamerlynck (Eds.), *Designs for excellence in education: The legacy of B. F. Skinner* (pp. 113-146). Longmont, CO: Sopris West.

West, R. P., Young, K. R., & Spooner, F. (1990). Precision Teaching: An introduction. *Teaching Exceptional Children, 22* (3), 4-9.

Wheatley, G. H. (1991). Constructivist perspectives in science and mathematics learning. *Science Education, 75,* 9-21.

White, O. R. (1986). Precision Teaching—Precision learning. *Exceptional Children, 52,* 522-534.

Winett, R. A., & Winkler, R. C. (1972). Current behavior modification in the classroom: Be still, be quiet, be docile. *Journal of Applied Behavior Analysis, 5,* 499-504.

Zeiler, M. D. (1996). Whither behaviorism? [A review of *Modern perspectives on B. F. Skinner and contemporary behaviorism*]. *The Behavior Analyst, 19,* 301-309.

Subject Index